MEMORY RESIDENT UTILITIES, INTERRUPTS, AND DISK MANAGEMENT
WITH MS AND PC DOS

Michael I. Hyman

Management Information Source, Inc.

COPYRIGHT

ACKNOWLEDGEMENTS

There are many people to whom I am indebted for help with this
project. I would especially like to thank my parents, Richard and
Roberta Hyman; my sister, Betsy Hyman; Chris Williams at MIS,
Inc.; Bob Smith of Qualitas, Inc., especially for his help in
Section III; Barbara Bakal, Rob DiGiacomo, Taylor Smith, and of
course, Mirna Goldberger.

TABLE OF CONTENTS

INTRODUCTION

Welcome to the world of advanced DOS programming. You will find this book to be the ultimate reference guide to getting the most out of your machine. As you read it, you'll learn how to use and enhance DOS to explore your computer and make mighty programs. Powerful examples will lead you along the way and provide models for later reference. You'll learn how to get back erased files, read hidden directories, protect disks from being reformatted, and much, much more. You'll also explore the new IBM keyboard, 3.5", 20, and 30 MB drives.

In Section 1, you'll discover how data is stored on disks. Step by step, you'll explore the partition table, the boot record, the FAT, the directory, and the data. You'll see how to read files, traverse paths, and retrieve erased files. You'll make a powerful disk utility, EXPLORER. Using it, you'll make disk titles, hide directories, and sneak through program files. Then, you'll make NEWCMMDS, a program to change the names of internal DOS commands.

In Section 2, you'll see how to use DOS and BIOS in your programs. You'll learn to use the keyboard, screen, and mouse. You'll learn to manipulate and create disk files and how to use conventional and expanded memory. You'll learn to get more out of the built-in DOS, learn about pitfalls to avoid, and discover the interrupts Microsoft won't tell you about. You'll see many examples, including MOVE--to move files and directories--and DIR2, an advanced directory command.

Section 3 presents the definitive guide to creating memory resident utilities. You'll learn about the different kinds of interrupts and how to divert them. You'll see how to make hot keys and screen windows. You'll learn about load detection, dormancy, and reentrancy. You'll see how to coexist with other resident utilities, with programs, and with DOS. You'll poll system status and learn the danger areas to avoid. You'll see powerful examples, including PROTECT--to prevent unauthorized reformatting of disks--and VIDEOTBL--to account for monitor characteristics.

What You'll Need

Section 1 uses Pascal; Sections 2 and 3 use Assembly Language. To get the most out of this book, I strongly recommend:

Turbo Pascal 3.0
Microsoft Macro Assembler 4.0

Program Disk to Accompany This Book

All program code is printed in this book; however, you may want to order the Advanced DOS Guide Diskette. It contains the source code for all the programs and gives you all the utilities, ready to run. If you don't have a Pascal compiler or an assembler, be sure to get this diskette. It'll save you much programming time and help you concentrate on what you are learning. Plus, you'll find that the Advanced DOS Guide Diskette contains a powerful set of utilities you will use over and over again.

You may also want to order FAILSAFE, a memory resident utility from the Princeton Software Group. FAILSAFE's UnLoop command lets you break out of any endless loop or hung program, and its Snoop feature lets you do full screen examining and editing of memory while a program is running. This is crucial for debugging resident programs or programs that contain interfaces between languages. FAILSAFE also gets back NEWed BASIC programs and lost text files.

An order form for these two programs is in the back of the book.

Note to Programmers:

The program listings in this book have been printed directly from the original program disks to ensure that no errors were introduced through rekeyboarding.

The letter "l" and the number "1" are represented in the program code by the same character. **In no case is the letter "l" used as a variable name.** This should eliminate any confusion.

SECTION I

EXPLORING DISKS

In this section, you will examine disks. You'll explore the boot record, FAT, directory, subdirectories, files, and partition. You'll see what they do, how to use them, and what they look like for the various types of disks. You will design a utility to probe and modify disks, and then examine some disk tricks. You'll wrap up the chapter by writing a program to modify DOS internal command names.

Understanding how disks work will help you in several ways. If you experience a disk problem, such as accidentally erasing a file, reformatting a hard disk, or damaging a directory, you'll know how to get the data back. Your knowledge will also help you develop or use applications that employ disks, such as databases or security systems.

Note: The letter "l" and the number "1" are represented in the program code by the same character. **In no case is the letter "l" used as a variable name.**

CHAPTER 1

FACTS ABOUT DISKS

Every time you use your computer, you use disks. You boot from a disk, load programs from disks, and save the results on disks. In the following few chapters, you'll examine how information is stored and organized on disks. This will help you write powerful utilities to enhance the way you use disks.

Normally, you think of disks as a collection of files. You might run the program files, edit the data files, or copy or erase them, but that's about all.

Actually, there is much more information on a disk. The disk needs to know what type of disk it is, what files it contains, where they are located, and where there is room to put more files. This information is stored in four basic structures that are mostly hidden from the user's view: the partition table, the boot record, the file allocation table, and the directory. The disk also has a physical structure of sides, tracks, and sectors. First, let's look at the physical structure of disks.

Disks are platters, flexible or hard, of a magnetic media. A hard disk is a set of these platters. Each platter has a top and a bottom side. The side of a disk being examined is referred to as the **side** or **head**. The head refers to the electromechanical device which does the actual reading. More or less, it is a little electromagnet which moves across the disk. Floppy disks have two sides. Hard disks usually have two sides for every platter they contain.

Each side is further broken down into concentric rings called **tracks** or **cylinders**. The disk head can be moved over any track on the disk. As the disk spins underneath it, the head can read the various pieces of information stored on the disk.

Each track is broken down into **sectors**. A sector is the smallest clump of information that can be read from or written to a disk.[1] Typically, each sector is 512 bytes long.

---

[1]Once the sector is read, you can look at the individual bytes.

There are many sectors on a disk to manage; therefore, sectors are grouped together into **clusters**. A cluster is simply a collection of contiguous sectors. There may be anywhere from two to eight sectors per cluster, depending upon the type of disk. Figure 1.1 shows a diagram of a disk.

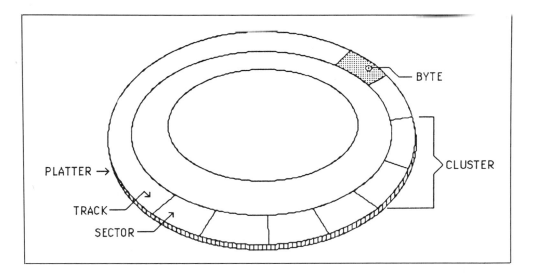

Figure 1.1 A Disk

This may sound complicated. Fortunately, DOS does most of the work for you. You usually don't need to worry about clusters or sectors and very rarely about tracks and sides.

Let's look at the four basic sections of information that tell how a disk is organized. You'll begin with the **partition table.** Most of the time, you only use one operating system (DOS), but some PC users also need CP/M or XENIX. If these users have a hard disk, they will surely want to use it to store files for all of these operating systems, which manipulate the disk in a way incompatible with DOS. In order to use a hard disk with more than one operating system, the hard disk is divided in up to four sections. Each can use a different operating system.

The partition table tells the location and size of each of these four sections, which section is to be used if the computer is booted from the hard disk,[2] and which sections use DOS as their operating system. This is very important. As you will see in the following chapters, DOS (and utility programs) expects to find certain types of information in certain places on the disk. On a hard disk, these predefined locations could be anywhere, depending on how the partitions are set up. DOS uses the partition table to see where the partition in use starts and uses this as an offset for all further accesses to the disk. This way, special information can always be found, and the partition setup is transparent to both DOS and the user.

When the computer is turned on, a program in ROM first tries to boot from whatever disk might be in drive A. If there isn't a disk in drive A, it sends control to a program preceding the partition table.[3] This program reads the partition table, and if the information it finds there is valid, finds the location of the boot record for the active partition and passes control there.

Remember, the partition table is only found on hard disks.

The **boot record** is the next important section on a disk. It contains the program to load and start the operating system. It also contains a table of information describing the disk: size, type, operating system, format, and vital information about the file allocation table and directory. DOS uses this information to determine how to read from and write to the disk.

Data is stored in a file in clusters. Often, these clusters do not occur one after another; the first part of a file could be somewhere near the beginning of the disk and the rest of the file in the middle or end of the disk. The **file allocation table** (FAT) tells which clusters each file uses. It also tells which sections of the disk are free for use and which sections of the disk are unusable because of a physical defect. The file allocation table is so important that usually two copies of it are kept on disks. Without it, all data on the disk would be a meaningless garble of randomly organized bytes.

---

[2]This section is called the **active partition.**

[3]On a system without a hard disk, ROM BASIC is started.

The **directory** is the final organizational structure. Among other things, it tells the names of the files, their size, when they were made, and how DOS can find them.

KEY PROGRAMMING POINTS

- Disks have sides, tracks, and sectors.

- Sectors are grouped into organizational units called clusters.

- The five basic parts of the disk are the partition table, boot record, file allocation table, directory, and data area.

CHAPTER 2

AN OVERVIEW OF EXPLORER

Let's begin a detailed examination of how disks work. You will not only learn how disks are structured and used; you will actually examine them. To do so, you will write a Pascal disk exploration utility. As different features of disks are discussed, you'll add modules to the program to examine them. Figure 2.1 shows the main menu from EXPLORER.

```
------------------------------MAIN MENU---------------
F1:    Dump and Modify Sectors
F2:    Examine Boot Record
F3:    Cluster by Cluster FAT Dump
F4:    Examine Root Directory
F5:    Examine File
F6:    Get Back Erased File
F7:    Examine Partition

F10:   Exit
```

Figure 2.1 EXPLORER's Main Menu

All of the code for the program appears in the text. It is written using Turbo Pascal 3.0. If you do not have this version of Pascal, you may have to make slight modifications. Consider getting the Advanced DOS Guide Diskette. It has all of the program source code and the ready-to-run programs. You don't have to type in all the code and worry about mistakes; you can use the already compiled programs. If you do not have a Pascal compiler, be sure to get this disk. The EXPLORER.COM program will be a valuable utility to you and used often throughout this book. Notes on using the diskette will be placed within boxes.

You will make EXPLORER as flexible as possible. It will be menu driven with full screen input routines. The main routine will read commands and pass control to more specialized procedures, each with their own sub-menus of commands. You will use text windows to keep the screen clean.

Because the code for EXPLORER is long, you must write it one section at a time and then use the include ($I) command to compile these sections along with the main module. The main module will be called explorer.pas.

You will run EXPLORER frequently throughout this section. Before you do so, you may want to leave Turbo Pascal. Turbo Pascal seems to occasionally cache disk information; this makes EXPLORER operate incorrectly. Compile EXPLORER as a COM file, leave Turbo Pascal, and then run it. It should work perfectly.

Throughout this book, we will use numbers from the binary, decimal, and hex numbering systems. Binary numbers will be written as 100111b, decimal numbers as 14, and hex numbers as $16 or 16h.

KEY PROGRAMMING POINTS

- You will create a disk exploration utility called EXPLORER.

- You will write the EXPLORER code as a series of modules. For each module, you will add an include command ($I) to explorer.pas. Then compile explorer.pas.

CHAPTER 3

GETTING COMMANDS
AND DISK I/O

To write EXPLORER, start with explorer.pas, the foundation. In explorer.pas, you will set up the constants and type definitions for the whole program and process commands for the main menu. Also in explorer.pas, you will put the elemental routines for reading from and writing to disk.

In order to get the flexibility and control you need, you will write your own routines to read commands from the keyboard and do disk I/O. The disk I/O routines are probably more complex than any of the routines in the next four chapters. This is because they require Assembly Language.

If you are not familiar with Assembly Language programming, you may find these routines rather confusing. To make the routines powerful, you need to use BIOS and DOS interrupts. If this is foreign to you, just skim along and use the code at the end of this chapter. You may not understand it perfectly but will at least have a sense of what it does.

READING COMMANDS

To make EXPLORER easy to use and professional looking, you want to be able to process function and cursor keys. Unfortunately, **readln** can't process these keys. You need to use a BIOS interrupt.[1]

BIOS interrupts are subroutines stored in ROM that perform the most elemental interactions with the hardware of the computer. For example, there are BIOS interrupts to print characters on the screen, to check the position of the light pen, and to send information to the printer. There are also BIOS interrupts to read strokes from the keyboard. Each interrupt has a number and set of parameters that it uses.

---

[1]BIOS and DOS interrupts are discussed in depth in Section II.

To call an interrupt from Pascal, pass the interrupt number and the parameters using the **intr** command. The parameters are set using the following data structure:

```
result = record
      ax,bx,cx,dx,bp,si,di,ds,es,flags: integer;
    end;
```

Each of the integer variables represents one of the 8086 registers.[2]   Sometimes, instead of referring to ax, bx, cx, or dx, you will refer to ah, al, bh, bl, ch, cl, dh, or dl. This just refers to the high and low order bytes of the corresponding register. For example, ah = ax div 256; al = ax mod 256.

To read the keyboard, use interrupt 16h. Call it with AH = 0. The interrupt routine then waits for a keystroke, and after one occurs, returns with AX containing the keystroke code. If AL is not 0, the key is one of the normal letter or number keys, and AL contains its ASCII code. But if AL is 0, AH contains a code for one of the function or cursor keys.

Interrupt 16h and the codes it returns will be discussed in detail in Chapter 15. For now, just look at the procedures that use interrupt 16h to see the type of values that it returns. For example, you can see from the main procedure that if the F10 key is pressed, the interrupt will return with AX = 4400h.

The Pascal code reading the keyboard will look something like this:

```
regs.ax := 0;        {regs is of type result.  AX = 0 means
                      read keyboard}
intr($16,regs);      {wait for a key and return the code}
if regs.ax and $ff = 0 then ... {key is a function or cursor
                      key}
```

You can check the value with the statement:

```
case (regs.ax) of .....
```

The code for explorer.pas is listed at the end of this chapter. Look through it for the routine that reads the keyboard.

---

[2]If you are not familiar with 8086 registers, don't worry. The concept isn't crucial here, and you'll always be told how to set the parameters.

READING FROM AND WRITING TO DISK

To read from and write to the disk, you will also use interrupts, but this time, use DOS interrupts. DOS interrupts are very similar to BIOS interrupts except that the DOS interrupt routines are not part of ROM. Instead, they are loaded when the computer is booted. As far as our program is concerned, there is no difference.

Use the interrupts 25h and 26h to read and write sectors. The sectors are referred to by their **logical sector number.** The first sector on a disk is numbered 0, the next 1, and so on, until there are no sectors left.

Sometimes, sectors are referred to by their **physical sector number** instead. In the physical numbering scheme, you must also specify the side and the track. Each track has sectors numbered from 1 to the last sector in the track. The DOS interrupts make it much easier for you. DOS worries about when to change tracks or sides. Just tell it a sector number and it finds it for you.[3]

You will almost always use the logical sector number when reading from and writing to disk.

Interrupt 25h is called with four parameters:

```
AL = drive number (0 = A, 1 = B, 2 = C, and so on)
CX = number of sectors to read
DS:BX = location where read data is to be placed
        (DS is the segment of the buffer address; BX is the
        offset.)
```

Interrupt 26h uses the same parameters, but CX is the number of sectors to write, and DS:BX points to the location where the data which is to be written can be found.

---

[3]By contrast, the BIOS disk interrupts use the side, track, sector reference scheme.

It would be nice if you could just call these interrupts using the
intr command, as you did to read the keyboard. Unfortunately,
these two interrupts are nasty. Unlike all the other interrupts,
they don't clean up after themselves before returning to the
calling program. Rather, they leave behind some data--a status
flag on the stack. If you used the **intr** command, everything would
be fine until the procedure which did the read or write was
finished. When it tried to return to the procedure which called
it, it would crash.

To get around this problem, you have to incorporate a small
Assembly Language program into explorer.pas using the **inline**
function.[4]   You'll examine this in detail for reading from disk.
The process for writing to disk is essentially the same.

You'll create a function called DiskRead to read from the disk.
The function will take as parameters the drive number, the
starting sector number, the number of sectors to read, and a
pointer to a buffer area in which the information will be stored.
If it can't read from the disk, it will return an error code.
You'll use the **inline** code to call the DOS interrupt, check for an
error, clean up, and return.

Note carefully the process of interfacing between Turbo Pascal and
Assembly Language. It is incorrectly documented in the Turbo
Pascal manual.[5]

When a function is called, it passes its parameters on the stack.
Value parameters are passed as data; variable parameters and
arrays are passed as pointers. The different types of data are
passed using different formats. Bytes and integers are passed as
words; pointers are passed as an offset and segment. For details
on the other types, see the Turbo Pascal manual.

---

[4]If you are not using Turbo Pascal, you will have to use an
equivalent command. The format in which variables are passed on
the stack may be slightly different. Consult your compiler's
manual.

[5]Versions 2.0 and 3.0.

After the function declaration, space is pushed on the stack for the function result. For integers, booleans, bytes, and chars, this is one word. The parameters are pushed after this, from the left side of the declaration to the right. Then, three more words are pushed on.[6] Finally, the **inline** code is called.

To read the parameters, first save the bp register by pushing it on the stack. Next, move the sp value to bp and add eight to it to point to the parameter area (two for the just pushed bp and six for the three words pushed on the stack). Add to bp to get to the next parameter. Remember, since the parameters were pushed onto the stack from left to right, as you add to bp you will encounter them from right to left.

For our function, you are passing a byte, two integer values, and a pointer. The function result is an integer. Thus, after pushing bp, setting it to the sp value, and adding eight:

```
bp will point to the pointer offset value
bp + 2 will point to the pointer segment value
bp + 4 will point to an integer
bp + 6 will point to an integer
bp + 8 will point to a byte (stored as a word)
bp + 10 will point to the function result
```

Remember to account for any values you push onto the stack in your inline code. You add eight because you push bp, and Turbo Pascal pushes three extra words.

To return a function result, place the value you wish to return in the stack location corresponding to the return value.

You can modify any of the 8086 registers in the **inline** code. Before exiting, you must restore bp, sp, ds, and ss.

Let's look at the Assembly Language program to read a sector from disk. This program reads the parameters, calls the DOS disk read interrupt, checks for an error, cleans up the stack, and returns the error code (0 if there was no error). Note: a **ret** instruction is not needed at the end of the code--that is done by

---

[6]This is not documented in the Turbo Pascal manuals.

the end in the Turbo Pascal function. To use the Assembly
Language program in the Pascal program, assemble it, and read the
assembled values from the .LST file. This has been done in the
explorer.pas listing. (Before proceeding with program code, see
special note on letter "l" and number "1" at the beginning of this
section.)

```
; Reads sectors from disk using DOS interrupt 25h.  Assumes used
; within a function xxx(drive: byte; sector,no_sects: integer;
;       var buffer:array): integer
; Drive is a number indicating the disk drive, where 0=A, 1=B, ...
; Sector is the starting sector, no_sects tells how many sectors to
; read, and buffer is the disk buffer where the data will be stored.
;
; Returns a zero if the read was successful, otherwise returns a
; number telling an error code.

            push    bp              ;save bp register
            mov     bp,sp           ;get pointer to stack
            add     bp,8            ;point to parameters
            push    ds              ;save ds register
            mov     bx,[bp]         ;offset of disk buffer
            mov     ax,[bp+2]       ;segment of disk buffer
            mov     ds,ax           ;point to buffer for interrupt
            mov     cx,[bp+4]       ;number of sectors to read
            mov     dx,[bp+6]       ;first sector to read
            mov     al,[bp+8]       ;drive
            push    bp              ;save bp because it is destroyed
                                    ;by the interrupt
            int     25h             ;issue the DOS disk read
                                    ;interrupt
            jnc     ok              ;if there is no carry, the read
                                    ;was successful
            popf                    ;Was no good--pop disk flags
            pop     bp              ;restore bp
            mov     [bp+10],ax      ;Use error code for return
                                    ;value
            jmp     cont
ok:         popf                    ;Was good read--pop disk flags
            pop     bp              ;restore bp
            xor     ax,ax           ;Use 0 for error code and use
            mov     [bp+10],ax      ;it as the function return
                                    ;value
cont:       pop     ds              ;restore ds
            pop     bp              ;restore bp
                                    ;and continue with the code in
                                    ;the function
```

EXPLORER.PAS

Now that you can read keyboard commands and read from and write to the disk, let's examine the whole explorer.pas code. Note how the disk read and write routines are entered with the **inline** command. Also note the keyboard reading lines.

Many of the constants deal with window locations. Windows will be used much more in the later modules. Note that the disk buffer has been set up large enough to read in nine sectors at a time. The reason for this will be discussed in Chapter 5.

Also note that global variables are used to indicate the drive and sector being examined. This is so that you can locate a specialized sector in one module, and then modify it from another.

```
      Code for this section is found in
      explorl.pas.  Copy it to
      explorer.pas.
```

```
{.....................DISK EXPLORER.........................
.
. This is a program to explore disks. It has commands for decoding
. the partition, boot record, FAT, and directory, for examining
. and modifying data sectors and directories, for displaying
. files, and for getting back erased files.
.
. This is the main body of code--the one to be compiled. Because
. of the length of the code, each section is kept in a separate
. disk file which is included into the listing.
.
.........................................................}

program DiskExplorer;


{
.................................................
.
. Constant definitions
.
.................................................
}
```

```
const
   BUFLEN = 4096;          {size in bytes in disk buffer}
   BUFSECT = 9;            {number of sectors in the disk buffer}
   COMMANDX = 1;           {these four constants define the location}
   COMMANDY = 20;          {of the window for displaying command menus}
   COMMAND_RT = 79;
   COMMAND_BOT = 24;
   STATUSX = 1;            {these four constants define the location}
   STATUSY = 18;           {of the window for displaying the status}
   STATUS_RT = 79;
   STATUS_BOT = 19;
   LFTSCRN = 1;            {these four constants define the location}
   TOPSCRN = 1;            {of the main display window}
   RTSCRN = 80;
   BOTSCRN = 17;
   ERROR = -1;             {this constant is for parameter passing}



{
.....................................
.
. Type declarations
.
.....................................
}


type

   {for DOS interrupts}
   result = record
       ax,bx,cx,dx,bp,si,di,ds,es,flags: integer;
     end;

   {buffer for reading in disk sectors}
   buf = array[0..BUFLEN] of byte;



{
.....................................
.
. Global variables
.
.....................................
}
```

```
var
   finished: boolean;
   glbl_drive: byte;            {drive in use}
   glbl_sector: integer;        {sector read}
   buffer: buf;                 {buffer for disk info}
   regs: result;                {for DOS interrupts}

{
................................
.
. General subroutines
.
................................
}


{
: DiskRead
:
: This function reads sectors from disk using DOS interrupt 25h.
: Drive is a number indicating the disk drive, where 0 = A,
: 1 = B, ...  Sector is the starting sector, no_sects tells how
: many sectors to read, and buffer is the disk buffer where the
: data will be stored.
:
: Returns a zero if the read was successful, otherwise returns a
: number telling an error code.
}

function DiskRead(drive:byte; sector,no_sects:integer;
               var buffer:buf):integer;
   begin
   inline ($55/            {    push  bp}
           $8B/$EC/        {    mov   bp,sp}
           $83/$C5/$08/    {    add   bp,8      ;pt to vars}
           $1E/            {    push  ds}
           $8B/$5E/$00/    {    mov   bx,[bp]    ;offset of buff}
           $8B/$46/$02/    {    mov   ax,[bp+2]  ;segment of buf}
           $8E/$D8/        {    mov   ds,ax}
           $8B/$4E/$04/    {    mov   cx,[bp+4]  ;number of sect}
           $8B/$56/$06/    {    mov   dx,[bp+6]  ;first sector}
           $8A/$46/$08/    {    mov   al,[bp+8]  ;drive}
           $55/            {    push  bp         ;save bp}
           $CD/$25/        {    int   25h        ;read it}
           $73/$08/        {    jnc   ok}
           $9D/            {    popf             ;pop disk flags}
           $5D/            {    pop   bp         ;restore bp}
           $89/$46/$0A/    {    mov   [bp+10],ax ;return error code}
           $EB/$08/$90/    {    jmp   cont}
           $9D/            {ok: popf             ;pop disk flags}
           $5D/            {    pop   bp         ;restore bp}
           $33/$C0/        {    xor   ax,ax      ;0}
           $89/$46/$0A/    {    mov   [bp+10],ax ;return no error}
           $1F/            {cont:pop  ds         ;restore ds}
           $5D);           {    pop   bp         ;restore bp}
   end;
```

```
{
: DiskWrite
:
: This function writes sectors to disk using DOS interrupt 26h.
: The parameters and return value are the same as for DiskRead.
}

function DiskWrite(drive:byte; sector,no_sects:integer;
                   var buffer:buf):integer;
    begin
      inline ($55/               {      push  bp}
              $8B/$EC/            {      mov   bp,sp}
              $83/$C5/$08/        {      add   bp,8        ;pt to vars}
              $1E/                {      push  ds}
              $8B/$5E/$00/        {      mov   bx,[bp]      ;offset of buff}
              $8B/$46/$02/        {      mov   ax,[bp+2]    ;segment of buf}
              $8E/$D8/            {      mov   ds,ax}
              $8B/$4E/$04/        {      mov   cx,[bp+4]    ;number of sect}
              $8B/$56/$06/        {      mov   dx,[bp+6]    ;first sector}
              $8A/$46/$08/        {      mov   al,[bp+8]    ;drive}
              $55/                {      push  bp          ;save bp}
              $CD/$26/            {      int   26h         ;write it}
              $73/$08/            {      jnc   ok}
              $9D/                {      popf              ;pop disk flags}
              $5D/                {      pop   bp          ;restore bp}
              $89/$46/$0A/        {      mov   [bp+10],ax  ;return error code}
              $EB/$08/$90/        {      jmp   cont}
              $9D/                {ok:   popf              ;pop disk flags}
              $5D/                {      pop   bp          ;restore bp}
              $33/$C0/            {      xor   ax,ax       ;0}
              $89/$46/$0A/        {      mov   [bp+10],ax  ;return no error}
              $1F/                {cont:pop   ds           ;restore ds}
              $5D);              {      pop   bp          ;restore bp}
    end;


{
: beep
:
: Makes an error tone.
}

procedure beep;
    begin
        sound(400);
        delay(500);
        sound(300);
        delay(500);
        nosound;
    end;
```

```
{
: display_start_screen
:
: Displays the main menu.
}

procedure display_start_screen;
   begin
      window(1,1,80,25);
      clrscr;
      writeln('================Disk Examiner=================');
      writeln;
      writeln;
      writeln;
      writeln;
      writeln('-------------------MAIN MENU--------------------');

      { Add command information for later modules here.
        For example:

        writeln('F1:   Dump and Modify Sectors');    }

      writeln;
      writeln('F10:  Exit');
   end;



{
...................................
.
. Load in other DiskExplorer files
.
...................................
}

{add $I statements for later modules here}



{
...................................
.
. Main
.
...................................
}
```

```
begin
   glbl_drive := 0;          {initialize global drive and sector}
   glbl_sector := 0;
   finished := false;

   while not finished do begin
      display_start_screen;               {display menu}
      regs.ax := 0;                       {wait for key}
      intr($16,regs);
      if regs.ax and $ff = 0 then begin {is it a function key?}
         clrscr;
         case (regs.ax) of

            {add commands for calling other modules here}

            $4400:  {F10}
                    finished := true;
         end;
      end;
   end;
end.
```

Enter this code and save it as explorer.pas. You may also want to compile and run it.

KEY PROGRAMMING POINTS

- Use interrupts to read the keyboard and read and write disk sectors.

- Use the **inline** and **intr** commands to interface Turbo Pascal with Assembly Language.

- DOS references sectors by their logical sector number.

CHAPTER 4

EXPLORING SECTORS

Now that you know how to read and write sectors from disk, let's add a module that will let you choose a sector, display the data it contains, and modify it. Then, you will be able to explore the disk.

Each sector is composed of 512 bytes. These bytes could be text data, a program, or some type of encoded information. You'll write your program to print out the hex and ASCII values for each of these bytes. That will give you a good idea of what type of information is on the disk. Later, you will add another way of displaying the data.

You'll display 256 bytes at a time. This makes an attractive screen display of 16 rows with 16 bytes each. Display the hex values on the left side of the screen and the ASCII values on the right. To make it easier to read the hex values, separate each by a space. (See Figure 4.1.)

```
0F 03 00 00 00 00 FF FF 05 02 06 02 07 02 FF FF    . . . . . . . . . . . .
FF FF 0A 02 0B 02 0C 02 0D 02 0E 02 FF FF FF FF    . . . . . . . . . .
11 02 12 02 13 02 14 02 15 02 16 02 FF FF 18 02    . . . . . . . . . . . . .
19 02 1A 02 FF FF FF FF 1D 02 1E 02 1F 02 20 02    . . . . . . . . . .   .
FF FF 22 02 23 02 24 02 FF FF FF FF FF FF 28 02    ".#.$.(.
29 02 2A 02 2B 02 2C 02 2D 02 2E 02 2F 02 30 02    ).*.+.,.-...0.
31 02 32 02 33 02 34 02 35 02 36 02 37 02 38 02    1.2.3.4.5.6.7.8.
39 02 3A 02 3B 02 3C 02 3D 02 3E 02 3F 02 40 02    9.:.;.<.=.>.?.@.
41 02 42 02 43 02 44 02 FF FF 46 02 47 02 48 02    A.B.C.D.F.G.H.
49 02 4A 02 4B 02 4C 02 4D 02 4E 02 4F 02 50 02    I.J.K.L.M.N.O.P.
51 02 52 02 53 02 54 02 55 02 56 02 FF FF 58 02    Q.R.S.T.U.V.X.
59 02 FF FF FF FF FF FF FF FF FF FF FF FF FF FF    Y.
FF FF FF FF FF FF FF FF FF FF 66 02 FF FF 68 02    f.h.
69 02 6A 02 6B 02 6C 02 6D 02 FF FF 6F 02 FF FF    i.j.k.l.m.o.
71 02 72 02 73 02 74 02 75 02 76 02 77 02 FF FF    q.r.s.t.u.v.w.
FF FF FF FF FF FF 7C 02 7D 02 7E 02 FF FF 6C 02    {.}.~.l.

Drive: 2    Sector: 3

--------------------SECTOR DISPLAY--------------------
F1: Change Drive    F2: Read Sector    F3: Read Previous
F4: Read Next       sh-F5: Write       F6: Toggle Style
F10: Exit
```

Figure 4.1 A Sector Dump

Because only 256 bytes are displayed at a time, you'll need a command to flip between the first and last 256 bytes in the sector. Use the PgUp and PgDn keys.

You'll also need commands to change the drive and sector number.

Finally, you'll want to be able to modify the data on the disk. You'll need to have a cursor that you can move around the screen, a way to input new values, a way to figure which byte in the sector should be changed, and a way to write new values to disk.

Let's outline some of these requirements more closely, put the program together, and then experiment with it.

To display the data, divide the screen in half--the hex side and the ASCII side. Start the ASCII display at column 50. For each byte you want to display, print its two byte hex representation on the left side, skip over to the proper column on the right, and display its ASCII value. If the byte is a control code, that is, less than 32, just print a period. Thus, the screen spacing won't be messed up if you try to print characters with special meanings, such as tab or line feed.

Use variables to store the x and y location of the cursor and the **gotoxy** command to position it. Use the four arrow keys to move the cursor around. If a regular key--one that is not a cursor or function key--is pressed, the program assumes you want to change the value of the byte at the cursor location to that indicated by the key struck. If the cursor is in the hex side of the display, you'll see what hex number it is over, see if the key struck was a valid hex digit, and modify either the high or low digit of the number. Then, advance the cursor to the right to make it easier to enter several numbers in succession. If the cursor is in the ASCII side of the screen, you'll see what character it is over and change it to the character of the key just pressed.

As you can see, you'll need routines to determine whether the cursor is in the hex or ASCII side of the screen and to convert from hex characters to numbers, from hex numbers to hex characters, and from numbers to ASCII characters. You'll also need a routine to loop through 256 bytes in the disk buffer.

Begin by reading sector 0 from disk 0. Then, you'll have commands to enter a new sector number, read the previous sector, and read the next sectors. Note that you are using the disk numbers instead of letters (0=A, 1=B, 2=C, etc.). You may want to change this.

Let's go through and examine the code. Put it into a program module called sector.pas. You'll also make a few additions to explorer.pas.

> The code for this module is found in
> sector1.pas. Copy it to sector.pas.

```
{......................SECTOR.PAS......................
.
. This file contains routines for reading, decoding, and
. writing disk sectors.
.
..................................................}

{
..................................
.
. General subroutines
.
..................................
}

{
: hex
:
: Returns the hex character corresponding to num.
: Returns ERROR if num >= 16.
:
}
function hex(num:byte): char;
   begin
      if (num <= 0) or (num > 15) then
         hex := '0'
      else if (num > 0) and (num <= 9) then
         hex := chr(ord('1') + num - 1)
      else
         hex := chr(ord('A') + num - 10);
   end;



{
: unhex
:
: Returns the number corresponding to a hex character.
: Returns ERROR if not a hex character.
:
}
```

```
function unhex(letter:char): byte;
    begin
        if letter in ['0'..'9'] then
            unhex := ord(letter) - ord('0')
        else if letter in ['A'..'F'] then
            unhex := ord(letter) - ord('A') + 10
        else if letter in ['a'..'f'] then
            unhex := ord(letter) - ord('a') + 10
        else
            unhex := ERROR;
    end;

{
: get_new_drive
:
: Reads in the number for a new drive. Tries to read in a sector
: to see if it is a valid drive.  Continues prompting for a
: drive number until the read is good.
:
: Sets glbl_drive to the new drive number.
:
}

procedure get_new_drive(var data:buf);
    var
        fin: boolean;
    begin
        window(COMMANDX,COMMANDY,COMMAND_RT,COMMAND_BOT);
        clrscr;
        fin := false;
        {  note - when switching from hard drive to
            floppy, will have to first move sector no. to
            a decent sector number, or else will give errors}
        while not fin do begin
            write('Drive: ');
            readln(glbl_drive);
            if diskread(glbl_drive,glbl_sector,1,data) <> 0 then
                writeln('ERROR -- try again')
            else
                fin := true;
        end;
    end;

{
.................................
.
. Routines to figure cursor location
.
.................................
}
```

```
{
:  in_hex_side
:
:  Returns true if the cursor is in the hex display side and is
:  over a hex digit during a hex dump.
:
}

function in_hex_side(curs_x,curs_y: integer): boolean;
    begin
        if (curs_x >= LFTSCRN) and (curs_x div 3 < 16) {on ASCIISIDE}
            and (curs_y <= BOTSCRN) and (curs_y >= TOPSCRN)
            and (curs_x mod 3 <> 0) then          {not blank space}
          in_hex_side := true
        else
          in_hex_side := false;
    end;


{
:  in_ascii_side
:
:  Returns true if the cursor is in the ASCII display side during
:  a hex dump.
:
}

function in_ascii_side(curs_x,curs_y: integer): boolean;
    begin
        if (curs_x >= ASCIISIDE) and (curs_x <= ASCIISIDE + 15)
            and (curs_y <= BOTSCRN) and (curs_y >= TOPSCRN) then
          in_ascii_side := true
        else
          in_ascii_side := false;
    end;

{
.................................
.
. Routines to display data
.
.................................
}

{
:  display_status
:
:  Prints the drive and sector being examined.
:
}

procedure display_status;
    begin
        window(STATUSX,STATUSY,STATUS_RT,STATUS_BOT);
        clrscr;
        writeln('Drive: ',glbl_drive,'   Sector: ',glbl_sector);
    end;
```

```
{
: prt_data
:
: Prints a byte in hex and the corresponding ASCII value.  Puts
: the hex number in the left side of the screen, and the ASCII
: value in the right.
:
}

procedure prt_data(row,column:integer;value:byte);
   begin
     gotoxy(column,row);
     write(hex(value shr 4));        {high hexit}
     write(hex(value and $f));       {low hexit}
     gotoxy((column div 3)+ASCIISIDE,row);{to right side of screen}
     if value < 32 then
        write('.')
     else
        write(chr(value));
   end;


{
: display_page
:
: Displays the hex and ASCII values of 256 bytes from the data
: buffer. The values are displayed in 16 rows, each containing
: 16 values.  The hex numbers are displayed in the left side of
: the screen, each as two digits followed by a space. The ASCII
: characters are displayed in the right side of the screen, with
: no separator.  That is, a display may look like:
:
: 41 42 43  ... ...   ... ... ...    ABC ... ...
: 70 6f  ..   ..    ..    ..     .    po ... ..
:
: The values are taken starting with the offset-th byte.
:
}


procedure display_page(data:buf;offset:integer);
   var
     row,column:integer;
     value:byte;
   begin
     window(LFTSCRN,TOPSCRN,RTSCRN,BOTSCRN);
     clrscr;
     for row := 0 to 15 do
        for column := 0 to 15 do begin
           value := data[offset + row*16 + column];
           prt_data(row+1,3*column+1,value);
        end;
   end;
```

```
{
...................................
.
. Routines to change data in the buffer
.
...................................
}



{
: adjust_hex_data
:
: This routine is called to change the data in the buffer during a
: hex dump.  It determines whether the cursor is over a hex byte
: or an ASCII character, adjusts the old value according to the
: input_data, and then writes that into the proper location in the
: data buffer.
}
procedure adjust_hex_data(var curs_x,curs_y,input_data:integer;var
            data:buf; offset: integer);
   var
      d_loc,d_val: integer;
   begin
      if in_hex_side(curs_x,curs_y) then begin {cursor is in hex side}
         d_loc := (curs_x - 1) div 3 + (curs_y - 1)*16;
         {.....what was the old value?.....}
         d_val := unhex(chr(input_data and $ff));
         if d_val <> ERROR then begin
            if curs_x mod 3 = 1 then      {high hexit}
               data[d_loc + offset] := (data[d_loc + offset] and $f)
                  + d_val*16
            else   {low hexit}
               data[d_loc + offset] := (data[d_loc + offset]and $f0)
                  + d_val;
            prt_data(1 + d_loc div 16,(d_loc mod 16)*3 + 1,
                  data[d_loc + offset]);   {update the display}
            curs_x := curs_x + 1;   {advance the cursor}
         end
      end
      else if in_ascii_side(curs_x,curs_y) then begin {ascii side}
         d_loc := curs_x - 50 + (curs_y - 1)*16;
         data[d_loc + offset] := input_data and $ff;
         prt_data(1 + d_loc div 16,(d_loc mod 16)*3 + 1,data[d_loc +
          offset]);
         curs_x := curs_x + 1;
      end;
   end;
```

```
{
: display_data
:
: This procedure checks the style value to see whether to do a
: hex dump.  Later on, you'll make an addition to it.
:
}

procedure display_data(data: buf;offset,style: integer);
   begin
      if style = HEX_DUMP then
         display_page(data,offset*256)
      end;



{
...................................
.
. Main sector examining routines
.
...................................
}


{
: display_dump_commands
:
: This procedure displays the sector examining menu.
:
}

procedure display_dump_commands;
   begin
      window(COMMANDX,COMMANDY,COMMAND_RT,COMMAND_BOT);
      clrscr;
      writeln('----------------SECTOR DISPLAY----------------');
      writeln('F1: Change Drive F2: Read Sector F3: Read Previous');
      writeln('F4: Read Next      sh-F5: Write');
      writeln('F10: Exit');
   end;


{
: sector_dump
:
: This procedure is the main sector examining procedure.  It
: initializes some variables, then reads and acts upon the sector
: examining commands.
:
}
```

```
procedure sector_dump(var data: buf);
  var
    fin,finished: boolean;
    offset,curs_x,curs_y,style: integer;
    regs: result;
  begin
    finished := false;
    curs_x := ASCIISIDE;    {start cursor in the ASCII section}
    curs_y := 1;
    offset := 0;
    style := HEX_DUMP;        {initially, do hex dumps}
    if diskread(glbl_drive,glbl_sector,1,data) <> 0 then
      {read sector} beep;
    display_dump_commands;
    display_status;
    display_page(data,offset);
    while not finished do begin
      gotoxy(curs_x,curs_y);
      regs.ax := 0;
      intr($16,regs);              {get command}
      if regs.ax and $ff = 0 then      {is it a function key?}
        case (regs.ax) of
          $4800:  {up arrow -- move cursor up one row}
                  if curs_y > TOPSCRN then
                    curs_y := curs_y - 1;
          $4b00:  {left arrow -- move cursor left}
                  if curs_x > LFTSCRN then
                    curs_x := curs_x - 1;
          $4d00:  {right arrow -- move cursor right}
                  if curs_x < RTSCRN then
                    curs_x := curs_x + 1;
          $5000:  {down arrow -- move cursor down one row}
                  if curs_y < BOTSCRN then
                    curs_y := curs_y + 1;
          $4900,$5100:  {page up,down}
                  begin
                    offset := (offset + 1) mod 2;
                    display_data(data,offset,style);
                  end;
          $3b00:  {F1  change drive}
                  begin
                    get_new_drive(data);
                    display_dump_commands;
                    display_status;
                    display_data(data,offset,style);
                  end;
```

```
$3c00:   {F2  read sector}
         begin
             window(COMMANDX,COMMANDY,COMMAND_RT,
                     COMMAND_BOT);
             clrscr;
             fin := false;
             while not fin do begin {read in new number}
                 write('Sector: ');
                 readln(glbl_sector);
                 if diskread(glbl_drive,glbl_sector,1,
                         data)<>0 then {check for validity}
                     writeln('ERROR -- try again')
                 else
                     fin := true;
             end;
             display_dump_commands;
             display_status;
             display_data(data,offset,style);
         end;
$3d00:   {F3  read previous sector}
         if glbl_sector > 0 then begin
             glbl_sector := glbl_sector - 1;
             if diskread(glbl_drive,glbl_sector,1,data)
                 <>0 then beep;
             display_status;
             display_data(data,offset,style);
         end;
$3e00:   {F4  read next sector}
         begin
             glbl_sector := glbl_sector + 1;
             if diskread(glbl_drive,glbl_sector,1,data)
                 <>0 then {invalid or bad sector} beep;
             display_status;
             display_data(data,offset,style);
         end;
$5800:   {Shift-F5  write sector to disk}
         if diskwrite(glbl_drive,glbl_sector,1,data)
                 <>0 then beep;
$4400:   {F10 exit}
         finished := true;
    end
  else if style = HEX_DUMP then     {not a command}
      adjust_hex_data(curs_x,curs_y,regs.ax,data,offset*256)
   end;
end;
```

Note how windows are used in display_status, display_page, and display_dump_commands. Also, note how function keys and arrow keys are used as commands. Look at how the global values glbl_drive and glbl_sector are used, and how the disk information is passed in a buffer. Check how DiskRead and DiskWrite are used, and how the display procedures operate. Work through all of the procedures to make sure you have an idea of how they operate.

Before you can use this new module, you need to make some changes to explorer.pas. Save this module as sector.pas, load explorer.pas, and make the following modifications:

Code for these changes is found in expmdc4.pas (explorer modifications from Chapter 4). You can move them into explorer.pas, or just type in the additions.

In the constant declaration section, add:

```
ASCIISIDE = 50;
HEX_DUMP = 2;
```

In display_start_screen add:

```
writeln('F1:   Dump and Modify Sectors');
```

In the area for including other DiskExplorer files, add:

```
{$I b:sector.pas}
```

If you keep your source disk in a different drive, such as A or C, modify this line appropriately.

In the case statement in the main code section, add:

```
$3b00:  {F1}
      sector_dump(buffer);
```

USING THE PROGRAM

After making these changes, save the program, compile it, correct
any typos, and run it. Remember, always compile explorer.pas,
even if you are only fixing errors in sector.pas.

When you run EXPLORER, you'll see the start up menu on the screen.
Press F1 to dump and modify sectors. Next, explore your disks.
Read through the different sectors. Look at sector 0. Try sector
5. Look at sectors 23 and 35. Look at a different disk or at a
different drive. Be sure to look at both the first and last 256
bytes in each sector.

You'll probably find a variety of interesting text messages. For
example, when you look at sector 0, you'll find the DOS version
the disk was formatted with. If you look at sector 7 on a floppy
disk, you'll see the names of the files on the disk. In the next
few chapters, you'll explore these areas in more detail.

If you feel adventurous, make a backup copy of the Advanced DOS
Guide Diskette. Find the message in sector 0 (it will be in the
second half) that says "Non-System disk or disk error." Replace
this message with a different one. Make sure that it is not any
longer than the original message, and don't change any periods
that may be representing control codes. Next, use shift-F5 to
save the changes to this sector. Put the disk in drive A and
press Ctrl-Alt-Del. You'll see your new error message. You may
want to search through your disk for other messages to change.
There will be many of them on a system disk. Be very careful about
changes that you make. Don't make any changes (at least not yet)
to a hard disk or to data that isn't part of a text message.

KEY PROGRAMMING POINTS

- Sectors are the smallest disk organizational unit. They
  contain 512 bytes.

- You can find interesting messages and modify programs by
  editing sectors.

- EXPLORER uses the arrow keys to move the cursor.

CHAPTER 5

THE BOOT RECORD

You are now ready to examine the boot record--one of the disk's four organizational structures. The boot record is always located at sector 0. It contains a set of parameters that describe the diskette and a routine to boot the computer. Look at the boot record with EXPLORER.

The first three bytes contain a machine language command to jump to the booting program. This program resets the disk, examines the boot record parameters, loads in part of the root directory to check that IBMBIO.COM and IBMDOS.COM are the first files, and then reads and activates these programs. The program is followed by text messages. The boot record is terminated by the bytes 55h and AAh.

Following the jump instruction is a set of parameters which describe the disk:

Boot Record Parameters

Byte	Contents
(0)	(Jump instruction)
3-10	8 letter ASCII name of the DOS with which the disk was formatted
11-12	Bytes per sector
13	Sectors per cluster
14-15	Sectors in boot record
16	Copies of FAT
17-18	Root directory entries
19-20	Sectors per disk
21	Disk type
22-23	Sectors per FAT
24-25	Sectors per track
26-27	Sides per disk
28-29	Number of reserved sectors

The disk type byte will be:

Value	Type of Disk
F8h	Hard disk
F9h	Quad density or 3.5"
FCh	Single-sided, 9 sectors per track
FDh	Double-sided, 9 sectors per track
FEh	Single-sided, 8 sectors per track
FFh	Double-sided, 8 sectors per track

Use EXPLORER to examine the boot record of several disks. Examine as many different types as you can. Typically, you will find:

Sample Boot Record Parameters

Type	Sect	Sect/clust	Root ent	FAT sect	Sect/trk
ss, 8/trk	320	1	64	1	8
ds, 8/trk	640	2	112	1	8
ss, 9/trk	360	1	64	2	9
ds, 9/trk	720	2	112	2	9
quad. dens.	2400	1	224	7	15
3.5"	1440	2	112	3	9
10MB hard	20740	8	512	8	17
20MB hard	41752	4	512	41	17
30MB hard	62203	4	512	61	17
RAM	1984	1	128	6	9

The parameters for hard disks vary according to the partition set up and the type of hard disk. For all of the disks, there are 512 bytes per sector and 2 copies of the FAT. The flexible disks all have 2 sides and have no reserved sectors. RAM disk parameters vary widely.

By reading the boot record, a utility can learn important information about the format of the disk. For example, the first sector of the root directory can be computed from the size of the boot record, the size of the FAT, and the number of copies of the FAT. The first data sector starts after the root directory and the reserved sectors. The number of sectors tells the size of the disk or the partition. If a routine changes the FAT, it can look at the boot record to see how many copies it needs to change. You will use the information in the boot record quite frequently as you build EXPLORER.

THE BOOT RECORD AND IBM PC COMPATIBLES

The format of the boot record differs slightly on some IBM PC Compatibles. With DOS 2.11-1.03, a DOS version used by some Leading Edge computers, the eight letter name of the DOS version is missing. The rest of the disk information is the same, but it starts with byte 3. This is corrected with DOS 2.11-1.04. If you use EXPLORER with compatibles and get strange results when reading the boot record, check the boot record format to see if the eight-byte name is missing. If so, modify EXPLORER appropriately. You can also modify EXPLORER to use interrupt 21h, function 50 (see Chapter 21) to get disk information rather than reading the boot record.

BOOT.PAS

Let's add a module to EXPLORER to decode the information in the boot record. This module, boot.pas, will read in sector 0 of the disk and print out a table of the information it finds there.

```
The code for this section is found in
boot.pas.
```

```
{......................BOOT.PAS......................
.
. This file contains routines for decoding the boot record
.
..................................................}


{
: display_boot_data
:
: This procedure decodes the data in the boot record.
: See the text for an explanation of the boot record format.
:
}

procedure display_boot_data(data: buf);
   var
      i: integer;
   begin
      window(LFTSCRN,TOPSCRN,RTSCRN,BOTSCRN);
      clrscr;
      write('Formatted with ');
      for i := 3 to 10 do
         write(chr(data[i]));
      writeln;
      writeln('There are ',data[11] + 256*data[12],' bytes per ',
              'sector');
      writeln('There are ',data[13],' sectors per cluster');
      writeln('There are ',data[14] + data[15]*256,' sectors in ',
              'the boot record');
      writeln('There are ',data[16],' copies of the FAT');
      writeln('Can be up to ',data[17] + data[18]*256,' entries in ',
              'the root directory');
      writeln('There are ',data[19] + int(data[20])*256:6:0,
              'sectors');
      write('The disk is ');
      case data[21] of
         $f8:  writeln('a hard disk');
         $f9:  writeln('a quad density or 3.5 inch');
         $fc:  writeln('single-sided, 9 sectors/track');
         $fd:  writeln('double-sided, 9 sectors/track');
         $fe:  writeln('single-sided, 8 sectors/track');
         $ff:  writeln('double-sided, 8 sectors/track');
         else writeln;
      end;
      writeln('There are ',data[22] + data[23]*256,' sectors in ',
              'the FAT');
      writeln('There are ',data[24] + data[25]*256,' sectors/ ',
              'track');
      writeln('There are ',data[26] + data[27]*256,' sides');
      writeln('There are ',data[28] + data[29]*256,' reserved ',
              'sectors');
   end;
```

```
{
: display_boot_commands
:
: This procedure displays the boot record examining commands.
:
}

procedure display_boot_commands;
    begin
        window(COMMANDX,COMMANDY,COMMAND_RT,COMMAND_BOT);
        clrscr;
        writeln('------------------BOOT DISPLAY------------------');
        writeln('F1: Change Drive                    F10: Exit');
    end;


{
: boot_dump
:
: This is the main routine.  It displays the menus, and reads and
: acts upon commands.
:
}

procedure boot_dump(var data: buf);
    var
        finished:boolean;
        regs: result;
    begin
        finished := false;
        glbl_sector := 0;                       {boot record starts here}
        if diskread(glbl_drive,glbl_sector,1,data) <> 0 then {read it}
            beep;
        display_boot_commands;
        while not finished do begin
            display_boot_data(data);            {display data}
            display_status;
            regs.ax := 0;                       {get command}
            intr($16,regs);
            if regs.ax and $ff = 0 then
                case (regs.ax) of
                    $3b00:  {F1 new drive}
                            begin
                                get_new_drive(data);
                                display_boot_commands;
                                display_status;
                            end;
                    $4400:  {F10 exit}
                            finished := true;
                end;
        end;
    end;
```

After you have entered and saved this program, you need to make the following additions to explorer.pas:

> The code for these changes is found in expmdc5.pas. You will need to move the code to the appropriate part of explorer.pas or just type in the changes.

In display_start_screen, add:

writeln('F2:   Examine Boot Record');

Add:

{$I b:boot.pas}

Change the drive name if necessary.

In the main code, add:

```
$3c00:   {F2}
         boot_dump(buffer);
```

After making these additions, resave explorer.pas, compile, and correct any typos. Then run it. Use the F2 command to explore the boot record data for the same disks that you looked at before.

KEY PROGRAMMING POINTS

- The boot record contains important information about the disk's type and the size of the disk's organizational structures.

- The boot record contains a short program to start DOS.

- Utilities can learn important information about a disk by reading the boot record.

- The boot record format may vary for IBM compatible computer DOS versions, such as DOS 2.11-1.03.

CHAPTER 6

THE FILE ALLOCATION TABLE

In a moment you will examine the file allocation table--the table
DOS uses to determine what parts of the disk each file uses, what
parts are free, and what parts are bad. First, you need to
examine the way DOS stores files on the disk.

The beginning sectors of the disk are reserved for the boot
record, file allocation table, and directory. The rest of the
disk, called the **data area,** is used for storing files. DOS
divides the data area into contiguously numbered groups of
sectors, called **clusters.** DOS knows which of these clusters are
not being used. When a file is created, DOS finds a free cluster
and allocates it to the file. This is where the file will begin
to store its data. If the file is longer than that one cluster,
DOS searches for the next free cluster and also allocates it to
the file. This continues as long as the file needs more space.

A cluster is the smallest allocation unit. Even if a file is only
three bytes long, it will still use a whole cluster on the disk.
As you saw in Chapter 5, cluster size varies between one and eight
sectors. DOS chooses the size to make a trade-off between the
number of clusters DOS needs to keep track of and the amount of
space that is wasted by partially filled clusters.

The FAT is a table with an entry for each cluster. Each entry
tells whether the cluster is free, part of a file, reserved, or
bad. If the cluster is part of a file, the entry tells the
cluster number of the next cluster in the file or an end-of-file
value. The values that indicate free, reserved, or bad sectors
are outside the range of valid cluster numbers for a file. That
is, they are greater than the number of clusters on the disk or
less than the first cluster number, so there is never any
confusion.

Let's look at an example. Suppose you create a new file and the
first cluster it is given is number 10. As you write data to the
file, you will write it to the sectors contained in cluster 10.
Meanwhile, the FAT entry for cluster 10 will contain an end-of-
file marker, as it is the last cluster in the file. Suppose your
file needs more room than that in one cluster. DOS searches the

FAT, starting with the 10th entry, for the next free cluster. Suppose this is cluster 15. Your file will begin writing data to the sectors belonging to cluster 15. The FAT entry for cluster 10 will be changed to the number 15, and the entry for cluster 15 will be changed to the end-of-file marker.

To determine the clusters a file uses, trace it through the FAT, jumping from cluster entry to cluster entry. The list this creates is called the **file chain**.

The first group of sectors in the data area is called cluster 2, the next group, cluster 3, and so forth. For example, on double-sided floppies having 9 sectors per track, the data space starts with sector 12. There are 2 sectors per cluster. Thus, sectors 12-13 are cluster 2, sectors 14-15 are cluster 3, and so on. The first cluster is numbered 2 to make accessing the file allocation table easier. You'll see this in a moment.

To determine the start of the data area, look at the boot record. The first sector in the data area is:

(sectors in the boot record) + (copies of the FAT) * (sectors in the FAT) + (entries in the root directory) * 32 / (bytes per sector) + (reserved sectors)

THE 12 AND 16-BIT FATS

Let's examine the FAT in more detail. There are two styles of FATs, the **12-bit** and the **16-bit**. The 12-bit FAT is used for "small disks" such as floppies and 10MB hard drives. The 16-bit FAT is used for "large disks" such as 20MB and 30MB hard drives. The 12-bit FAT uses 12 bits to store each cluster code. Thus, it can address up to 4096 clusters (minus a few clusters for status codes). The 16-bit FAT uses a word for each cluster code. Thus, it can address almost 65,536 clusters. The 16-bit FAT was developed so that a disk with as many sectors as a 20MB hard disk could be used without having to make the cluster size incredibly large.

DOS decides whether the disk should use a 12 or 16-bit FAT when the disk is formatted. There are two ways this can be determined. In the first, check the nymber of sectors on the disk. If there are more than 31,110 sectors, a 16-bit FAT is used.[1] This corresponds to a 15M disk. If the disk is smaller, a 12-bit FAT is used. The second way is outlined in Chapter 10.

Interestingly, FDISK, the program to set up partitions on the hard disk, also decides what FAT style the DOS partition should use, but it uses a different criterion. It chooses the 16-bit FAT for any disks having more than 20,740 sectors. When the partition is formatted, DOS changes the FAT style according to the FORMAT criterion.

In the 12-bit FAT, every 3 bytes stores information for two clusters. The very first byte in the FAT contains the disk type code--the same as in the boot record. The next two bytes are ffh's. The next byte starts file information for the first cluster: number 2. Note that if you considered the first 3 bytes as containing information for clusters 0 and 1, the information for cluster 2 would start at the cluster 2 table entry. This is why clusters are numbered starting with 2. Information for the next clusters follows sequentially.

Because each cluster entry takes up one and one half bytes, cluster entries are encoded in groups of three bytes. To decode the value:

1)   Multiply the cluster value by 3

2)   Integer divide the result by 2

This gives an offset into the FAT.

---

[1]This is documented incorrectly in the DOS manual. The 15 megabyte number was derived experimentally. The actual sector cut off may be slightly different because it is not possible to choose the number of individual sectors per partition. The DOS technical manual prints the FDISK cutoff value. The method used to compute the FORMAT cutoff gets the same number as the DOS manual when the FDISK cutoff was computed.

3) If the cluster number is even:

Load the word pointed to in the FAT, and AND it with fffh.

If the cluster number is odd:

Load the word pointed to in the FAT, and shift it right four bits.

Schematically, the FAT looks like this:

```
xx ff ff      yy yy yy      yy yy yy      yy yy yy  .....
Disk type     group 1       group 2       group 3
```

For each group:
```
yy yy yy
23 x1 xx          even cluster
xx 3x 12          odd cluster
```

where 1 is the most significant hexit; 3, the least.

The cluster entry means:

Value (hex)	Meaning
000	Cluster is free.
001	Cluster is in use. Invalid chain number because clusters start with number 2.
002-fef	Cluster is in use. Entry points to next cluster in chain.
ff0-ff6	Cluster is reserved (not free, not part of file chain).
ff7	Cluster is bad.
ff8-fff	Cluster is the last cluster in a file chain (end-of-file marker).

The 16-bit FAT format is simpler. One word is used for each cluster entry. As with the 12-bit format, the first two entries identify the type of disk. The first byte is the disk type code, as used in the boot record; the next three bytes are ffh's. Every following word contains the cluster entry code.

To decode the value, multiply the cluster number by two. Read in the FAT word at this offset. This is the value.

The meaning of cluster entry values is similar to that for 12-bit FATs:

Value (hex)	Meaning
0000	Cluster is free.
0001	Cluster is in use. Invalid chain number because clusters start with number 2.
0002-ffef	Cluster is in use. Entry points to next cluster in chain.
fff0-fff6	Cluster is reserved (not free, not part of file chain).
fff7	Cluster is bad.
fff8-ffff	Cluster is the last cluster in a file chain (end-of-file marker).

For both the 12 and 16-bit file allocation tables, the first sector in a cluster is:

(cluster number - 2) * (sectors per cluster) + (number of first sector in the data area)

The FAT always begins immediately following the boot record. You can find its location by reading the boot record data table to determine the size of the boot record. Usually, the FAT begins at sector one. Because the FAT is so important, DOS keeps copies of it immediately following the original. The number of copies is also found in the boot record. Usually there are two copies: the original and a backup.

For a double-sided disk,[2] the FAT begins at sector one, is two sectors long, and is followed by one copy. Use EXPLORER to examine the file allocation table on a double-sided disk. Then, look at the copy. Try to decode a few cluster entries. Note the disk type code which starts the FAT.

---

[2]From now on, a double-sided disk will refer to a double-sided, 9 sector per track disk.

FAT.PAS

Let's look at a program to examine the FAT. It will determine where the FAT starts, its style, and its size by looking at the boot record. Then it will scan through the FAT, one sector at a time, to decode the cluster entries. You'll use characters to represent the status of each cluster.

Since the file allocation tables can be quite large, you'll read them in groups of nine sectors at a time. This is what the BUFSECT constant stands for. Use nine sectors so that for both 12 and 16-bit FATs, the last byte in your group will be a complete entry (9*512 is evenly divisible by 1.5 and 2).

The tricky part is decoding 12-bit FATs. FAT entries don't divide evenly across sector bounds, so you need to compute an adjusting factor to start your scan at the beginning of a cluster entry group. Skip over the disk type bytes (cluster entries 0 and 1).

The code for fat.pas follows. Type it in and save it as fat.pas.

```
The code for this section is found in
fat.pas.
```

```
{............................FAT.PAS......................
.
. This file contains routines for reading and decoding the
. FAT.  It will work with both the 12 and 16-bit formats.
.
....................................................}
```

```
{
.................................................
.
. General subroutines
.
.................................................
}
```

```
{
: get_disk_info
:
: This procedure reads the boot record to get information about
: the disk's format
:
}

procedure get_disk_info(var info:disk_info;var data:buf);
   begin
      if diskread(glbl_drive,0,1,data) <> 0 then {read boot record}
         beep;
      info.fat_start := data[14] + data[15]*256;
      info.fat_copies := data[16];
      info.root_entries := data[17] + data[18]*256;
      info.sect_in_fat := data[22] + data[23]*256;
      info.fat_type := 12;
      if (data[21] = $f8) and (int(data[19] + data[20]*256)>31110)
         then info.fat_type := 16;
      info.sect_per_clust := data[13];
   end;




{
..................................
.
. Main fat examining routines
.
..................................
}




{
: display_fat_data
:
: This routine graphically displays the usage of one sector from
: the FAT.  For 12-bit FATS, it computes an offset so that the data
: examined will not start in the middle of a cluster number. It
: then reads through the sector  and displays a symbol to represent
: used, free, bad, or reserved clusters.  It skips over the disk
: id code.
:
: 12-bit FATs are displayed in 10 rows of up to 35 symbols.
:
: 16-bit FATs are displayed as 8 rows of up to 32 columns.  The
: disk id bytes are skipped.
:
}
```

```
procedure display_fat_data(data:buf;offset,fat_type:integer);
  var
    row,column,off_adj,fat_off,clust_val: integer;
  begin
    window(LFTSCRN,TOPSCRN,RTSCRN,BOTSCRN);
    clrscr;
    if fat_type = 12 then begin        {12-bit}
      off_adj := -(512*offset mod 3);   {don't break a clust num}
      for row := 0 to 9 do begin
        for column := 0 to 34 do
          if (row*35 + column < 512/(3/2)) and {just display 1 sect}
          not ((row = 0) and (column < 2) and (offset = 0)){not id}
          then begin
            fat_off := 3*(row*35 + column) div 2 + off_adj +
                       (offset mod BUFSECT)*512;
            if not odd(row*35 + column) then        {even cluster}
              clust_val := data[fat_off]*16 + data[fat_off + 1]mod 16
            else            {odd cluster}
              clust_val := (data[fat_off] div 16)*256 +
                  data[fat_off+1];
            case clust_val of        {print code}
              0:              write('.');
              1:              write('1');
              2..4079:        write('*');
              4080:           write('B');
              4081..4087:     write('R');
              4088..4095:     write('*');
            end;
          end;
        writeln;
      end;
    end
    else begin {16-bit fat}
      for row := 0 to 7 do begin
        for column := 0 to 31 do
          if not ((row = 0) and (column < 2) and (offset = 0))
          then begin
            fat_off := row*8 + column + (offset mod BUFSECT)*512;
            clust_val := data[fat_off] + data[fat_off+1]*256;
            case clust_val of
              0:              write('.');
              1:              write('1');
              2..$ffef:       write('*');
              $fff0..$fff6:   write('R');
              $fff7:          write('B');
              $fff8..$ffff:   write('*');
            end;
          end;
        writeln;
      end;
    end;
  end;
```

```
{
: display_fat_exm_commands
:
: Display the FAT examination menu.
:
}

procedure display_fat_exm_commands;
   begin
      window(COMMANDX,COMMANDY,COMMAND_RT,COMMAND_BOT);
      clrscr;
      writeln('------------------FAT DISPLAY------------------');
      writeln('F1: Change Drive                    F10: Exit');
      writeln;
      writeln('. FREE  * IN USE  B BAD  R RESERVED  1 SPECIAL');
   end;




{
: fat_dump
:
: This is the main procedure.  It displays menus and data, and
: reads and acts upon commands.
:
: Because the FAT can be very large on hard disks, only a portion
: of the FAT (BUFSECT sectors) is read at a time.  The code to
: move through the FAT checks when a new section of the FAT needs
: to be read in.
:
}

procedure fat_dump(var data:buf);
   var
      finished:boolean;
      regs: result;
      offset_sector: integer;     {how many sectors into FAT}
      info: disk_info;
   begin
      finished := false;
      offset_sector := 0;         {start at beginning of FAT}
      get_disk_info(info,data);
      display_fat_exm_commands;
      glbl_sector := info.fat_start;
      if diskread(glbl_drive,glbl_sector,BUFSECT,data) <> 0 then
               {read FAT}
         beep;
      display_status;
```

```
while not finished do begin
  display_fat_data(data,offset_sector,info.fat_type);
  display_status;
  regs.ax := 0;
  intr($16,regs);          {read command}
  if regs.ax and $ff = 0 then
    case (regs.ax) of
       $4900:  {page up -- go to previous sector}
               if offset_sector <> 0 then begin
                  offset_sector := offset_sector - 1;
                  {check to see if need to read in another
                  set of sectors from disk.}
                  if offset_sector mod BUFSECT=BUFSECT - 1
                       then
                      if diskread(glbl_drive,info.fat_start
                          + offset_sector - (BUFSECT - 1),
                          BUFSECT,data) <> 0 then
                            beep;
                  {set glbl_sector to the sector being
                  examined}
                  glbl_sector := info.fat_start +
                       offset_sector;
               end;
       $5100:  {page down -- go to next sector}
               if offset_sector <> info.sect_in_fat - 1 then
                       begin
                  offset_sector := offset_sector + 1;
                  {see if need to read in another set of
                  sectors from disk}
                  if offset_sector mod BUFSECT = 0 then
                      if diskread(glbl_drive,info.fat_start +
                          offset_sector,BUFSECT,data)
                          <> 0 then
                          beep;
                  glbl_sector := info.fat_start +
                       offset_sector;
               end;
       $3b00:  {F1  new drive}
               begin
                  glbl_sector := 0;
                  get_new_drive(data);
                  offset_sector := 0;
                  get_disk_info(info,data);
                  glbl_sector := info.fat_start;
                  if diskread(glbl_drive,glbl_sector, {read FAT}
                    BUFSECT,data) <> 0 then
                      beep;
                  display_fat_exm_commands;
                  display_status;
               end;
       $4400:  {F10  exit}
               finished := true;
    end;
  end;
end;
```

You will also need to make the following additions to explorer.pas:

```
Code for these changes can be found
in expmdc6.pas
```

In the type definitions, add:

```
{stores important facts about the disk format}
disk_info = record
    fat_start: integer;
    fat_copies: byte;
    root_entries: integer;
    sect_in_fat: integer;
    fat_type: byte;
    sect_per_clust: byte;
  end;
```

To display_start_screen add:

```
writeln('F3:   Cluster by Cluster FAT Dump');
```

Also add:

```
{$I b:fat.pas}
```

and change the drive location as necessary.

To the case statement in the main routine, add:

```
$3d00:  {F3}
        fat_dump(buffer);
```

Save the changes, compile, and correct any typos. Then run EXPLORER. Use the new FAT examine feature to examine the FATs of several disks. Page through the FAT for a while, then return to the main menu and select the Sector Dump feature. You will see the actual hex information for the FAT sector you were just examining.

KEY PROGRAMMING POINTS

- Sectors are grouped into clusters. Files are composed of groups of clusters. The clusters in a file are not necessarily contiguous.

- The file allocation table tells what clusters a file uses and what clusters are unusable.

- There are two types of FATs: the 12-bit and the 16-bit. The 16-bit FAT is used for 20 and 30 megabyte drives.

- The FAT is stored after the boot record. Usually, there are two copies of the FAT.

CHAPTER 7

THE ROOT DIRECTORY

The next organizational structure is the root directory. The root directory contains information about all of the files in the root level, including volume names and root-level subdirectories. Use information in the root directory to trace files and get back erased files. By tinkering with it, you can change a file's attributes, add volume names, and prevent files from being accessed.

The root directory appears immediately following the FAT. To find its location, read the boot record and compute:

(size of boot record) + (sectors in the FAT) * (copies of the FAT)

The number of entries in the root directory is also stored in the boot record. Each entry takes up 32 bytes. Thus, the size of the root directory in sectors is:

(entries in the root directory) * 32 / (bytes per sector)

In all normal DOS disks, there are 512 bytes per sector. This formula simplifies to:

(entries in the root directory) / 16

Use EXPLORER to look at the first sector in the root directory. A double-sided diskette will start at sector 5. You will see the names of all your files, plus a lot of gibberish.

Here's what the 32 bytes in a directory entry mean:

Byte	Contents

0-10 File name and extension, in ASCII characters. Spaces are padded before the three extension letters. The period separating the name and extension is not included.

If the first byte is 0, the entry and all following directory entries are unused.

If the first character is a period (2eh) and the second is a space, the entry is for the current directory. This is used as a pointer for accessing the subdirectory.

If the first and second characters are periods followed
by a space, the entry is for the parent directory.
This is used as a pointer to move from a subdirectory
to its parent directory.

If the first byte is e5h, the file corresponding to the
entry is erased. All other file name characters and
information are unchanged. Erased directory positions
are the first to be used when a new file is added.

11   File attribute. This entry indicates certain
characteristics of the file, as follows:

Bit Position	Meaning
01	Read-only
02	Hidden
04	System
08	Volume label
10	Subdirectory
20	Archive
40	Unused
80	Unused

Hidden, system, volume, and subdirectory entries are
hidden from normal directory searches. The archive
bit is set when a file has been modified, and is
used when making backup copies of a hard disk.
The volume label only has meaning in the root
directory.

12-21   Currently unused. Reserved for future use.

22-23   Time the file was created or last changed. The word
is encoded as:

```
15 14 13 12 11   10 9 8 7 6 5   4 3 2 1 0
<  hour      >   <minute    >   <seconds / 2>
```

To decode the information:

Hour = (byte 23) SHR 3
Minute = ((byte 23) AND 111b) SHL 3 +
    ((byte 22) SHR 5)
Second = 2 * ((byte 22) AND 11111b)

24-25   Date the file was created or last changed. The word is
          encoded as:

15 14 13 12 11 10 9   8 7 6 5   4 3 2 1 0
< year - 1980   >   <month>   < day   >

To decode the information:

Year = 1980 + ((byte 25) SHR 1)
Month = 8 * ((byte 25) AND 1) + ((byte 24) SHR 5)
Day = (byte 24) AND 11111b

26-27   This word tells the first cluster allocated to the file.
          It is the starting cluster of the file chain.

28-31   A double word telling the size of the file in bytes. The
          first word is the least significant word. Note that this
          length is set by the last program to modify the file. It
          does not necessarily represent the actual length of the
          file, nor is the length necessarily computed the same way
          by different programs. Also, some programs use this
          length to determine where a program ends. Others search
          for an end-of-file character or do both.

ROOT.PAS

Let's write a program to decode the information in the root
directory. It will determine the root directory's location and
size by reading the boot record and decode the entry information
one sector at a time. An output appears in Figure 7.1.

```
     IBMBIO   .COM   RHS...    12: 0: 0   12/30/1985        2    16369
     IBMDOS   .COM   RHS...    12: 0: 0   12/30/1985       10    28477
     BOOKS    .      ....D.    13:21:44    7/ 4/1986      280        0
     COMM     .      ....D.    13:22:10    7/ 4/1986      539        0
     CONFIG   .      ....D.    13:22:16    7/ 4/1986      611        0
     DOS      .      ....D.    13:22:18    7/ 4/1986      633        0
     ED       .      ....D.    13:22:32    7/ 4/1986      750        0
     FASTBACK.       ....D.    13:18:30    7/ 4/1986      192        0
     LANGUAGE.       ....D.    13:22:46    7/ 4/1986      870        0
     MOUSE1   .      ....D.    15:21:46    8/ 1/1986       32        0
     PCPAINT  .      ....D.    18:33:20    8/ 1/1986      361        0
     PSG      .      ....D.    10: 8:10    7/18/1986       67        0
     UTILITY  .      ....D.    13:24:20    7/ 4/1986     1842        0
     WINDOWS  .      ....D.    20:42:38    8/11/1986     4397        0
     WP       .      ....D.    13:24:28    7/ 4/1986     1921        0
     AUTOEXEC.BAT    ......    10: 0:18    9/ 4/1986       47      207

     Drive: 2    Sector: 123

     ---------------ROOT DIRECTORY DISPLAY-----------------
     F1: Change Drive                        F10: Exit
```

Figure 7.1 The Root Directory

```
    The code for this section is located
    in root.pas.
```

```
{........................ROOT.PAS.........................
.
. This file contains routines for reading and decoding
. the disk directory.
.
..............................................................}


{
: display_dir_data
:
: This procedure decodes directory data.  Offset tells the number
: of sectors into the directory to start decoding.
:
}
```

```
procedure display_dir_data (data:buf;offset:integer);
  var
    entry,i,data_start: integer;
  begin
    window(LFTSCRN,TOPSCRN,RTSCRN,BOTSCRN);
    clrscr;
    for entry := 0 to 15 do begin     {16 entries per sector}
      data_start := entry*32 + (offset mod BUFSECT)*512;{find start}
      if data[data_start] = 0 then
        writeln('...UNUsED...')
      else begin   {entry is used}
        case data[data_start] of       {filename}
          $e5:  begin    {erased}
                  write('*');
                  for i := 1 to 7 do
                    write(chr(data[data_start + i]));
                  write('.');
                  for i := 8 to 10 do
                    write(chr(data[data_start + i]));
                  write(' ');
                end;
          $2e:  if data[data_start + 1] = $2e then
                  {data for parent}
                  write('...PARENT... ')
                else
                  write('...CURRENT.. ');
          else begin    {normal file}
                  for i := 0 to 7 do
                    write(chr(data[data_start + i]));
                  if (data[data_start + 11] and 8) = 0 then
                    write('.');
                  for i := 8 to 10 do
                    write(chr(data[data_start + i]));
                  if (data[data_start + 11] and 8) <> 0 then
                    write(' ');
                  write(' ');
                end;
      end;
```

```
write(' ');
{file attribute}
if (data[data_start + 11] and 1) <> 0 then   {read only}
   write('R')
else
   write('.');
if (data[data_start + 11] and 2) <> 0 then   {hidden}
   write('H')
else
   write('.');
if (data[data_start + 11] and 4) <> 0 then   {system}
   write('S')
else
   write('.');
if (data[data_start + 11] and 8) <> 0 then   {volume}
   write('V')
else
   write('.');
if (data[data_start + 11] and $10) <> 0 then   {directory}
   write('D')
else
   write('.');
if (data[data_start + 11] and $20) <> 0 then   {archive}
   write('A')
else
   write('.');
write('  ');
{time created}
write((data[data_start + 23] shr 3):2);
write(':');
write(((data[data_start + 23] and 7) shl 3 +
      (data[data_start + 22] shr 5)):2);
write(':');
write((data[data_start + 22] and 31)*2:2);
write(' ');
{date created}
write((((data[data_start + 25] and 1) shl 3) +
      (data[data_start + 24] shr 5)):2);
write('/');
write((data[data_start + 24] and 31):2);
write('/');
write((data[data_start + 25] shr 1) + 1980);
write('  ');
{first cluster}
write(data[data_start + 26] + int(data[data_start + 27])*
      256:6:0);
write('  ');
{size}
```

```
         writeln(data[data_start + 28] + int(data[data_start + 29])*
              256 + int(data[data_start + 30])*256*256 +
              int(data[data_start + 31])*256*256*256:8:0);
     end;
   end;
 end;




{
: display_root_dir_commands
:
: This procedure displays the root directory examining menu.
:
}

procedure display_root_dir_commands;
   begin
      window(COMMANDX,COMMANDY,COMMAND_RT,COMMAND_BOT);
      clrscr;
      writeln('------------ROOT DIRECTORY DISPLAY--------------');
      writeln('F1: Change Drive                F10: Exit');
   end;




{
: root_dir_dump
:
: This is the main procedure.  It displays menus and data, and
: reads and acts upon commands.  Because the directory files can
: be very large, only a portion (BUFSECT sectors) is read in at a
: time.  The commands for moving through the directory check to
: see when another section needs to be read in.
:
}

procedure root_dir_dump(var data:buf);
  var
    finished:boolean;
    regs: result;
    offset_sector,direct_start,direct_size: integer;
    info: disk_info;
  begin
    finished := false;
    offset_sector := 0;    {start at beginning}
    get_disk_info(info,data);
```

```
display_root_dir_commands;
{find start and size}
direct_start := info.fat_start + info.fat_copies*info.
   sect_in_fat;
direct_size := info.root_entries * 32 div 512;
{read in first chunk of info}
glbl_sector := direct_start;
if diskread(glbl_drive,glbl_sector,BUFSECT,data) <> 0 then
   beep;
display_status;
while not finished do begin
   display_dir_data(data,offset_sector);
   display_status;
   regs.ax := 0;
   intr($16,regs);    {get command}
   if regs.ax and $ff = 0 then
     case (regs.ax) of
        $4900:  {page up -- look at previous sector}
                if offset_sector <> 0 then begin
                   offset_sector := offset_sector - 1;
                   {see if need to read in new section
                      of directory}
                   if offset_sector mod BUFSECT = BUFSECT - 1
                      then
                      if diskread(glbl_drive,direct_start +
                         offset_sector - (BUFSECT - 1),
                         BUFSECT,data)
                         <> 0 then
                            beep;
                   glbl_sector := direct_start + offset_sector;
                end;
        $5100:  {page down -- look at next sector}
                if offset_sector <> direct_size - 1 then begin
                   offset_sector := offset_sector + 1;
                   {see if need to read in new section
                      of directory}
                   if offset_sector mod BUFSECT = 0 then
                      if diskread(glbl_drive,direct_start +
                         offset_sector,BUFSECT,data)
                         <> 0 then
                            beep;
                   glbl_sector := direct_start + offset_sector;
                end;
```

```
    $3b00:   {F1  new drive}
             begin
                glbl_sector := 0;
                get_new_drive(data);
                offset_sector := 0;
                get_disk_info(info,data);
                direct_start := info.fat_start +
                    info.fat_copies*info.sect_in_fat;
                direct_size := info.root_entries * 32 div 512;
                glbl_sector := direct_start;
                if diskread(glbl_drive,glbl_sector,
                    {read in direct}
                    BUFSECT,data) <> 0 then
                    beep;
                display_root_dir_commands;
                display_status;
             end;
    $4400:   {F10  exit}
             finished := true;
        end;
    end;
end;
```

Enter this program and save it as root.pas. Then make the following changes to explorer.pas:

```
        The code for these changes is found
        in expmdc7.pas
```

To display_start_screen add:

```
    writeln('F4:   Examine Root Directory');
```

Add:

```
{$I b:root.pas}
```

and change the drive letter if necessary.

To the case statement in the main section add:

```
$3e00:  {F4}
        root_dir_dump(buffer);
```

Save these changes, compile the program, and correct any typos. Then run it. Examine the directories of several disks.

CHANGING DIRECTORY INFORMATION

Even more useful than decoding the directory information is
modifying it. This allows you to hide a file, change a
subdirectory to a normal file so that you can process it with
editors and normal DOS file commands, or change the time and date
of a file's creation. You can also change the volume name or make
files inaccessible. In Chapter 11, you'll explore several tricks
that can be done by modifying the directory information.

With your current program, you can modify directory entries by
using the root directory examining function, then switching to the
sector dump and modify feature. You must, however, modify the
encoded information.

Let's add routines to make changing the directory entries easier.
You'll give your sector dump procedure the option to decode data
as if it were a directory sector instead of just in hex format.
You'll add routines to change the directory-decoded information.
If the cursor is over part of the file name, typing in a character
will change the file name. If the cursor is over a file
attribute, pressing any key will toggle the status of the
attribute. You may want to enhance the code so you can easily
change the time and date stamp as well. Do not add routines to
change the length and starting cluster.

To add these changes, you'll slightly alter root.pas and make some
major additions and revisions to sector.pas.

In root.pas, change the procedure declaration for display__dir__data
to:

```
procedure display_dir_data;
```

```
    Make the above change to display_dir_
    data.  The revised sector.pas is in
    sector2.pas.  Copy it to
    sector.pas
```

Make the following changes in sector.pas:

In display_data, add:

```
else
    display_dir_data(data,0);
```

In display_dump_commands, change:

```
writeln('F4: Read Next     sh-F5: Write');
```

to:

```
writeln('F4: Read Next     sh-F5: Write     F6: Toggle Style');
```

In the case statement in sector_dump add:

```
$4000:  {F6 toggle display style}
        begin
          style := (style mod 2) + 1;
          display_data(data,offset,style);
        end;
```

And change:

```
        else if style = HEX_DUMP then    {not a command}
          adjust_hex_data(curs_x,curs_y,regs.ax,data,offset*256)
```

to:

```
        else if style = HEX_DUMP then    {not a command}
          adjust_hex_data(curs_x,curs_y,regs.ax,data,offset*256)
        else  {style = DIRECT_DUMP}
          adjust_direct_data(curs_x,curs_y,regs.ax,data);
```

Add the following before the display_data procedure:

```
{
: Forward declare this procedure from root.pas so that you can
: decode sectors as portions of directory files.
}


procedure display_dir_data(data:buf;offset:integer); forward;
```

In the section containing routines to change data in the buffer,
add:

```
{
: adjust_direct_data
:
: This procedure is for adjusting data during a directory dump.
: Only the name and attributes can be modified. Modification of
: other parameters is left to the reader. To change a character
: in the name, type in the new character over that to be changed.
: To change the setting of an attribute, move to the position for
: that attribute and hit any key to toggle it.
:
}

procedure adjust_direct_data(var curs_x,curs_y,input_data:
          integer; var data: buf);
  begin
    input_data := input_data and $ff;
    case (curs_x) of
      1..8:  {name}
              begin
                data[(curs_y - 1)*32 + curs_x - 1] := input_data;
                curs_x := curs_x + 1;
              end;
      10..12: {ext}
              begin
                data[(curs_y - 1)*32 + curs_x - 2] := input_data;
                curs_x := curs_x + 1;
              end;
      16..21: {attributes}
              begin
                data[(curs_y - 1)*32 + 11] := data[(curs_y - 1)*32
                  + 11] xor (1 shl (curs_x - 16));
                curs_x := curs_x + 1;
              end;
    end;
    display_dir_data(data,0);
  end;
```

Make these changes, save them, and recompile EXPLORER, correcting any typos. Then run it. Look at the directory with Sector Dump. Toggle the display to decode directory format. Move the cursor to one of the file names and type over it. Perhaps put in lower-case characters. Try changing some attributes. Use the shift-F5 command to write these changes to disk. Make sure that you remember what you have changed. Don't make changes to important files unless you have a backup. Exit EXPLORER and use **dir** to look at the disk you have changed.

In Chapter 11, you'll modify the directory to perform some interesting tricks. In Chapter 18 (Section II), you'll modify the file attributes to move subdirectories.

KEY PROGRAMMING POINTS

- The root directory tells the names, size, and location of files and directories in the root level.

- The information for each file is stored in a 32 byte entry.

- The root directory occurs after the FAT.

- You can modify the directory to hide files and perform other tricks.

CHAPTER 8

FILES

You have already learned much about files: a file's data is stored in the data area, the directory tells the first cluster a file uses, and the file chain is stored in the FAT.

To examine a file, scan the directory until you find the file's name. Then read the starting cluster. From here, trace the file through the FAT, saving the file chain in an array. To look at a cluster, examine the sectors corresponding to the cluster. To look at the previous or next cluster in the file, simply look in the previous or next array location to see what cluster to load. This way, you avoid reading in the FAT sectors every time you want to switch clusters.

You can't just read through the chain blindly. Since you are using an array, it is possible that the number of clusters in the file will exceed the bounds of the array, though you can make the array large enough so that this is unlikely. It's also possible, though unlikely, that the file allocation table was damaged and that there is a **circular chain**. When this happens, one cluster in the file points to a previous cluster in the file, resulting in an endless loop. To prevent these occurrences, simply check that you don't exceed the array's bounds.

Once you know a file's clusters, convert the cluster numbers to sector numbers. Cluster 2 is the first sector in the data space. The start of the data space is computed from the boot record, as discussed in Chapter 6.

FILE.PAS

Let's add a module to EXPLORER to examine files. You'll begin by only examining files in the root directory. Then, you'll examine files in subdirectories as well.

There are many routines you need. You need to read in the name of the file to search for. To convert it to the directory format, you need to capitalize it, remove the extension period, and pad it with spaces. You have to read in sections of the root directory and compare their file name entries to the name of the file you're looking for. You need to trace through the FAT to read the file

chain. To do this, you need to keep track of what part of the FAT
you just read and what part contains the next file chain
information. You also need a routine to decode the information
for a given cluster in the FAT.

Let's look at the code to do this:

```
The code for this section is located
in file.pas.
```

```
{.........................FILE.PAS.........................
.
. This file contains routines for reading and displaying files
.
.........................................................}
```

```
{
.......................................
.
. General name subroutines
.
.......................................
}
```

```
{
: buf_strcmp
:
: This procedure compares the name in fn to that in the data
: buffer pointed to by offset.  Returns true if there is a match.
:
}
```

```
function buf_strcmp(fn:file_name;offset:integer;data:buf): boolean;
    var
        i: integer;
        match: boolean;
    begin
        match := true;
        i := 0;
        while match and (i < 11) do         {11 chars in a filename}
            if ord(fn[i + 1]) <> data[offset + i] then
                match := false
            else
                i := i + 1;
        if match = true then
            buf_strcmp := true
        else
            buf_strcmp := false;
    end;


{
: get_file_name
:
: This procedure reads in a file name.
:
}

procedure get_file_name(var fn: file_name);
    begin
        window(COMMANDX,COMMANDY,COMMAND_RT,COMMAND_BOT);
        clrscr;
        write('Name: ');
        readln(fn);
    end;



{
: convert_file_name
:
: This procedure takes a file name in xxx.yyy format and converts
: it to the form names stored in the directory.  That is, it
: pads out spaces and removes the '.'.  For example, MIRNA.COM is
: converted to MIRNA    COM
:
}
```

```
procedure convert_file_name(var fn:file_name);
    var
       i,fn2_ptr: integer;
       fn2: file_name;
    begin
       fn2 := '            ';
       fn2_ptr := 1;                    {pts to position in new string}
       for i := 1 to length(fn) do
          if fn[i] = '.' then
             fn2_ptr := 9
          else begin
             fn2[fn2_ptr] := upcase(fn[i]);
             fn2_ptr := fn2_ptr + 1;
          end;
       fn := fn2;
    end;
```

```
{
..................................
.
. Information printing subroutines
.
..................................
}
```

```
{
: display_status2
:
: This procedure prints information about the current sector and
: file being examined.
:
}

procedure display_status2(fn: file_name; f_length: integer);
   begin
     window(STATUSX,STATUSY,STATUS_RT,STATUS_BOT);
     clrscr;
     writeln('Drive: ',glbl_drive,'  Sector: ',glbl_sector,
             '  Name: ', fn,'  Length: ',f_length);
   end;
```

```
{
: display_file_use
:
: This procedure prints out a list of the clusters used by a file,
: in the order that they are used (the file chain).  This
: procedure is called after an attempt to move before the
: beginning of a file.  (That is, after a PREV CLUSTER command is
: entered while the beginning of the file is being examined.)
:
}

procedure display_file_use(ft:file_trace);
    var
        i: integer;
    begin
        window(LFTSCRN,TOPSCRN,RTSCRN,BOTSCRN);
        clrscr;
        writeln('File uses clusters: ');
        for i := 1 to ft.length  do
            write(ft.chain[i],' ');
        writeln;
    end;



{
: print_end_of_file
:
: This procedure prints a message to indicate that the end of the
: file being examined has been reached.
:
}

procedure print_end_of_file;
    var
        i: integer;
    begin
        window(LFTSCRN,TOPSCRN,RTSCRN,BOTSCRN);
        clrscr;
        gotoxy(20,8);
        writeln('End Of File');
    end;




{
.....................................
.
. Routines for converting between sectors and clusters,
. and for determining FAT sectors to use
.
.....................................
}
```

```
{
:  fat_sector_for
:
:  This procedure determines which section, i.e., which set of
:  BUFSECT sectors, in the FAT contains the information for a
:  particular cluster. Returns the sector number of the first
:  sector in that section.
:
:  For example, if the cluster information is contained in the
:  first BUFSECT set of FAT sectors, it will return 0; in the
:  second set, BUFSECT; and so forth.
:
}

function fat_sector_for(clust,fat_type: integer): integer;
   begin
      if fat_type = 12 then      {12 bit format}
         fat_sector_for := (round(clust * 3 / (2 * 512)) div
            BUFSECT) * BUFSECT
      else    {16 bit format}
         fat_sector_for := (round(clust * 2 / 512) div BUFSECT) *
            BUFSECT;
   end;
```

```
{
:  cluster_to_sector
:
:  This procedure returns the number of the sector at which a
:  cluster begins.
:
}

function cluster_to_sector(cur_cluster: integer;info: disk_info):
      integer;
   var
      data_area: integer;
   begin
      data_area := info.fat_start + info.fat_copies*info.sect_in_fat
                  + info.root_entries * 32 div 512;
      cluster_to_sector := (cur_cluster - 2) * info.sect_per_clust
                  + data_area;
   end;
```

```
{
: next_cluster
:
: This function returns the number of the next cluster in a file
: chain.  It does so by reading the value stored in the FAT for
: the cur_cluster location.  If the value is an end of file code,
: it returns ERROR.
:
:
}

function next_cluster(cur_cluster: integer;info: disk_info;
            var data:buf;var cur_FAT_clust:integer): integer;
  var
    new_clust_off,new_clust,next_FAT_clust: integer;
  begin
    {both 1.5 and 2 byte clusters divide evenly across 9 sectors}
    next_FAT_clust :=  fat_sector_for(cur_cluster,info.fat_type);
    if next_FAT_clust <> cur_FAT_clust then begin {read in proper}
      cur_FAT_clust := next_FAT_clust;             {section of FAT}
      if diskread(glbl_drive,info.fat_start+cur_FAT_clust,BUFSECT,
          data) <> 0 then
        beep;
    end;
    if info.fat_type = 12 then begin
      new_clust_off := (cur_cluster * 3 div 2) mod (BUFSECT*512);
           {loc}
      new_clust := data[new_clust_off] + 256*data[new_clust_off
          + 1]; {val}
      if odd(cur_cluster) then        {decode value}
        new_clust := new_clust shr 4
      else
        new_clust := new_clust and $fff;
      if (new_clust >= $ff8) and (new_clust <= $fff) then
           {eof marker}
        next_cluster := ERROR
      else
        next_cluster := new_clust;
    end
    else begin {16 bit fat}
      new_clust_off := (cur_cluster * 2) mod (BUFSECT*512);
      new_clust := data[new_clust_off] + 256*data[new_clust_off
          + 1];
      if (new_clust > $fff8) and (new_clust <= $ffff) then
           {eof marker}
        next_cluster := ERROR
      else
        next_cluster := new_clust;
    end;
  end;
```

```
{
 ................................
 .
 . Routines for finding and tracing files
 .
 ................................
}


{
: trace_file
:
: Traces the file chain through the FAT, saving the results in the
: file_trace array.
:
: The size of the array imposes an arbitrary limit on the maximum
: file size which can be examined.  This can be changed by altering
: the CHAINSIZE constant.  Using an array with a length pointer is
: much more efficient in this case than a more flexible list
: structure.
:
}
procedure trace_file(var ft:file_trace; first_cluster:integer; var
          data:buf);
   var
     info: disk_info;
     cur_loc,next_loc: integer;
   begin
     get_disk_info(info,data);
     ft.length := 1;
     ft.chain[ft.length] := first_cluster;{starts at first_cluster}
     cur_loc := -1;    {indicates FAT sector.  -1 => none was read}
     repeat     {traverse chain through FAT}
        ft.chain[ft.length + 1] := next_cluster(ft.chain[ft.length],
           info, data,cur_loc);
        ft.length := ft.length + 1;
     until (ft.chain[ft.length] = ERROR) or (ft.length = CHAINSIZE);
     ft.length := ft.length - 1;
   end;


{
: search_for_sub_file
:
: Searches through the data buffer, which contains a section of
: a directory, for an entry which matches the file name.
: Num_entries imposes a limit on the number of entries searched.
: If a matching name is found, returns an offset into the buffer.
: If not, returns ERROR.
:
}
```

```
function search_for_sub_file(fn:file_name;num_entries:integer;
        data:buf): integer;
    var
        i: integer;
        finished: boolean;
    begin
        finished := false;
        i := 0;
        while not finished and (i < num_entries) do
            {search through data}
            if buf_strcmp(fn,i*32,data) then
            {look for matching name}
                finished := true
            else
                i := i + 1;
        if finished then
            search_for_sub_file := i*32
        else
            search_for_sub_file := ERROR;
    end;



{
: search_for_file
:
: Searches through the root directory to find the information
: for a file.
:
: Will find the information for files with any attributes,
: including hidden or subdirectory.
:
: Assumes that it is called with the first BUFSECT sectors of the
: root directory in the data buffer.
:
: Returns an offset into the data buffer for the file information,
: if the file is found, or else returns ERROR.
:
}
```

```
function search_for_file(full_name: file_name; info: disk_info;
         var data: buf): integer;
    var
        found_it: boolean;
        first_cluster,i,root_size,search_size,direct_start: integer;
        ft: file_trace;
    begin
        convert_file_name(full_name);
        root_size := (info.root_entries * 32 div 512) div BUFSECT;
        direct_start := info.fat_start + info.fat_copies*info.
            sect_in_fat;
        i := 0;
        found_it := false;
        if root_size > 0 then       {number of entries to examine}
            search_size := BUFSECT * 512 div 32
        else
            search_size := info.root_entries;
        while (i <= root_size) and not found_it do begin
                {search through root}
            first_cluster := search_for_sub_file(sub_name,search_size,
                data);
            if first_cluster <> ERROR then
                found_it := true
            else begin
                i := i + 1;
                {not found, so read next section of the root}
                if diskread(glbl_drive,direct_start + i*BUFSECT,
                 BUFSECT,data) <> 0 then
                    beep;
            end;
        end;
        {root search is finished}
        search_for_file := first_cluster;
    end;


{
...................................
.
. Main routines
.
...................................
}
```

```
{
: display_file_commands
:
: This procedure displays the menu for examining files.
:
}
procedure display_file_commands;
  begin
    window(COMMANDX,COMMANDY,COMMAND_RT,COMMAND_BOT);
    clrscr;
    writeln('--------------ROOT FILE DISPLAY----------------');
    writeln('F1: Change Drive  F2: Change File  F3: Prev ',
    'Cluster');
    writeln('F4: Next Cluster  F5: Toggle Style F10: Exit');
  end;


{
: file_dump
:
: This is the main procedure.  It displays menus and data and
: reads and processes commands.  File data can be displayed as hex
: data or as directory data.
:
}

procedure file_dump(var data:buf);
   var
     finished:boolean;
     regs: result;
     offset_sector,direct_start,style,cur_sector,
         new_sector,file_ptr,first_cluster: integer;
     info: disk_info;
     fn: file_name;
     ft: file_trace;
  begin
     finished := false;
     display_file_commands;
     offset_sector := 0;
     cur_sector := 0;
     style := HEX_DUMP;
     fn := '';
     ft.length := 0;
     get_disk_info(info,data);
     direct_start := info.fat_start + info.fat_copies*info.
           sect_in_fat;
     while not finished do begin
```

```
if cur_sector <> 0 then          {display data}
    if style = DIRECT_DUMP then
        display_dir_data(data,offset_sector)
    else
        display_page(data,offset_sector*256);
display_status2(fn,ft.length);
regs.ax := 0;
intr($16,regs);                  {get command}
if regs.ax and $ff = 0 then
    case (regs.ax) of
        $4900: {page up--display previous sector in cluster}
                begin
                    if offset_sector = 0 then
                        offset_sector := style * info.sect_per_clust
                            - 1   {move two sectors at a time if
                                    displaying directory info.}
                    else
                        offset_sector := offset_sector - 1;
                    glbl_sector := cur_sector + (offset_sector
                        div style);
                end;
        $5100: {page down -- display next sector in cluster}
                begin
                    offset_sector := (offset_sector + 1) mod
                        (style * info.sect_per_clust);
                    glbl_sector := cur_sector +
                        (offset_sector div style);
                end;
        $3b00: {F1  new drive}
                begin
                    glbl_sector := 0;
                    get_new_drive(data);
                    offset_sector := 0;
                    get_disk_info(info,data);
                    direct_start := info.fat_start +
                        info.fat_copies*info.sect_in_fat;
                    display_file_commands;
                    fn := '';
                    ft.length := 0;
                    display_status2(fn,ft.length);
                end;
```

```
$3c00: {F2  new file}
       begin
         get_file_name(fn);
         display_file_commands;
         {read in start of directory info}
         if diskread(glbl_drive,direct_start,BUFSECT,
           data) <> 0 then
           beep
         else begin
           {find start of file info}
           first_cluster := search_for_file(fn,info,
           data);
           if first_cluster = ERROR then
             beep
           else begin  {file found}
             {find where it begins}
             first_cluster := data[first_cluster +
             26] + 256*data[first_cluster + 27];
             {trace the chain through the fat}
             trace_file(ft,first_cluster,data);
             {start displaying it from the
              beginning}
             file_ptr := 0;
             cur_sector := 0;
             display_file_use(ft);
           end;
         end;
       end;
$3d00: {F3  previous cluster}
       begin
         if file_ptr > 0 then begin
           file_ptr := file_ptr - 1;   {move back
                                        in chain}
           if file_ptr = 0 then begin
           {if move before start, display file use}
             cur_sector := 0;
             display_file_use(ft);
           end
           else begin
             {find start of cluster}
             cur_sector := cluster_to_sector(ft.
               chain[file_ptr],info);
             glbl_sector := cur_sector;
             offset_sector := 0;
             if diskread(glbl_drive,glbl_sector,
               info.sect_per_clust,data) <> 0 then
                 beep;
           end;
         end;
       end;
```

```
     $3e00:  {F4   next cluster}
             begin
               if file_ptr <= ft.length then begin
                 file_ptr := file_ptr + 1;
                   {move forward in chain}
                 if file_ptr > ft.length then begin
                   cur_sector := 0;
                   print_end_of_file;
                 end
                 else begin
                   {find where cluster starts}
                   cur_sector := cluster_to_sector(ft.
                     chain [file_ptr],info);
                   glbl_sector := cur_sector;
                   offset_sector := 0;
                   if diskread(glbl_drive,glbl_sector,
                     info.sect_per_clust,data) <> 0 then
                     beep;
                 end;
               end;
             end;
     $3f00:  {F5   switch style}
             style := (style mod 2) + 1;

     $4400:  {F10   exit}
             finished := true;
       end;
   end;
end;
```

Type in this code, and save it as file.pas.

There are a few things to note. When you specify a file name, it must not include the drive letters first. That is, use FAILSAFE.COM, not A:FAILSAFE.COM. Use the change drive command to change the drive. If the file can't be found, the program will beep.

If you press the display previous cluster command when the first cluster of the file is being displayed, instead of an error appearing, a screen will come up listing all the clusters that the file uses. If you press the next cluster command when the last cluster of the file is being displayed, a message will come up that the end of file has been reached. The first time you examine a file, the chain display will come up. The file can also be displayed in hex or directory format. You'll use these features in a moment.

You will also need to make some additions to explorer.pas.

```
These changes are found in expmdc8.pas
```

In the type declarations, add:

```
{a list for tracing the clusters that a file uses}
file_trace = record
    chain: array[1..CHAINSIZE] of integer;
    length: integer;
  end;


{string for filename.ext}
file_name = string[12];
```

In display_start_screen add:

```
writeln('F5:   Examine File');
```

Add:

```
{$I b:file.pas}
```

and change the drive letter if necessary. In the case statement in the main section, add:

```
$3f00:  {F5}
        file_dump(buffer);
```

Save these changes, compile the program, and correct any typos. Then run it. Examine some of the files in the root directory. Move back and forth through the clusters and the sectors in the clusters. Try some program files. If you are looking at a system disk, look at IBMBIO.COM--one of the hidden system files. Look at some text files, such as letters or batch files.

SUBDIRECTORIES

Next, look at a subdirectory. For example, if you have a subdirectory called DOS, examine it with EXPLORER by using DOS as the file name to study. Note that a file will be found. Look at its first cluster. Now toggle the display style to directory decode. It contains the same type of directory information as the root directory. In fact, subdirectories are just a blend of files and the root directory. They are files of arbitrary length containing many directory entries. As with the root directory, they can also contain entries that indicate another subdirectory.

If you want to examine a file in a subdirectory, first search through the root directory until you find an entry for the first subdirectory in the file's path. Then, search through that subdirectory file--reading each cluster in its file chain--until you come to an entry for the next subdirectory in the file's path. Continue this search until you come to the directory entry for the file itself. From here, find the starting cluster, trace the file through the FAT, and examine it, just as before.

CHANGING FILE.PAS TO WORK WITH SUBDIRECTORIES

Let's make some changes to file.pas so that it can examine files contained in subdirectories.

```
These modifications are found in
filemd.pas.  For major changes, the
whole procedure is repeated with the
changes installed.  Simply replace
old procedures with these.
```

In get_file_name, change:

```
var fn: file_name
```

to:

```
var fn: long_name
```

In display_status2, change:

```
fn: file_name
```

to:

```
fn: long_name
```

In file_dump, change:

```
fn: file_name
```

to:

```
fn: long_name
```

Then, change the function search_for_file to:

```
{
: search_for_file
:
: Searches through the directory structure to find the information
: for a file.  Starts by looking through the root directory for
: the first subdirectory, searches through that subdirectory for
: the next subdirectory entry, and so on, until the desired file
: is found.
:
: Subdirectories are searched by examining them cluster by cluster,
: using their file chain.
:
: Will find the information for files with any attributes,
: including hidden or subdirectory.
:
: Assumes that it is called with the first BUFSECT sectors of the
: root directory in the data buffer.
:
: Returns an offset into the data buffer for the file information,
: if the file is found, or else returns ERROR.
:
}
```

```
function search_for_file(full_name: long_name; info: disk_info;
          var data: buf): integer;
    var
        an_error,found_it: boolean;
        first_cluster,i,root_size,search_size,direct_start: integer;
        sub_name: file_name;
        ft: file_trace;
    begin
        an_error := false;
        parse_name(full_name,sub_name);{find first file to look for}
        convert_file_name(sub_name);
root_size := (info.root_entries * 32 div 512) div BUFSECT;
direct_start := info.fat_start + info.fat_copies*info.
    sect_in_fat;
i := 0;
found_it := false;
if root_size > 0 then      {number of entries to examine}
    search_size := BUFSECT * 512 div 32
else
    search_size := info.root_entries;
while (i <= root_size) and not found_it do begin
    {search through root}
    first_cluster := search_for_sub_file(sub_name,search_size,
     data);
    if first_cluster <> ERROR then
        found_it := true
    else begin
        i := i + 1;{not found, so read next section of the root}
        if diskread(glbl_drive,direct_start + i*BUFSECT,BUFSECT,
         data) <> 0 then
            beep;
    end;
end;
{root search is finished}
if first_cluster = ERROR then   {file not found}
    an_error := true;
while not an_error and (full_name <> '') do begin
    first_cluster := data[first_cluster + 26] + 256*
        data[first_cluster + 27];
        {find where file (next directory) begins}
    trace_file(ft,first_cluster,data);     {trace it}
    parse_name(full_name,sub_name);
        {begin looking for next file}
    convert_file_name(sub_name);
    found_it := false;
    i := 1;
```

```
      while not found_it and not an_error and (i <= ft.length)
         do begin
         glbl_sector := cluster_to_sector(ft.chain[i],info);
         if diskread(glbl_drive,glbl_sector,info.sect_per_clust,
            data) <> 0 then
            an_error := true
         else begin    {read through subdirectory chain}
            first_cluster := search_for_sub_file(sub_name,
                  info.sect_per_clust * 16, data);   {16=512/32}
            if first_cluster <> ERROR then
               found_it := true;
         end;
         i := i + 1;
      end;
      if not found_it then {file (or subdir) not there, so quit}
         an_error := true;
   end;
   if not an_error then
      search_for_file := first_cluster
   else begin
      beep;
      search_for_file := ERROR;
   end;
end;
```

In the general name subroutines, after the get_file_name
procedure, add:

```
{
: parse_name
:
: This procedure removes the first name from a file name path,
: given by full_name, and returns it in sub_name.  If full_name
: is only a file name (not a path), then returns that name and
: clears full_name.
:
: For example, if called with:    full_name = sub1\sub2\file
: would return with:              full_name = sub2\file
:                                 sub_name = sub1
:
:
}
```

```
procedure parse_name(var full_name: long_name; var sub_name:
    file_name);
    var
        slash_pos: integer;
    begin
        slash_pos := pos('\',full_name);
        if slash_pos = 0 then begin
            sub_name := full_name;
            full_name := '';
        end
        else begin
            sub_name := copy(full_name,1,slash_pos - 1);
            delete(full_name,1,slash_pos);
        end;
    end;
```

After making these changes to file.pas, save them. Then, add the following to the type definitions in explorer.pas:

```
{string for pathname\filename.ext}
long_name = string[64];
```

Save explorer.pas, compile it, and correct any typos. Then run it. Examine some files contained in subdirectories. Remember to supply the full path name but not the drive name. For example, use UTILITIES\FAILSAFE.COM, not C:UTILITIES\FAILSAFE.COM. Also, don't start file names with a \. EXPLORER will always start its search from the root directory.

KEY PROGRAMMING POINTS

- Files are groups of clusters. The first cluster number is stored in the directory. The FAT contains a list of the remaining clusters.

- To look at data in a file, find the clusters in the file chain and look at the sectors in those clusters.

- Subdirectories are files containing information in directory format. To find a file in a subdirectory, scan through each subdirectory in the path, looking for the entry for the next subdirectory in the path.

CHAPTER 9

ERASED FILES

When a file is erased, the first character in its directory entry is set to e5h, and all clusters in its file chain are marked free (0). No information is changed in the data clusters, and no other information is changed in the directory entry. If another directory entry does not use the erased entry's position, you can find the erased file's starting cluster and length. If no other files have been added to disk, all of the erased file's data will be intact; you just have to figure out how to put it together. Depending upon disk fragmentation and size, if a few files have been added, there is still a good chance that all or most of the erased file's data will be intact.

To get back an erased file, find its directory entry. From here, find its old size and first cluster. Try to piece together the file chain by looking at the data stored in clusters marked free, starting with what used to be the file's first cluster. Because DOS tries to save files contiguously, it is very likely that the clusters for the file start with and follow the first cluster. If you find a cluster with part of the file in it, add it to the chain. Of course, the cluster must be free and not previously added to the chain. After finding as much of the file as possible, write the file chain to the FAT and the FAT copies, and restore the directory entry. You also have to update the first cluster pointer and size in the directory entry.

If the subdirectory containing the file has been destroyed, first get back the subdirectory, then the file. If this is not possible, but the entry for the file can still be found--that is, that part of the subdirectory was not written over--copy down the information for that entry. Then type it in as the last entry in the root directory (or some subdirectory). Make sure the first character stays e5h. Then use the procedure outlined above to retrieve the file.

If no information about the file is left, add an entry to the root directory that has the file's name with the first character e5h. Don't worry about the file time or date. Set the attribute byte to zero, the first cluster to two, and the size to zero. Then go through the above procedure. To help you find the clusters containing the lost information, you may want to write a utility to search the disk for sectors containing particular text or byte strings.

You can also use this procedure to get back information from a hard disk that has been reformatted. It could be quite time-consuming to locate file fragments unless you write a searching utility.

ERASED.PAS

Several features are needed for a utility that retrieves erased files. It must display how many clusters the old file had and how many the rebuilt file has. It must be able to search forward and backward through the FAT for free clusters. It must be able to jump to the cluster containing any particular sector and display what has been recovered so far. Most of these features are just bookkeeping. When as much of the file is recovered as possible, the utility must be able to write changes to the disk.

Let's look at a module to do this. This module asks you for the name of the file to recover. Find the first character in the file name portion, remember it, and change it to e5h. This way, your directory search routines can find it. Use find_pos to locate the last \ in a string. The first character in the file name will follow it.

The routines next_avail_cluster and prev_avail_cluster just search through the FAT until they find a free cluster.

Because the FAT is used constantly by these routines, a separate buffer is kept just to hold a piece of the FAT. As the FAT can be much larger than this buffer, keep track of the portion of the FAT in the buffer.

One procedure in the ERASED.PAS module selects the drive and file, then calls up the procedure with the full menu of recovery commands. This is to prevent the user from accidentally reselecting a different file or drive during the middle of recovery, and to make the recovery command section simpler.

> The code for this section is located in
> erased.pas.

```
{.........................ERASED.PAS........................
.
. This file contains routines for recovering erased files.
.
........................................................}
```

```
{
....................................
.
. Routines to display information
.
....................................
}
```

```
{
: display_status3
:
: This procedure prints information about the current information
: being displayed and about the file that is being recovered.
:
}
procedure display_status3(fn:long_name;f_length,old_length:
      integer);
  begin
    window(STATUSX,STATUSY,STATUS_RT,STATUS_BOT);
    clrscr;
    writeln('Drive: ',glbl_drive,' Sector: ',glbl_sector,' Name: ',
            fn,' Length: ',f_length,' Old length: ',old_length);
  end;
```

```
{
: display_in_use_error
:
: This procedure displays a message that the cluster cannot be
: added to a file because it is already in use.
:
}
```

```
procedure display_in_use_error;
   var
      i: integer;
   begin
      window(LFTSCRN,TOPSCRN,RTSCRN,BOTSCRN);
      clrscr;
      writeln('Cluster in use, cannot chain');
      delay(2000);
   end;




{
.................................
.
. Name processing routines
.
.................................
}


{
: last_pos
:
: This procedure returns the last position where the character obj
: occurs in the string.  It is used to find the first character in
: the name of the file that was erased.
:
}

function last_pos(obj:char;str:long_name): integer;
   var
      final_pos,next_obj: integer;
      new_str: long_name;
   begin
      final_pos := 0;
      new_str := str;
      repeat   {search until there are no more obj's}
         next_obj := pos(obj,new_str);
         final_pos := final_pos + next_obj;
         delete(new_str,1,next_obj);
      until next_obj = 0;
      last_pos := final_pos;
   end;
```

```
{
.................................
.
. Conversion routines
.
.................................
}


{
: sector_to_cluster
:
: This function returns the number of the cluster containing a
: particular sector.
:
}

function sector_to_cluster(cur_sector: integer;info: disk_info):
    integer;
  var
    data_area: integer;
  begin
    data_area := info.fat_start + info.fat_copies*info.sect_in_fat
        + info.root_entries * 32 div 512;
    sector_to_cluster := (cur_sector - data_area) div info.
        sect_per_clust + 2;
  end;


{
.................................
.
. FAT processing routines
.
.................................
}


{
: next_avail_cluster
:
: This function returns the cluster number of the first free
: cluster following the cluster passed in variable cluster. It
: examines each cluster entry in the FAT following the passed
: cluster until one is found that is unused (cluster value
: will be 0).  If there are no more free clusters on the disk,
: returns ERROR.  (Note: will search through FAT until comes
: back to original cluster.)  There is no need to worry about
: which section of the FAT to examine;  next_cluster takes
: care of that.
:
}
```

```
function next_avail_cluster(cluster:integer;info: disk_info;var
      FAT:buf; var cur_FAT:integer):integer;
   var
      i,max_search: integer;
      finished: boolean;
   begin
      i := 0;
      finished := false;
      if info.fat_type = 12 then   {12 bit format}
         max_search := (info.sect_in_FAT * 512 * 2 div 3) - 2
      else    {16 bit format}
         max_search := (info.sect_in_FAT * 512 div 2) - 2;


         {Note: max_search tells the number of cluster entries in
          the FAT. i indicates how many clusters have been
          examined, so after i > max_search, have examined the
          whole FAT.  Cluster tells the current cluster being
          examined, so when cluster > max_search, have wrapped
          around from the end of the FAT to the beginning.}

      while (i < max_search) and not finished do begin
         i := i + 1;
         cluster := cluster + 1;    {look at next cluster}
         if cluster > max_search + 2 then   {wrap around FAT}
            cluster := 2;
         if next_cluster(cluster,info,FAT,cur_FAT) = 0 then
            {check value}
            finished := true;
      end;
      if finished then
         next_avail_cluster := cluster
      else
         next_avail_cluster := ERROR;
   end;




{
: prev_avail_cluster
:
: This procedure is like next_avail_cluster, except that it
: returns the cluster number for the first free cluster that is
: before the passed cluster.
:
}
```

```
function prev_avail_cluster(cluster:integer;info: disk_info;var
          FAT:buf; var cur_FAT: integer):integer;
   var
      i,max_search: integer;
      finished: boolean;
   begin
      i := 0;
      finished := false;
      if info.fat_type = 12 then
         max_search := (info.sect_in_FAT * 512 * 2 div 3) - 2
      else {16-bit FAT}
         max_search := (info.sect_in_FAT * 512 div 2) - 2;
      while (i < max_search) and not finished do begin
         i := i + 1;
         cluster := cluster - 1;
         if cluster < 2 then
            cluster := max_search + 2;
         if next_cluster(cluster,info,FAT,cur_FAT) = 0 then
            finished := true;
      end;
      if finished then
         prev_avail_cluster := cluster
      else
         prev_avail_cluster := ERROR;
   end;
```

```
{
: change_cluster_num
:
: This procedure changes the FAT to update a file chain.  new_val
: contains the number of the cluster which is to follow the cluster.
: The offset in the FAT that contains the cluster's information is
: computed and then changed. Note: nothing is written to disk.
:
: This procedure is used when writing a new chain to disk after an
: erased file has been recovered or when a new cluster has been
: added to the file chain as a file is being recovered.
:
}
```

```
procedure change_cluster_num(cluster,new_val: integer;info:
               disk_info; var FAT:buf);
   var
      clust_off: integer;
   begin
      if info.fat_type = 12 then begin   {12-bit FAT}
         clust_off := (cluster * 3 div 2) mod (BUFSECT * 512);
               {compute loc}
         if new_val = EOCHAIN then
               {use this value to indicate file end}
            new_val := $fff;
         if odd(cluster) then begin
            FAT[clust_off] := (FAT[clust_off] and $f) + ((new_val
               and $f) shl 4);
            FAT[clust_off+1] := new_val shr 4;
         end
         else begin
            FAT[clust_off] := new_val and $ff;
            FAT[clust_off + 1] := (FAT[clust_off + 1] and $f0) +
               new_val shr 8;
         end;
      end
      else begin {16-bit FAT}
         clust_off := (cluster * 2) mod (BUFSECT * 512);
         if new_val = EOCHAIN then
            new_val := $ffff;
         FAT[clust_off] := new_val and $ff;   {low byte}
         FAT[clust_off+1] := new_val shr 8;   {high byte}
      end;
   end;
```

```
{
:  write_chain_to_FAT
:
:  This procedure takes a file chain passed in ft, writes it into
:  the FAT, and writes the FAT to disk.  Because the FAT may be
:  very large, it is updated in groups of BUFSECT sectors.  Any
:  duplicate copies of the FAT are also updated.
:
}
```

```
procedure write_chain_to_FAT(ft:file_trace;info: disk_info;var
               FAT:buf);
  var
    i,fat_part,fat_size,save_size: integer;
  begin
    fat_size := info.sect_in_fat div BUFSECT; {sections in FAT}
    for fat_part := 0 to fat_size do begin {for each section..}
       if diskread(glbl_drive,info.fat_start + fat_part*BUFSECT,
              {read it}
              BUFSECT,FAT) <> 0 then
         beep;
       for i := 1 to ft.length - 1 do    {add all file chain
             elements which occur in this section}
          if fat_sector_for(ft.chain[i],info.fat_type) =
             fat_part*BUFSECT then
             change_cluster_num(ft.chain[i],ft.chain[i+1],info,
             FAT);
       {now for the end of chain marker}
       if fat_sector_for(ft.chain[ft.length],info.fat_type) =
             fat_part*BUFSECT then
          change_cluster_num(ft.chain[ft.length],EOCHAIN,info,FAT);
       {write this updated section to disk for each FAT copy}
       for i := 1 to info.fat_copies do begin

          {if the part of the FAT to be saved is the very last
          section, then all BUFSECT sectors need not be written.
          (In fact, doing so would overwrite part of the directory
          and part of the duplicate FAT.)  save_size is the number
          of sectors to save.}

         if fat_part <> fat_size then
            save_size := BUFSECT
         else
            save_size := info.sect_in_fat - BUFSECT*fat_part;
          if diskwrite(glbl_drive,info.fat_start + (i - 1)*info.
             sect_in_fat + fat_part*BUFSECT,save_size,FAT) <> 0 then
             beep;
       end;
    end;
  end;
```

```
{
..................................
.
. Procedures for getting back a particular file
.
. Note:  there are two large procedures, recover_erased_file and
. get_back files.  get_back_files is used to choose the drive and
. file to be recovered.  If the name entered was in fact erased,
. then  recover_erased_file is called.  It contains the routines
. to find free clusters, display them, add them to the chain, and
. review the clusters added to the file being erased.
.
..................................
}




{
: display_recover_commands
:
: This procedure displays the menu for getting back a particular
: erased file.
:
}

procedure display_recover_commands;
 begin
  window(COMMANDX,COMMANDY,COMMAND_RT,COMMAND_BOT);
  clrscr;
  writeln('-----------RECOVERING ERASED FILE--------------');
  writeln('F1: Add to File F2: Prev Free Clust F3: Next Free ',
  'Clust');
  writeln('F4: Toggle Style F5: Prev in File   F6: Next in File');
  writeln('F7: Goto Sector  sh-F8: Save File    F10: Exit');
 end;


{
: recover_erased_file
:
: This is the most important procedure. It processes commands
: to find free clusters, to display the data they contain in
: either hex/ASCII format or in directory format, to add clusters
: to the file being recovered, to review the progress so far, to
: move to any part of the disk (to either add that cluster or
: continue searching from there), and to save the recovered
: information from the file that was erased.
:
}
```

```
procedure recover_erased_file(fn:long_name;first_clust: integer;
          first_let:char;num_clust,direct_sect,entry_offset: integer;
          var data:buf;var cur_FAT_clust:integer);
   var
      ft: file_trace;
      FAT: buf;
      fin,finished: boolean;
      new_size: real;
      style,cur_sector,offset_sector,cur_cluster,file_ptr,i: integer;
      sect_to_read:integer;
      info: disk_info;
   begin
      FAT := data;        {this buffer just stores FAT info}
      ft.length := 0;     {file length is initially 0}
      finished := false;
      display_recover_commands;
      offset_sector := 0;
      file_ptr := 0;
      style := HEX_DUMP;
      get_disk_info(info,data);
      cur_sector := cluster_to_sector(first_clust,info);
                        {read in info from}
      glbl_sector := cur_sector;
                        {the first cluster}
      if diskread(glbl_drive,glbl_sector,info.sect_per_clust,data)
         <> 0 then
        beep;
      while not finished do begin
        if cur_sector <> 0 then      {display info}
           if style = DIRECT_DUMP then
              display_dir_data(data,offset_sector)
           else
              display_page(data,offset_sector*256);
        display_status3(fn,ft.length,num_clust);
        regs.ax := 0;        {get command}
        intr($16,regs);
        if regs.ax and $ff = 0 then
           case (regs.ax) of
              $4900:  {page up -- display prev sector in cluster}
                      begin
                         if offset_sector = 0 then
                            offset_sector := style * info.
                                  sect_per_clust - 1
                         else
                            offset_sector := offset_sector - 1;
                         glbl_sector := cur_sector + (offset_sector
                                 div style);
                      end;
```

```
$5100:   {page down -- display next cluster in sector}
         begin
             offset_sector := (offset_sector + 1) mod
                     (style * info.sect_per_clust);
             glbl_sector := cur_sector +
                     (offset_sector div style);
         end;
$3b00:   {F1  Add cluster to file}
         begin
             {compute the cluster number}
             cur_cluster := sector_to_cluster
                     (cur_sector,info);
             {is it used by another file?}
             if next_cluster(cur_cluster,info,FAT,
             cur_FAT_clust) <> 0 then
                 display_in_use_error

             {Now check if the cluster has already been
              added to the file. Note: even though you
              mark clusters in the FAT as used after
              they are added (see code which follows),
              these changes are only temporary. If the
              FAT is very large, then these changes may
              have been lost when a new FAT section was
              read in. Therefore, need to double check
              by looking through the file chain.}

             else begin
                 fin := false;
                 for i := 1 to ft.length do
                     if ft.chain[i] = cur_cluster then
                         fin := true;
                 if fin then
                     display_in_use_error
                 {cluster unused, so add it}
                 else begin
                     ft.length := ft.length + 1;
                     ft.chain[ft.length] := cur_cluster;
                     change_cluster_num(cur_cluster,
                         EOCHAIN,info, FAT);
                         {mark in FAT that cluster is}
                         {in use. This is temporary}
                 end;
             end;
         end;
```

```
$3c00:   {F2 Find previous available cluster}
         begin
             {find it}
             cur_cluster := prev_avail_cluster
                 (sector_to_cluster(cur_sector,info),info,
                 FAT,cur_FAT_clust);
             if cur_cluster <> ERROR then begin
                 cur_sector := cluster_to_sector
                     (cur_cluster, info);
                 offset_sector := 0;
                 glbl_sector := cur_sector;
                 if diskread(glbl_drive,glbl_sector,
                         {read it}
                         info.sect_per_clust,data) <> 0
                     then beep;
             end;
         end;


$3d00:   {F3 Find next available cluster}
         begin
             {find it}
             cur_cluster := next_avail_cluster
                 (sector_to_cluster(cur_sector,info), info,
                         FAT,cur_FAT_clust);
             if cur_cluster <> ERROR then begin
                 cur_sector := cluster_to_sector
                     (cur_cluster, info);
                 offset_sector := 0;
                 glbl_sector := cur_sector;
                 if diskread(glbl_drive,glbl_sector,
                     {read it} info.sect_per_clust,data)
                     <> 0 then
                         beep;
             end;
         end;


$3e00:   {F4 Toggle display style}
         style := (style mod 2) + 1;


$3f00:   {F5 Display previous cluster in file}
         begin
             {Note: the file pointer is initially set
             to 0. Thus, if this command is used
             before an F6 command, nothing will happen.
             Once F6 has been pressed, it will operate
             normally.  It is the same in function as
             the corresponding function in the display
```

```
            if file_ptr > 0 then begin
                file_ptr := file_ptr - 1;
                if file_ptr = 0 then begin
                    cur_sector := 0;
                    display_file_use(ft);
                end
                else begin
                    cur_sector := cluster_to_sector(ft.
                        chain[file_ptr],info);
                    glbl_sector := cur_sector;
                    offset_sector := 0;
                    if diskread(glbl_drive,glbl_sector,
                        info.sect_per_clust,data)
                        <> 0 then
                            beep;
                end;
            end;
        end;

$4000:  {F6 Display next cluster in file}
        begin
            {Note: file_ptr is initially set to 0, not
            to the last cluster added to a file.  So
            the first time this command is used, will
            display the very first sector added to the
            file.  Works just as the corresponding
            feature in file.pas}

            if file_ptr <= ft.length then begin
                file_ptr := file_ptr + 1;
                if file_ptr > ft.length then begin
                    cur_sector := 0;
                    print_end_of_file;
                end
                else begin
                    cur_sector := cluster_to_sector(ft.
                        chain[file_ptr],info);
                    glbl_sector := cur_sector;
                    offset_sector := 0;
                    if diskread(glbl_drive,glbl_sector,
                        info.sect_per_clust,data) <> 0 then
                        beep;
                end;
            end;
        end;
$4100:  {F7  input a sector number and go to that
        cluster. This is especially useful when the
        file may be very fragmented, and it is known
        in advance where certain sections of the
        file are.}
```

```
      begin
        window(COMMANDX,COMMANDY,COMMAND_RT,
            COMMAND_BOT);
        clrscr;
        fin := false;
        while not fin do begin
          write('Sector: ');
          readln(cur_sector);{read sector number}
          {find the sector which begins the
           cluster containing cur_sector}
          cur_sector := cluster_to_sector
              (sector_to_cluster(cur_sector,info),info);
          glbl_sector := cur_sector;
          offset_sector := 0;
          {read It}
          if diskread(glbl_drive,glbl_sector,
              info.sect_per_clust,data) <> 0 then
            writeln('ERROR -- try again')
          else
              fin := true;
        end;
        display_recover_commands;
      end;
$5b00: {shft-F8  save file}
      if ft.length <> 0 then begin
        write_chain_to_FAT(ft,info,FAT);{update FAT}
        sect_to_read := entry_offset div 512;
        if diskread(glbl_drive,direct_sect +
            sect_to_read,1, data) <> 0 then
          beep;
        {update directory}
        entry_offset := entry_offset mod 512;
        {first, fix the first letter in the
         filename}
        data[entry_offset] := ord(upcase
            (first_let));
        {now, put in the (possibly changed) first
         cluster entry}
        data[entry_offset+26] := ft.chain[1] and $ff;
        data[entry_offset+27] := ft.chain[1] shr 8;

        {if the file size was changed, update it
         to the approximate new size.  Calculate
         the new size as the number of bytes per
         cluster times the number of clusters added.
         (may be off by several bytes.)}
```

```
                    if ft.length <> num_clust then begin
                        new_size := ft.length * 512 *
                            info.sect_per_clust;
                        data[entry_offset+31] := round(new_size
                            / (256*256*256));
                        data[entry_offset+30] := round
                            ((new_size - 256*256*256*data
                            [entry_offset+31]) / (256*256));
                        data[entry_offset+29] := round((new_size
                            - 256*(data[entry_offset+30] + 256*
                            data[entry_offset+31])) / 256);
                        data[entry_offset+28] := round(new_size -
                            256*(data[entry_offset+29] + 256*data
                            [entry_offset+30] + 256*256*data
                            [entry_offset+31]));
                    end;
                    if diskwrite(glbl_drive,direct_sect +
                        sect_to_read,1, data) <> 0 then
                        beep;
                end;

        $4400:   {F10  exit}
                 finished := true;
            end;
    end;
end;



{
.................................
.
. Main routine
.
.................................
}



{
: display_get_back_files_commands
:
: This procedure displays the menu for choosing erased files
: to recover.
:
}

procedure display_get_back_files_commands;
    begin
        window(COMMANDX,COMMANDY,COMMAND_RT,COMMAND_BOT);
        clrscr;
        writeln('----------GET BACK AN ERASED FILE--------------');
        writeln('F1: Change Drive   F2: Choose File    F10: Exit');
    end;
```

```
{
: get_back_files
:
: This procedure processes commands to choose an erased file.
: If the directory entry is found for the erased file, then this
: procedure calls recover_erased_file.
:
}

procedure get_back_files(var data:buf);
  var
     finished:boolean;
     regs: result;
     direct_start,first_let_pos,file_loc,direct_sect,old_size,
         first_clust: Integer;
     info: disk_info;
     fn: long_name;
     first_let: char;
     FAT_clust: integer;
  begin
     finished := false;
     display_get_back_files_commands;
     fn := '';
     get_disk_info(info,data);
     direct_start := info.fat_start + info.fat_copies*info.
         sect_in_fat;
     while not finished do begin
        display_status;
        regs.ax := 0;
        intr($16,regs);     {get commands}
        if regs.ax and $ff = 0 then
           case (regs.ax) of
              $3b00:  {Fl new drive}
                      begin
                      glbl_sector := 0;
                      get_new_drive(data);
                      get_disk_info(info,data);
                      direct_start := info.fat_start +
                          Info.fat_copies*info.sect_in_fat;
                      display_get_back_files_commands;
                      display_status;
                  end;
```

```
$3c00:   {F2 new file}
         begin
             get_file_name(fn);
             display_get_back_files_commands;
             {find first letter in filename}
             first_let_pos := last_pos('\',fn) + 1;
             first_let := fn[first_let_pos];
             {change it to the erased indicator}
             fn[first_let_pos] := chr($e5);
             {search for the directory entry}
             glbl_sector := direct_start;
             if diskread(glbl_drive,glbl_sector,
                 BUFSECT,data) <> 0 then
                 beep;
             file_loc := search_for_file(fn,info,data);
             if file_loc = ERROR then   {not found}
                 beep
             else begin
                 {directory entry found.  Find its old
                  size and old first cluster}
                 FAT_clust := -1;
                 clrscr;
                 direct_sect := glbl_sector;
                 first_clust := data[file_loc+26] + 256*
                         data[file_loc + 27];
                 old_size := ((data[file_loc+28] +
                             data[file_loc+29]*256 +
                             data[file_loc+30]*256*256 +
                             data[file_loc+31]*256*256)
                             shr 9) + 1;
                 {bytes divided by 512 = sectors}
                 old_size := round(old_size/info.
                     sect_per_clust);  {= number of clusters}
                 writeln('Need to get ',old_size,
                     ' clusters');
                 {if first cluster is in use, then the
                  file is damaged}
                 if next_cluster(first_clust,info,data,
                     FAT_clust) <> 0 then
                     writeln('File is Partly Damaged');
                 delay(2000);
                 recover_erased_file(fn,first_clust,
                         first_let, old_size,direct_sect,
                         file_loc,data,FAT_clust);
                 display_get_back_files_commands;
                 display_status;
             end;
         end;

$4400:   {F10  exit}
         finished := true;
     end;
  end;
end;
```

Type in this module, and save it as erased.pas. Then, make the following changes to explorer.pas.

```
Code for these changes is found in
expmdc9.pas.
```

In display_start_screen, add:

```
writeln('F6:   Get Back Erased File');
```

Add:

```
{$I b:erased.pas}
```

and change the drive letter as necessary.

In the case statement in the main section of code, add:

```
$4000:  {F6}
        get_back_files(buffer);
```

Save these changes, compile the code, and correct any typos. Then, try it out. Format a disk and copy a few text and program files to it. Start by erasing one of the text files. Use EXPLORER to retrieve it. Next, try one of the program files. You may also want to make, fill, and remove some subdirectories and then try to retrieve them. Erase a few text files at once, and then try to retrieve them.

Note: this routine changes the FAT. Test it on a trial disk before you use it for a real application. This way, if you made a mistake while typing in the code, you will be able to catch it before modifying the FAT on an important disk.

KEY PROGRAMMING POINTS

- When a file is erased, the first byte in the directory entry is changed to e5h. All entries in the file chain are set to zero.

- You can attempt to recover an erased file by manually examining all free clusters and piecing together a file chain.

CHAPTER 10

THE PARTITION TABLE

Only hard disks have a partition table. This table tells where each partition begins, its size, whether it is a DOS partition and, if so, the type of FAT, and whether it is the **active partition**. There is also a small program which checks through the partition table to verify that it is valid, then loads in and executes the boot record of the active partition.

The partition table is located on the very first sector of the hard disk: head 0, track 0, sector 1. Note that you are using the head, track, sector numbering scheme, not the DOS numbering scheme. DOS disk calls treat the first sector of the active partition as sector 0. The partition table is located before the start of all partitions, so you cannot read the information in the partition table with DOS calls. You need to use the BIOS disk calls. The BIOS calls can access any sector on the disk, regardless of the partition it is in.

You'll first see how the partition information is stored, then how to use the BIOS disk calls, and finally, how to write a module to examine the partition table.

The partition table starts at the 446th (1beh) byte of the first sector and is 64 bytes long. It is followed by the bytes 55h aah. It contains four identical contiguous 16 byte blocks. The first block is for partition one, the second is for partition two, and so on.

The format of each block is:

Byte	Meaning
0	Boot indicator. Contains 80h for the active partition, 0 for all others. Only onc partition can be active at a time.
1	Side where the partition begins.
2	The low six bits are the sector where the partition begins. The high two bits are the high two bits of the track where the partition begins. This is the format that the BIOS call uses.

3	Low order eight bits of the track where the partition begins.
4	System indicator. Contains 4 if the partition is a DOS partition that uses a 16-bit FAT, 1 if the partition is a DOS partition that uses a 12-bit FAT, and 0 otherwise.
5	Side where partition ends.
6	Low order six bits are the sector where the partition ends. The high two bits are the high two bits of the ending track number.
7	Low eight bits of the track number where the partition ends.
8-11	Double word containing the number of sectors preceding the partition. Low order word is stored first.
12-15	Double word containing the number of sectors in the partition. Low order word is stored first.

FDISK sets up the partition table. FORMAT sometimes modifies it.

READING THE PARTITION TABLE WITH BIOS

In order to read the partition table, you need to use a BIOS disk read. As mentioned, BIOS specifies sectors with the drive, side, track, sector format. Floppy drives and hard drives are numbered separately. Floppy drives are 0-3, and hard drives are 80h-87h. Thus, the B drive is drive 1 while the C drive (assuming it is a hard drive) is drive 80h. The side normally ranges between 0 and 7. The track is a 10-bit number; the sector number is 6 bits.

To read from a disk, use BIOS interrupt 13h. You can call it with the **intr** instruction. Set up the parameters so that:

AH	=	2
AL	=	number of sectors to read (must not be 0)
CL	=	low 6 bits are the sector number
	=	high 2 bits are high 2 bits of the track
CH	=	low 8 bits of the track
DL	=	drive
DH	=	side
ES:BX	=	pointer to buffer where the read information will be stored

This interrupt is discussed in detail in Section II.

PART.PAS

Here's the code for a module to examine the partition table. Note that it asks for the number of the hard disk to examine where 0 is the first hard disk, 1 the second, and so on. The program adds 80h to this to convert it to the BIOS disk numbering scheme.

```
The code for this section is found in
part.pas.
```

```
{ ........................PART.PAS........................
.
. This file contains routines for reading and decoding
. the partition.
.
.................................................................}
```

```
{
: get_new_hard_drive
:
: This procedure reads in the number of the hard disk from
: which the partition information is read.  0 is for the first
: hard drive, 1 the second, and so on.
:
}
procedure get_new_hard_drive(var disk_num:integer);
   begin
      window(COMMANDX,COMMANDY,COMMAND_RT,COMMAND_BOT);
      clrscr;
      write('Number of hard drive: ');
      readln(disk_num);
   end;


{
: decode_partition
:
: This procedure decodes the partition information.  See the text
: for details.
:
}
procedure decode_partition(disk:integer;data: buf);
   const
      TABLE_OFF = $1be;
   var
      i: integer;
   begin
      window(LFTSCRN,TOPSCRN,RTSCRN,BOTSCRN+1);
      clrscr;
      writeln('Hard disk: ',disk,' Sector: 0  Track: 0  Head: 0');
      for i := 0 to 3 do begin
         write('Partition ',i+1,' is ');
         if data[TABLE_OFF + i*16] <> $80 then
            write('not ');
         writeln('active');
         write('It is ');
         if data[TABLE_OFF + i*16 + 4] = 1 then
            write('a 12-bit FAT ')
         else if data[TABLE_OFF + i*16 + 4] = 4 then
            write('a 16-bit FAT ')
         else
            write('not a ');
         writeln('DOS partition');
         writeln('It starts at head ',data[TABLE_OFF + i*16 + 1],'
            sector ',
            data[TABLE_OFF + i*16 + 2],' track ',
            data[TABLE_OFF + i*16 + 3]);
```

```
        writeln('It ends at head ',data[TABLE_OFF + i*16 + 5],
                ' sector ',
            data[TABLE_OFF + i*16 + 6],' track ',
            data[TABLE_OFF + i*16 + 7]);
    end;
  end;



{
: display_part_commands
:
: This procedure displays the partition examining menu.
:
}

procedure display_part_commands;
    begin
        window(COMMANDX,COMMANDY,COMMAND_RT,COMMAND_BOT);
        clrscr;
        writeln('------------EXAMINE PARTITION TABLE------------');
        writeln('F1: Choose Drive                    F10: Exit');
    end;



{
: partition_dump
:
: This is the main procedure.  It reads and displays data and
: processes commands.
:
: Because the partition record cannot be accessed through DOS,
: this procedure uses a BIOS disk read call.
:
}

procedure partition_dump(var data:buf);
    var
        finished: boolean;
        regs: result;
        disk: integer;
    begin
        finished := false;
        clrscr;
        display_part_commands;
        while not finished do begin
            regs.ax := 0;
            intr($16,regs);            {get command}
            if regs.ax and $ff = 0 then
                case (regs.ax) of
```

```
                $3b00:    {F1 new drive}
                      begin
                        get_new_hard_drive(disk);
                        display_part_commands;
                        {set up registers to read the disk using
                         a BIOS call.  Note that hard disks are
                         numbered starting with $80}
                        regs.ax := $201;
                        regs.dx := $80 + disk;
                        regs.cx := 1;
                        regs.es := seg(data);
                        regs.bx := ofs(data);
                        intr($13,regs);    {read it}
                        decode_partition(disk,data);
                      end;
                $4400:    {F10   exit}
                        finished := true;
                  end;
         end;
      end;
```

Enter this code and save it as part.pas. Then make the following changes to explorer.pas.

```
The changes in this section are found
in expmdc10.pas.
```

In display_start_screen, add:

writeln('F7:   Examine Partition');

Add:

{$I b:part.pas}

and change the drive if necessary.

In the case statement in the main section, add:

```
$4100:  {F7}
        partition_dump(buffer);
```

Save these changes, compile EXPLORER, and correct any typos. Then, look at the partition table on your hard disk.

KEY PROGRAMMING POINTS

- Only hard disks have partitions.

- The partition table tells the location of each partition. For DOS partitions, it tells the FAT type. The table also indicates which partition will be used for booting.

- The partition table is located at head 0, track 0, sector 1. To read it, you must use a BIOS interrupt.

CHAPTER 11

DISK PROBLEMS
AND DISK TRICKS

Several problems, although rare, can occur with the FAT. They result when the FAT is not updated properly, as can occur if a disk is removed in the middle of a FAT write, if the media degrades, or by general program malfunction, such as a partial overwrite of the FAT. These problems are cross-linked, circularly-linked, and partially-linked files and orphaned clusters. Another problem is file fragmentation.

Cross-linked files occur when the file chain for one file points into the file chain for another file. Both files end up sharing a group of clusters. To write a program to check for cross links, set up a buffer, called COUNT, that is the same size as the FAT, and fill it with zeros. Then, read the file chain for each file on the disk. This will require some sort of tree search, such as a depth-first sort, to read through all the directory structures. Every time you use a cluster in a file chain, increment the cluster value in COUNT. When you are finished, any entries in COUNT greater than one indicate cross-links. You might want to print out the name of the files that cause cross-links. To fix cross-links, decide which file gets the clusters in the overlapping area and break the other file chains at that point. You may also need to search through the disk to attach the end of the chain to other clusters. You can fix cross-links with EXPLORER but may wish to enhance the code before doing so.

Circularly-linked files are files that are cross-linked with themselves. That is, a cluster in the chain points to an earlier cluster in the chain. The file has no end. A very high number for an entry in COUNT indicates a circularly-linked file. To correct it, find where the circle starts and break the link. Again, you may have to attach the end of the chain to other clusters in order to repair the file.

You might like to experiment with a circularly-linked file. Make a copy of a text file that is over a cluster long. Use EXPLORER to find its first cluster. Change the FAT entry for this cluster to point to itself. Next, leave EXPLORER and TYPE the file. The first cluster will keep repeating until enough bytes have been printed to satisfy the file length. Now, use EXPLORER to change the directory length entry to make the file seem much longer. TYPE the file again.

Partially-linked files have their file chain broken before the end-of-file marker is reached. The last cluster has either a free or bad entry. To correct them, change the last entry or the one before it to the end-of-file marker. You may also have to chain in more clusters to fully repair the file.

Orphaned clusters are clusters that are marked as used but are not part of any file chain. Thus, they are never read, but they prevent the disk space from being used. To detect them, compare COUNT with the FAT. Any entries that are 0 in COUNT but not free or bad in the FAT correspond to orphaned clusters. To fix the problem, you can either change the orphaned clusters to free clusters or create a new file and attach them to it. CHKDSK does this.

File fragmentation causes performance problems. When a new cluster is needed for a file, the next free cluster is used. If a file was written after the first file was created but before the first file needed a new cluster, the new cluster will not be contiguous to the rest of the file. In fact, after heavy disk use, files can become very spread out across disks. This is a particular problem for hard disks. When a file is fragmented, it takes more time to access it because the disk head needs to travel a lot. Looking at the file chain will show how a file is fragmented. So will CHKDSK. To defragment a file, read through the file chain until you come to a cluster discontinuity. Then, reorganize the file to remove this discontinuity.

For example, suppose the cluster at the end of the contiguous section is 7 and the next cluster is 20. Move the data in cluster 8 to a different location and fix the file chain which points to it. Move the data in cluster 20 to cluster 8. Also fix that file chain. Continue this process with each file until they are all contiguous. This will take a great deal of time.

The algorithm as outlined is a bit crude; giving it more intelligence will improve its speed. For example, if the disk is not very full, you could search for a contiguous set of free clusters the length of the fragmented file and move the whole file to that section. The best way to defragment files on a floppy disk is to COPY them to a blank disk. Unfortunately, this means rebuilding the directory structure.

DISK TRICKS

Now that you have thoroughly examined disks and problems they can have, try some simple tricks. To start, try changing the date and time entries in the directory to a very large value. See how DOS lists them. Next, hide a subdirectory and DIR the disk. Use the ALT key to put the extended characters, such as the British pound sign, into a file name. Also, try putting lowercase characters in a file name and the volume. They will show up in the directory listing, but you will be unable to access the files. You could make a very simple security program based on this feature.

Make a title for your disk. The title is a block of text, perhaps several lines long, that gives more information than the volume label does. Using a hex display with the sector dump feature of EXPLORER, set up several dummy subdirectory entries in a directory. Type messages in the file name space. Be sure to use some lowercase characters in them; this way, the fake files can never be accessed. You can use tabs, carriage returns, and line feeds to clean up the display. For example, put tab characters in the extension and a few line feeds on the very last line. The result result could look like:

```
Volume in drive B has no label
Directory of  B:\

COMMAND  COM    23210   3-07-85   1:43p
*******           <DIR>   15-31-0107  19:63p
This is           <DIR>    7-22-0103  18:55p
a disk            <DIR>    7-22-0103  18:55p
title             <DIR>    7-22-0103  18:55p



                  <DIR>    7-22-0103  18:55p
PART     COM    30549   6-05-86   1:46p
       7 File(s)    308224 bytes free
```

To get rid of a disk title, make the first character of each title entry e5h.

In Chapter 18, you'll learn to reorganize your disk by moving whole directories from one directory to another. You'll also learn to set up several directory names for one directory. For example, you can have a directory called \BOOKPROG and one called \PROGRAMS\DOSBOOK\UTILITY that both contain the same files.

KEY PROGRAMMING POINTS

- Several disk problems can arise. The most serious stem from FAT damage.

- You can achieve several interesting effects by modifying the information stored in the disk organizational structures.

CHAPTER 12

CHANGING DOS
INTERNAL COMMANDS

You'll use EXPLORER for one more trick--changing DOS internal commands. Using EXPLORER, examine COMMAND.COM. After the first few clusters, you will find the DOS error messages and a list of the DOS internal commands. Each command appears as ASCII text followed by a four-byte jump pointer to its code. If you want to change the name for a DOS internal command, just change its name here and save the changes to disk. Get back to DOS and type COMMAND. This will reload the command shell with your changes. Be sure that you do not change the four-byte pointer. If you want to make a command unusable, use lower-case letters. For example, you could change DEL to del.

Of course, making this change is a bit dangerous. You might accidentally change part of the pointer or forget how you changed the commands if you ever wanted to get them back. Let's write a program to get around these problems. It will know what the old commands were, and it will read COMMAND.COM to see how they were changed. You can tell it the command you want to change and type in the new command word. It will truncate it and update the file. You can also tell it to revert to DOS's settings.

The only problem is that COMMAND.COM is different for each version of DOS. Fortunately, the command list is the same in each; only its location and the four-byte pointers change. Your program must know how to tell which version of COMMAND.COM it is examining, the offset of the commands in that version, and the offset of each command in the command table.

Each version of COMMAND.COM has a text string which identifies its version. A simple program was written to scan COMMAND.COM for this message, print its location, and then print the offset of the command table. The offset of the commands within the table is the same for each version.

DOS Version	Identifier	Offset	Command Table Offset
2.0	2.00	3839	14794
2.1	2.10	3839	14813
3.0	3.00	3993	18794
3.1	3.10	4283	19473
3.2	3.20	4571	20017

The identifier is an ASCII string. Look at the NEWCMMDS listing
to see the table of command offsets within the command table.

NEWCMMDS

Let's examine the program to change DOS internal commands.
It asks for the name of the command file--in case you have
renamed it so as not to change the original COMMAND.COM--
and scans it for the version identifier. From this, it
determines the offset of the command table and reads the
file up to this point. It then reads in the current command
names and displays them along with the original DOS command
names. It asks for the number of and new text for the
command to change, and, as an option, will restore the
original command name. New command names are converted to
uppercase. Changes can be saved or abandoned.

```
The code for this section is found in
newcmmds.pas.  newcmmds.com is ready
to run.
```

```pascal
{modifies the names of DOS internal commands}

program make_new_commands;
   const
      NUM_CMDS = 20;      {number of command names}
   type
     {stores a command name}
      name_str = string[6];

     {stores offset, original and new command names.  Original
      name is never changed.}
      command_info = record
         offset: integer;
         old_name: name_str;
         new_name: name_str;
       end;

     {stores info for each command}
      commands = array[1..NUM_CMDS] of command_info;

     {for checking DOS version}
      ver_str = string[4];

     {for reading from disk}
      buf = array[0..5119] of byte;      {40 blocks of 128 bytes}
```

135

```
var
    cmd_file: file;
    cmd_name: string[14];
    cnt: integer;
    cmd_list: commands;
    buffer: buf;
    cmd_offset,old_offset: integer;
    ver_num: ver_str;



{
: initialize_cmd_list
:
: This procedure sets up the offsets and original command names
: for the command list.
:
: Just uses the major commands.  Could be changed to modify all
: of the commands or error messages as well.
:
}

    procedure initialize_cmd_list(var cl:commands);
        begin
            cl[1].offset := 0;
            cl[1].old_name := 'DIR';
            cl[2].offset := 7;
            cl[2].old_name := 'RENAME';
            cl[3].offset := 17;
            cl[3].old_name := 'REN';
            cl[4].offset := 24;
            cl[4].old_name := 'ERASE';
            cl[5].offset := 33;
            cl[5].old_name := 'DEL';
            cl[6].offset := 40;
            cl[6].old_name := 'TYPE';
            cl[7].offset := 55;
            cl[7].old_name := 'COPY';
            cl[8].offset := 72;
            cl[8].old_name := 'DATE';
            cl[9].offset := 80;
            cl[9].old_name := 'TIME';
            cl[10].offset := 88;
            cl[10].old_name := 'VER';
            cl[11].offset := 95;
            cl[11].old_name := 'VOL';
            cl[12].offset := 102;
            cl[12].old_name := 'CD';
```

```
        cl[13].offset := 108;
        cl[13].old_name := 'CHDIR';
        cl[14].offset := 117;
        cl[14].old_name := 'MD';
        cl[15].offset := 123;
        cl[15].old_name := 'MKDIR';
        cl[16].offset := 132;
        cl[16].old_name := 'RD';
        cl[17].offset := 138;
        cl[17].old_name := 'RMDIR';
        cl[18].offset := 173;
        cl[18].old_name := 'PROMPT';
        cl[19].offset := 183;
        cl[19].old_name := 'PATH';
        cl[20].offset := 245;
        cl[20].old_name := 'CLS';
    end;
```

```
{
:  make_string
:
:  This procedure reads for bytes from the buffer and converts
:  them to string format.
:
}

 procedure make_string(var st: ver_str;buffer: buf;offset: integer);
     var
        i: integer;
        n: ver_str;
     begin
        for i := 1 to 4 do
           n[i] := chr(buffer[offset + i - 1]);
        st := copy(n,1,4);
     end;
```

```
{
:  get_ver_num
:
:  This procedure reads the command file and checks for the
:  version number identifier.  The identifier is returned in
:  ver_num.  Returns ERR! if no identifier found.
:
}
```

```
procedure get_ver_num(var ver_num:ver_str;var buffer:buf;var
    cmd_file:file);
  begin
    blockread(cmd_file,buffer,40);
    make_string(ver_num,buffer,3839);
    if (ver_num <> '2.00') and (ver_num <> '2.10') then begin
      make_string(ver_num,buffer,3993);
      if ver_num <> '3.00' then begin
        make_string(ver_num,buffer,4283);
        if ver_num <> '3.10' then begin
          make_string(ver_num,buffer,4571);
          if ver_num <> '3.20' then
            ver_num := 'ERR!';
        end;
      end;
    end;
  end;
```

```
{
: get_offset
:
: This function takes the version identifier as its argument and
: returns the location of the command table.  5120 bytes are
: subtracted because they have already been read in to determine
: the version number.
:
}

  function get_offset(ver_num: ver_str): integer;
    begin
      if ver_num = '2.00' then
        get_offset := 14794 - 5120
      else if ver_num = '2.10' then
        get_offset := 14813 - 5120
      else if ver_num = '3.00' then
        get_offset := 18794 - 5120
      else if ver_num = '3.10' then
        get_offset := 19473 - 5120
      else
        get_offset := 20017 - 5120;
    end;
```

```
{
: make_string2
:
: This procedure is exactly like make_string, except that it
: returns a string of type name_str.
:
}
```

```
procedure make_string2(var st: name_str;buffer: buf;offset,
    len: integer);
var
    i: integer;
    n: name_str;
begin
    for i := 1 to len do
        n[i] := chr(buffer[offset + i - 1]);
    st := copy(n,1,len);
end;
```

```
{
: read_commands
:
: This procedure reads through the command file until it comes to
: the portion containing the command table.  It then reads the
: names stored in the command table.
:
}

procedure read_commands(var offset:integer; var cmd_list:commands;
    var buffer:buf; var cmd_file: file);
var
    i: integer;
begin
    {read up to section with list}
    while offset > 5120 do begin
        blockread(cmd_file,buffer,40);
        offset := offset - 5120;
    end;
    {read section with list}
    blockread(cmd_file,buffer,(offset + cmd_list[NUM_CMDS].
        offset) div 128 + 1);
    {read command names}
    for i := 1 to NUM_CMDS do
        make_string2(cmd_list[i].new_name,buffer,offset +
            cmd_list[i].offset,length(cmd_list[i].old_name));
end;
```

```
{
: display_commands
:
: This procedure prints out the original and new command names.
:
}
```

```
procedure display_commands(cmd_list: commands);
   var
      i: integer;
   begin
      clrscr;
      writeln('#        Old Command       New Command');
      writeln;
      for i := 1 to NUM_CMDS do begin
         write(i);
         gotoxy(8,i+2);
         write(cmd_list[i].old_name);
         gotoxy(25,i+2);
         writeln(cmd_list[i].new_name);
      end;
   end;
```

```
{
: prepare_to_write
:
: This procedure repositions the file pointer to the beginning of
: the command table section.
:
}
```

```
procedure prepare_to_write(offset: integer;var cmd_file: file);
   var
      buffer: buf;
   begin
      offset := offset + 5120;
      close(cmd_file);
      reset(cmd_file);
      while offset > 5120 do begin
         blockread(cmd_file,buffer,40);
         offset := offset - 5120;
      end;
   end;
```

```
{
: modify_commands
:
: This procedure prompts for changes to command names.  It changes
: all new names to uppercase commands.  You may want to remove
: this feature.
:
}
```

```
procedure modify_commands(cmd_list:commands;var buffer:buf;
     var cmd_file: file; offset:integer);
  var
     i,j: integer;
     changed_name: string[6];
  begin
     repeat
        display_commands(cmd_list);
        write('Enter # to change, or 100 to write, or 200 to ',
            'exit: ');
        readln(i);
        if i = 100 then {write changes}
           blockwrite(cmd_file,buffer,(offset + cmd_list
              [NUM_CMDS].offset) div 128 + 1)
        else if (i > 0) and (i <= NUM_CMDS) then begin
              {change command}
           write('New name (<Return> to restore original): ');
           readln(changed_name);
           if length(changed_name) = 0 then {restore original}
              changed_name := cmd_list[i].old_name;
           for j := 1 to length(cmd_list[i].old_name) do begin
              {change command list}
              cmd_list[i].new_name[j] := upcase(changed_name[j]);
              {change buffer}
              buffer[offset + cmd_list[i].offset + j - 1] :=
                  ord(upcase(changed_name[j]));
           end;
        end;
     until i = 200;
  end;


begin   {main}
   clrscr;
   writeln('===============DOS Command Changer================');
   writeln;
   writeln;
   writeln;
   write('Enter the name of the COMMAND.COM file to change: ');
   readln(cmd_name);
   assign(cmd_file,cmd_name);
   reset(cmd_file);
   initialize_cmd_list(cmd_list);
   get_ver_num(ver_num,buffer,cmd_file);
   writeln('Version is DOS ',ver_num);
   delay(2000);
   if ver_num <> 'ERR!' then begin
      cmd_offset := get_offset(ver_num);
      old_offset := cmd_offset;
      read_commands(cmd_offset,cmd_list,buffer,cmd_file);
      prepare_to_write(old_offset,cmd_file);
      modify_commands(cmd_list,buffer,cmd_file,cmd_offset);
   end;
   close(cmd_file);
end.
```

Type in this code and save it as newcmmds.pas. Compile it and correct any typos. Then run it. The first time you run it, you may want to copy your COMMAND.COM to a different file, say COMMAND2.COM, so that if there are any typos, your file won't be damaged. Change some command names. Save the new version. Exit, then load the changed command file by typing COMMAND (or COMMAND2, etc.). Try using the original command names and the new ones.

One application of the program is to rename the DEL and erase commands to prevent accidental erasure of files. You may want to modify this program to give it fancier input and screen features.

KEY PROGRAMMING POINTS

- COMMAND.COM contains the DOS internal command names. Their location differs for each DOS version.

- You can change the DOS commands by editing COMMAND.COM.

SECTION II

BIOS AND DOS INTERRUPTS
AND UTILITY PROGRAMMING

In this section, we will learn how to use BIOS and DOS interrupts
to fully exploit the computer. We will see how to use the screen,
keyboard, disks, and memory, see how to set up utilities, and
explore many other useful interrupts--including those Microsoft
won't tell you about.

You'll use interrupts in most Assembly Language programs you write
and in high-level language programs as well. For example, you can
use interrupts to access disk files from Assembly Language or to
do graphics in C.

Note: The letter "l" and the number "1" are represented in the
program code by the same character. **In no case is the letter "l"
used as a variable name.**

CHAPTER 13

AN INTRODUCTION TO INTERRUPTS AND ASSEMBLY LANGUAGE PROGRAMMING

13 An Introduction to Interrupts and Assembly Language Programming

Interrupts[1] are a set of subroutines that perform elemental interactions between the computer and peripherals. Unlike normal subroutines that you include in programs, they are always present in the computer. There are basically two kinds of interrupts: **BIOS interrupts** and **DOS interrupts**. BIOS interrupts are coded in ROM. They perform the most basic interactions with hardware. For example, there are BIOS interrupts to read a sector from the disk, to write a character to the screen, and to read the position of the light pen.

Most **DOS interrupts** also deal with interactions between the computer and its peripherals, but they are at a much higher level. They deal with files and directories or input lines and memory allocation by building off of the BIOS interrupts. DOS interrupts are loaded every time DOS is booted. They change from DOS version to DOS version. Later DOS versions correct and enhance interrupts from the previous version and add new interrupts.

There is a special assembly language command--the int command-- that is used to call interrupts. Each interrupt has a number associated with it and uses a set of parameters which are passed in the 8086 registers.

Many interrupts have subfeatures. Each subfeature is called a **function**. When you call an interrupt that has several functions, you place the function number in the ah register. For example, interrupt 21h is the main DOS interrupt. It has close to a hundred functions. If you wanted to call interrupt 21h, function 1, you would:

```
{set parameters}
mov ah,1    ;select function
int 21h     ;do interrupt
```

As you can see, using interrupts is simple. When you need a service that an interrupt provides, simply set up the registers and call the interrupt.

---

[1]In this section, when we use the term **interrupt** we are referring only to **software interrupts**. In the next chapter we will also examine **hardware interrupts**.

Throughout this text, hexadecimal notation will be used for the interrupt numbers and decimal notation for the function values. This way, it will always be clear which is the interrupt number and which is the function number.

WHY USE INTERRUPTS?

Interrupts are very useful because they provide portability, speed software design and debugging, and provide an easy but powerful way to gain access to all hardware. As new types of hardware are introduced, the interrupts are updated to support them. This gives programs **portability**--the ability to be moved from one machine environment to another.

Interrupts also save much time and aggravation by taking care of all the nitty-gritty details of hardware. For example, BIOS worries about how to program the disk drive controller and compensate for errors. You simply ask to read a certain sector. This is crucial because there are so many hardware devices, and programs that deal directly with the hardware are very hard to debug.

Further, interrupts save program space; an interrupt call is short, and a subroutine is long. You also don't need to develop a library of standard routines to transport between programs.

By using DOS interrupts, you don't need to worry about any of the internal structures used to deal with files and devices. You simply say "look for this file" or "add this line to that file" instead of decoding file chains and directories.

INTERRUPTS AND UTILITIES

Interrupts are the heart of most utilities; they provide nearly complete control over all parts of the computer. In the following chapters, you will examine the different interrupts and see how to use them to add power to your programs. You will learn to deal with the screen, keyboard, disks, and memory. You will also discuss interrupts that deal with interrupts, with programs, and with a miscellany of important programming structures.

Note: There are several hundred functions which interrupts perform. Many later interrupts improve upon earlier interrupts. The earlier ones remain to insure upward compatibility. These early interrupts are not discussed if the later interrupts perform the same functions better and with less programming hassle.

THE STRUCTURE OF AN ASSEMBLY LANGUAGE PROGRAM

Throughout the rest of this book, you will learn many techniques to deal with Assembly Language programs. Assembly Language is the most elemental computer language.[2] It is composed of short mnemonics that translate directly into numbers. These numbers tell the computer to execute very basic instructions, such as "add two bytes" or "read a byte in memory."

Assembly Language programs are collections of Assembly Language instructions. Any set of numbers can be loaded into the computer's memory at any place and treated as an Assembly Language program. More than likely, such programs would hang the machine. When you write Assembly Language programs, you must give them a certain structure so that they behave properly.

The overall structure of an Assembly Language program has three parts: initialization, operation, and termination. The **initialization section** sets up all registers and data areas so that they are ready for program operation. Initialization code might also check what type of a computer and peripherals are being used. The **operation section** contains the main body of code--all the instructions for input, data processing, and output. The **termination section** contains instructions to fix any "messes" the program may have made and to return safely to DOS.

There are a few other concepts that must be discussed. BIOS and DOS reserve some sections at the bottom and top of memory addresses. DOS keeps track of what memory is free. When a program is run, it is usually loaded into the lowest available memory slot. When it finishes, the memory that it used is free again. Programs can be made **memory resident**. When they finish,

---

[2]I do not count microcode because it is not RAM executable.

the memory space they used is left reserved. Subsequent programs that run are loaded in the memory that follows them. Thus, the memory resident program is always loaded, and its instructions can be executed at any time they are branched to. You will examine this in detail in Section III.

Programs can also **spawn** children. The **parent** program tells DOS to execute the **child** program (or subprogram). It is loaded in memory following the parent, and when it terminates, control is returned to the parent. In a sense, all programs that you write are really children of DOS.

Spawning is a very powerful technique. It allows you to use any other program while your own is operating. For example, suppose you write a LISP[3] interpreter. LISP interpreters can read in several sets of definitions--LISP programs--at once. Suppose you need to make a small change in one of these files. The LISP interpreter could then spawn a text processor. When you exit the word processor, you return to LISP without needing to start over. You could also execute a DOS command, such as FORMAT, if you run out of disk space in the middle of a program.

Programs can also be loaded as overlays. They replace a section of code not currently in use. This can be used to operate programs too large to load in memory all at once.

Assembled and compiled programs are given the extension EXE or COM. COM programs must be smaller than 64K and can't have a stack segment. They take up less room on disk and load faster than EXE files. EXE files can be much longer than 64K and can use as many different types of segments as they like. When COM and EXE programs are executed, the segment registers are also set up in slightly different ways. It is best to make small utilities COM files. The easiest way to do this is to use only one segment and start the program with an **org 100h** command. After linking, use the EXE2BIN command.

DOS uses standard input and output devices. Normally, the input device is the keyboard, and the output device is the screen. These can be changed with the > and < DOS commands. Programs cannot tell if the input or output is redirected, and it really

---

[3]LISP is a computer language.

doesn't matter. Programs that are written using the DOS commands to read from and write to the standard input and output devices work just the same, no matter the redirection.

PROGRAMMING HINTS

Assembly Language programs can become quite difficult to understand unless a few precautions are taken. Use a structured style as much as possible. Have only one entrance and exit point in code blocks. Use subroutines. Give meaningful names to your variables. Thoroughly comment your programs while you are writing them.

Whenever possible, use interrupts rather than direct hardware programming. This makes your routines more readable and portable. Remember, interrupts often return results in the registers and flags. If you need one of the registers that is changed, be sure to save it before you call the interrupt.

If you write an EXE program, set up a stack of at least 800 bytes more than what your program needs. More is preferable. Your routine won't need this much, but memory resident utilities might. Don't assume that a particular peripheral is attached. If you need a device, such as a graphics board, check for it before you use it.

KEY PROGRAMMING POINTS

- Interrupts provide an easy-to-use link between the computer and its peripherals.

- Using interrupts makes programs shorter, more portable, easier to develop, and easier to update.

- Give Assembly Language programs a start, middle, and end.

- Use a structured programming style. Avoid assumptions.

- Creating child programs is a powerful technique.

- Make utility programs COM files if possible.

CHAPTER 14

OUTPUT: SCREEN CONTROL, TEXT, AND GRAPHICS

The computer can display information in several formats. With a color monitor and adaptor, it can display 40 or 80 columns of text or graphics. With a monochrome adaptor, it can display 80 columns of text. The display style is called the **screen mode**. When the computer is started, it always uses the 80 column text display format. If you want to use a different format, you must change the screen mode.

Set the screen mode with interrupt 10h, function 0. Setting the screen mode also clears the screen. (Before proceeding with program code, see special note on letter "l" and number "1" at the beginning of this section.)

```
-------------------------------------------------
Operation:  Set screen mode
Version:    BIOS
Interrupt:  10h
Function:   0
Called with:
    AH = 0
    AL = screen mode
Returns with:
    AX destroyed
-------------------------------------------------
```

The screen mode number is:

Number	Display Style	Adaptor
0	B & W 40 column text	CGA, EGA, 3270
1	color 40 column text	CGA, EGA, 3270
2	B & W 80 column text	CGA, EGA, 3270
3	color 80 column text	CGA, EGA, 3270
4	color medium resolution graphics	CGA, EGA, 3270
5	B & W medium resolution graphics	CGA, EGA, 3270
6	high resolution graphics	CGA, EGA, 3270
7	monochrome 80 column text	MONO, EGA, 3270
13	16 color medium resolution graphics	EGA
14	16 color high resolution graphics	EGA
15	4 shade monochrome graphics	EGA
16	4 or 16 color super high res graphics	EGA
48	3270 graphics	3270

CHOOSING THE VIDEO PAGE

With the CGA and EGA boards, text modes can have several pages. Each page contains a screen of data. Switching pages determines which screen of data is displayed. The page being displayed is called the **active page.** Pages are numbered starting with 0.

One page can be written to while another is displayed. This makes screen changes much smoother. Do all your updating on a non-displayed page. When you are finished, make it the active page. You can also store help information on one page and flip to it at your request.

When the screen mode is set, the active page is set to page 0. Unless you need to use more than one display page (most applications don't), don't worry about setting the active page. Just always use page 0.

The 40 column text screens have eight pages; the 80 column text screens have four. The monochrome 80 column text screen only has one page when used with the monochrome adaptor. When used with the EGA adaptor, it has eight pages.

```
-------------------------------------------------
Operation:  Sets active page
Version:    BIOS
Interrupt:  10h
Function:   5
Called with:
    AH = 5
    AL = page number
Returns with:
    AX destroyed
-------------------------------------------------
```

DETERMINING SCREEN MODE AND ACTIVE PAGE

When a program starts, it is usually a good idea to reset the screen mode. This way, the mode and active page are guaranteed. For some applications, such as pop-up memory resident utilities, you must know the old screen mode and active page before you change it.

```
--------------------------------------------------
Operation:  Determines screen mode and active page
Version:    BIOS
Interrupt:  10h
Function:   15
Called with:
    AH = 15
Returns with:
    AL = screen mode
    AH = characters columns on the screen
    BH = active page
--------------------------------------------------
```

CLEARING THE SCREEN

To clear all the display pages or to clear the screen when using the monochrome adaptor, reset the screen mode. To clear just one display page, print 50 line feeds and a carriage return.

PRINTING CHARACTERS

There are several different interrupts to print characters. Each is slightly different in how it processes control characters, attributes, and the cursor.

When printing out raw hex data, choose an interrupt that doesn't process control codes. This will keep your screen lined up. If you are printing out text data and do not need to keep track of lines or process control codes, use an interrupt that processes control codes. It will automatically account for carriage returns, tabs, and line feeds.

Interrupts that move the cursor place it at the end of the character last printed. If you use a non-cursor adjusting interrupt, you must set the cursor before you print each character.

The **attribute** is a byte that describes the character's color and intensity. On a color text screen, the low hexit controls the color of the character, the high hexit the color of the background. Usually, setting the background to an intense color causes the character to blink.

Hexit Value	Color
0	black
1	blue
2	green
3	cyan
4	red
5	purple
6	brown
7	white
8	gray
9	intense blue
10	intense green
11	intense cyan
12	intense red
13	intense purple
14	yellow
15	intense white

Attribute meaning is more complicated on a monochrome screen. Again, the low hexit controls the foreground, and the high hexit controls the background. If the low three bits of a hexit are 0, the character (or background) will be black; otherwise, it will be white. Setting the high bit of the low hexit makes the character more intense. Setting the high bit of the high hexit makes the character blink. The special combination of 001 for the low three bits makes the character underlined. The following table presents sample attributes. Use the intensity and blink bits to enhance them.

Value (hex)	Result
00	blank
01	underlined
07	normal
70	reversed
77	solid white

In graphics modes, the attribute selects the color of the character. If the high bit of the attribute is set, the character will be exclusive ORed (XORed) to the screen. Use the XOR mode if you want to recover what was stored underneath the characters. The first time you XOR it, the character will appear. The second time you XOR it, it will disappear.

Some interrupts ask which display page to write to. This parameter is ignored for modes, such as the graphics modes, that do not have multiple display pages.

```
----------------------------------------------------
Operation:  Print a character.
            Attribute set.
            Cursor not moved.
            Control characters not processed.
Version:    BIOS
Interrupt:  10h
Function:   9
Called With:
    AH = 9
    AL = character
    BL = attribute
    BH = page
    CX = number of times to repeat character.  Will not line feed
    in graphics modes.  Will line feed in text modes.
Returns With:
    AX destroyed
----------------------------------------------------
```

```
----------------------------------------------------
Operation:  Print a character.
            Attribute not changed.
            Cursor not moved.
            Control characters not processed.
Version:    BIOS
Interrupt:  10h
Function:   10
Called With:
    AH = 10
    AL = character
    BL = attribute if in graphics mode, otherwise unused.
    BH = page
    CX = number of times to repeat character.  Will not line feed
    in graphics modes.  Will line feed in text modes.
Returns With:
    AX destroyed
----------------------------------------------------
```

```
-------------------------------------------------
Operation:  Prints a character.
            Attribute not changed.
            Control codes processed.
            Cursor adjusted.
            Writes to active page.
Version:    BIOS
Interrupt:  10h
Function:   14
Called With:
    AH = 14
    AL = character
    BL = attribute if in graphics mode, otherwise unused
Returns With:
    AX destroyed
-------------------------------------------------


-------------------------------------------------
Operation:  Prints a character.
            Attribute not changed.
            Control codes processed.
            Cursor adjusted.
            Writes to active page.
            Output redirected to standard output device.
Version:    DOS 1.0 -
Interrupt:  21h
Function:   2
Called With:
    AH = 2
    DL = character
Returns With:
    AX destroyed
-------------------------------------------------
```

DISPLAYING STRINGS

A few interrupts print strings, but they do not use the standard
string format. They require the length to be known in advance or
use a $ as the terminator. Both are unnatural constraints. The
normal string terminator (that in C and Unix) is a 0; it is a
hassle for a programmer to have to count text length. You need to
write your own routine, which receives a pointer to a text string
and repeatedly calls interrupt 10h, 14 until a 0 is reached. If
you want the output to be redirected, replace the interrupt call
with one to interrupt 21h, function 2.

> The code for this routine is found in dispstr.asm.

```
;
;disp_msg
;
;       Displays an ASCIIZ string.
;       Called with:
;           DS:DX pointing to string
;       Returns with:
;           all registers preserved
;
;       The color for graphics modes is set up as a constant.  You
;       may wish to make this a passed parameter.
;
;       The characters will always be displayed on the screen.  To
;       allow for output redirection, change the interrupt 10h
;       call to an interrupt 21h, function 2 call, and set up the
;       registers appropriately.
;


disp_msg        proc        near
                push        ax
                push        bx
                push        si
                mov         bl,FORE_COLOR       ;color for graphics modes
                mov         si,dx               ;point to string
d_m_loop:       mov         al,[si]             ;load character
                cmp         al,0                ;check for end
                je          d_m_end
                mov         ah,0eh              ;print char service
                int         10h                 ;print it
                inc         si
                jmp         d_m_loop
d_m_end:        pop         si
                pop         bx
                pop         ax
                ret
disp_msg        endp
```

CONTROLLING THE CURSORS

If you use character printing services which do not adjust the cursors, or if you want to print to a screen location other than the current cursor position, you must be able to read and set the cursor position. A separate cursor is kept for each display page. The cursor calls apply to text and graphics screens.

```
-------------------------------------------------
Operation:  Set cursor position.
Version:  BIOS
Interrupt:  10h
Function:  2
Called With:
    AH = 2
    DH = row
    DL = column
    BH = page.  Set to 0 for graphics modes.
Returns With:
    AX destroyed
-------------------------------------------------
```

```
-------------------------------------------------
Operation:  Read cursor position.
Version:  BIOS
Interrupt:  10h
Function:  3
Called With:
    AH = 3
    BH = page number.  Set to 0 for graphics modes.
Returns With:
    AX destroyed
    CH = starting cursor line (see following interrupt)
    CL = ending cursor line
    DH = row
    DL = column
-------------------------------------------------
```

```
-----------------------------------------------
Operation:  Change cursor shape
Version:    BIOS
Interrupt:  10h
Function:   1
Called With:
    AH = 1
    CH = starting cursor line
    CL = ending cursor line
    The cursor lines are numbered starting with 0 at the top of a
    character block.  With the color graphics board, there are
    eight cursor lines; on the monochrome and EGA, fourteen.  If
    the starting line is below the ending line, the cursor will
    wrap around to the top of the character block.  Do not use
    numbers over 15.
Returns With:
    AX destroyed.
-----------------------------------------------
```

READING CHARACTERS FROM THE SCREEN

A fancy input routine or memory resident routine may need to read
what characters are displayed at a certain location on the screen.
The screen reading interrupt reads characters from graphics and
text screens. If you need to read a large area of the screen or
if speed is crucial, you may want to read the screen memory
directly (see Chapter 36).

```
-----------------------------------------------
Operation:  Reads character at cursor position.
        Will read from the graphics screen.
Version:    BIOS
Interrupt:  10h
Function:   8
Called With:
    AH = 8
    BH = display page.  Not used for graphics modes.
Returns With:
    AL = character
    AH = attribute
-----------------------------------------------
```

GRAPHICS

There are several interrupts which deal with graphics. For a complete discussion of graphics programming, see <u>Advanced IBM PC Graphics</u>. To display graphics, you must first choose one of the graphics modes, using the set mode interrupt.

```
-----------------------------------------------
Operation:  Select palette or background color.
         Use for medium resolution graphics.
Version:  BIOS
Interrupt:  10h
Function:  11
Called With:
    AH = 11
    BH = 0 to select background color
       = 1 to select palette
    BL = background color or palette number
Returns With:
    AX destroyed
-----------------------------------------------
```

Use this interrupt for medium resolution graphics. The background color can be any one of the 16 color values. There are four different palettes. Set the background color before choosing the palette. To select palette 0 or 1, use a background color from 0 -15 and select palette 0 or 1. To use palette 2 or 3, add 16 to the background color.

Palette No.	Color 1	Color 2	Color 3
0	green	red	brown
1	cyan	purple	white
2	int. green	int. red	yellow
3	int. cyan	int. purple	int. white

The following two interrupts are for setting and reading dots. The coordinate values are not range checked. They will wrap around if they exceed screen boundaries.

```
-------------------------------------------------------
Operation:  Set dot.
Version:  BIOS
Interrupt:  10h
Function:  12
Called With:
    AH = 12
    AL = dot color.  Set high bit to XOR.
    CX = x coordinate
    DX = y coordinate
Returns With:
    AX destroyed
-------------------------------------------------------

-------------------------------------------------------
Operation:  Read dot.
Version:  BIOS
Interrupt:  10h
Function:  13
Called With:
    AH = 13
    CX = x coordinate
    DX = y coordinate
Returns With:
    AL = color value of the dot
-------------------------------------------------------
```

KEY PROGRAMMING POINTS

- There are several text and graphics screen modes. Some modes have more than one page. The displayed page is called the active page.

- Characters can be read from and written to the text and graphics screens.

- The character printing interrupts differ in their processing of control codes, use of color, and movement of the cursor.

- There are several graphics-related interrupts.

CHAPTER 15

INPUT: THE KEYBOARD, LIGHT PEN, AND MOUSE

There are many interrupt functions to read from the keyboard. They differ in the way they report keystrokes, wait for keystrokes, echo keystrokes, and process Ctrl-Break. There are two types of keystrokes: **ASCII keys** and **extended keys**. The ASCII keys are the alphanumeric and control keys; the extended keys include the function and cursor keys. Some interrupts require two calls to report an extended key result. If your routine needs to take function and cursor keys for input, use an interrupt that returns extended character codes immediately.

Some interrupts wait for a keystroke before returning. Others report if a keystroke is ready and return right away. If you are using a routine that repeatedly performs an operation until a command modifies the operation, use an interrupt that doesn't wait for keyboard input. For example, you would not want to wait for input if you were rotating an object until a command changed the direction of rotation or if you were programming a video game.

Some interrupts echo the input character to the screen. This is useful for routines that read text character by character. If you do not want the keystroke to appear, as you would not in the two previous examples, use a non-echoing interrupt. Non-echoing interrupts are also good for reading passwords. Echoing interrupts do not print control codes.

If the BREAK ON command has not been given to DOS, some keyboard interrupts will still go to the Ctrl-Break routine after a Ctrl-Break has been pressed. Use these routines for input when you need the option to break out of a program at the time input is taken and are not sure if the BREAK switch will be set to ON or OFF.

The DOS interrupts read from the standard input device. This is normally the keyboard but can be redirected. The BIOS interrupts read from the keyboard.

The key that has been struck is indicated by a two-byte return code containing a normal byte and an extended byte. If the key is one of the extended keys, such as the function keys, then the normal byte is zero and the extended byte describes the struck key. For all other keys, the normal byte contains the ASCII code, and the extended byte contains a position code. The position code distinguishes between keys with identical ASCII codes, such as the two plus keys.

The DOS interrupts only return the ASCII code for normal keys. Extended keys require two calls. The first call returns a key code of zero (the normal byte). The second call returns the extended code. The zero byte indicates that an extended code is waiting.

The BIOS interrupts return both bytes immediately. If the normal byte is zero, the extended byte describes the struck key. If the normal byte is not zero, than the extended byte contains the position code.

Normal Codes

Key	Code (hex)	Code (decimal)
^A	01	1
^B	02	2
^C	03	3
^D	04	4
^E	05	5
^F	06	6
^G	07	7
^H, backspace	08	8
^I, tab	09	9
^J	0A	10
^K	0B	11
^L	0C	12
^M, enter	0D	13
^N	0E	14
^O	0F	15
^P	10	16
^Q	11	17
^R	12	18
^S	13	19
^T	14	20
^U	15	21
^V	16	22

Normal Codes

Key	Code (hex)	Code (decimal)
^W	17	23
^X	18	24
^Y	19	25
^Z	1A	26
^[, escape	1B	27
^/	1C	28
^]	1D	29
^^	1E	30
^_	1F	31
(space)	20	32
!	21	33
"	22	34
#	23	35
$	24	36
%	25	37
&	26	38
'	27	39
(	28	40
)	29	41
*	2A	42
+	2B	43
,	2C	44
-	2D	45
.	2E	46
/	2F	47
0	30	48
1	31	49
2	32	50
3	33	51
4	34	52
5	35	53
6	36	54
7	37	55
8	38	56
9	39	57
:	3A	58
;	3B	59
<	3C	60

Normal Codes

Key	Code (hex)	Code (decimal)
=	3D	61
>	3E	62
?	3F	63
@	40	64
A	41	65
B	42	66
C	43	67
D	44	68
E	45	69
F	46	70
G	47	71
H	48	72
I	49	73
J	4A	74
K	4B	75
L	4C	76
M	4D	77
N	4E	78
O	4F	79
P	50	80
Q	51	81
R	52	82
S	53	83
T	54	84
U	55	85
V	56	86
W	57	87
X	58	88
Y	59	89
Z	5A	90
[	5B	91
\	5C	92
]	5D	93
^	5E	94
	5F	95
`	60	96
a	61	97
b	62	98

Normal Codes

Key	Code (hex)	Code (decimal)
c	63	99
d	64	100
e	65	101
f	66	102
g	67	103
h	68	104
i	69	105
j	6A	106
k	6B	107
l	6C	108
m	6D	109
n	6E	110
o	6F	111
p	70	112
q	71	113
r	72	114
s	73	115
t	74	116
u	75	117
v	76	118
w	77	119
x	78	120
y	79	121
z	7A	122
{	7B	123
|	7C	124
}	7D	125
~	7E	126

codes 127-255 are generated by Alt 127-255

Extended Codes

Key	Code (hex)	Code (decimal)
^@	03	3
shift-tab	0F	15
alt-Q	10	16
alt-W	11	17
alt-E	12	18
alt-R	13	19
alt-T	14	20
alt-Y	15	21
alt-U	16	22
alt-I	17	23
alt-O	18	24
alt-P	19	25
alt-A	1E	30
alt-S	1F	31
alt-D	20	32
alt-F	21	33
alt-G	22	34
alt-H	23	35
alt-J	24	36
alt-K	25	37
alt-L	26	38
alt-Z	2C	44
alt-X	2D	45
alt-C	2E	46
alt-V	2F	47
alt-B	30	48
alt-N	31	49
alt-M	32	50
F1	3B	59
F2	3C	60
F3	3D	61
F4	3E	62
F5	3F	63
F6	40	64
F7	41	65
F8	42	66
F9	43	67
F10	44	68

Extended Codes

Key	Code (hex)	Code (decimal)
home	47	71
up arrow	48	72
PgUp	49	73
left arrow	4B	75
right arrow	4D	77
end	4F	79
down arrow	50	80
PgDn	51	81
insert	52	82
delete	53	83
shift-F1	54	84
shift-F2	55	85
shift-F3	56	86
shift-F4	57	87
shift-F5	58	88
shift-F6	59	89
shift-F7	5A	90
shift-F8	5B	91
shift-F9	5C	92
shift-F10	5D	93
ctrl-F1	5E	94
ctrl-F2	5F	95
ctrl-F3	60	96
ctrl-F4	61	97
ctrl-F5	62	98
ctrl-F6	63	99
ctrl-F7	64	100
ctrl-F8	65	101
ctrl-F9	66	102
ctrl-F10	67	103
alt-F1	68	104
alt-F2	69	105
alt-F3	6A	106
alt-F4	6B	107
alt-F5	6C	108
alt-F6	6D	109
alt-F7	6E	110
alt-F8	6F	111
alt-F9	70	112

Extended Codes

Key	Code (hex)	Code (decimal)
alt-F10	71	113
ctrl-PrtSc	72	114
ctrl-left arrow	73	115
ctrl-right arrow	74	116
ctrl-end	75	117
ctrl-PgDn	76	118
ctrl-home	77	119
alt-1	78	120
alt-2	79	121
alt-3	7A	122
alt-4	7B	123
alt-5	7C	124
alt-6	7D	125
alt-7	7E	126
alt-8	7F	127
alt-9	80	128
alt-0	81	129
alt- -	82	130
alt- =	83	131
ctrl-PgUp	84	132
F11	85	133
F12	86	134
shift-F11	87	135
shift-F12	88	136
ctrl-F11	89	137
ctrl-F12	8A	138
alt-F11	8B	139
alt-F12	8C	140

Position Codes

Key	Code (hex)	Code (decimal)
Normal Keys		
esc	01	1
1,!	02	2
2,@	03	3
3,#	04	4
4,$	05	5
5,%	06	6
6,^	07	7
7,&	08	8
8,*	09	9
9,(	0A	10
0,)	0B	11
-,_	0C	12
=,+	0D	13
backspace	0E	14
tab	0F	15
Q,q	10	16
W,w	11	17
E,e	12	18
R,r	13	19
T,t	14	20
Y,y	15	21
U,u	16	22
I,i	17	23
O,o	18	24
P,p	19	25
[,{	1A	26
],}	1B	27
enter, nmpd ent.	1C	28
A,a	1E	30
S,s	1F	31
D,d	20	32
F,f	21	33
G,g	22	34
H,h	23	35
J,j	24	36
K,k	25	37

Position Codes

<u>Key</u>	<u>Code (hex)</u>	<u>Code (decimal)</u>
L,l	26	38
;,:	27	39
',"	28	40
`,~	29	41
\,|	2B	43
Z,z	2C	44
X,x	2D	45
C,c	2E	46
V,v	2F	47
B,b	30	48
N,n	31	49
M,m	32	50
, <	33	51
. >	34	52
/ ?, numpad /	35	53
numpad *	37	55
(space)	39	57

Keypad keys

7, Home	47	71
8, up arrow	48	72
9, PgUp	49	73
-	4A	74
4, left arrow	4B	75
5	4C	76
6, right arrow	4D	77
+	4E	78
1, End	4F	79
2, down arrow	50	80
3, PgDn	51	81
0, Insert	52	82
. , Delete	53	83

The F11 and F12 key codes are for AT BIOS version 6/10/85.
Version 11/15/85 doesn't seem to support these function keys.

```
--------------------------------------------------
Operation:  Read character from keyboard.
            Waits for keystroke.
            Reports normal and extended codes immediately.
            No echo.
            Does not process Ctrl-Break.
Version:  BIOS
Interrupt:  16h
Function:  0
Called With:
    AH = 0
Returns With:
    AL = normal code
    AH = extended code (scan code if normal key)
--------------------------------------------------
```

```
--------------------------------------------------
Operation:  Read character from keyboard.
            Does not wait for keystroke.
            Reports normal and extended codes immediately.
            No echo.
            Does not process Ctrl-Break.
Version:  BIOS
Interrupt:  16h
Function:  1
Called With:
    AH = 1
Returns With:
    Zero flag = 0 if character ready
    Zero flag = 1 if character not ready
    AL = normal code if character ready
    AH = extended code if character ready
    If a character is ready, its code is reported, but it is not
    removed from the keyboard buffer.  This means that the next
    keyboard reading interrupt will return the same key code.  Use
    interrupt 16h, function 0 to remove the key code.
--------------------------------------------------
```

```
-------------------------------------------------
Operation:  Read character from standard input device.
            Waits for character.
            Reports normal and extended codes separately.
            Echoes.
            Processes Ctrl-Break.
Version:  DOS 1.0 -
Interrupt:  21h
Function:  1
Called With:
    AH = 1
Returns With:
    AL = key code.  Will be 0 for extended keys.  In this case,
    repeat the interrupt, and AL will contain the extended code.
-------------------------------------------------


-------------------------------------------------
Operation:  Read character from standard input device.
            Waits for character.
            Reports normal and extended codes separately.
            No echo.
            Processes Ctrl-Break if BREAK ON.
Version:  DOS 1.0 -
Interrupt:  21h
Function:  7
Called With:
    AH = 7
Returns With:
    AL = key code.  Will be 0 for extended keys.  In this case,
    repeat the interrupt, and AL will contain the extended code.
-------------------------------------------------


-------------------------------------------------
Operation:  Read character from standard input device.
            Waits for character.
            Normal and extended codes returned separately.
            No echo.
            Processes Ctrl-Break.
Version:  DOS 1.0 -
Interrupt:  21h
Function:  8
Called With:
    AH = 8
Returns With:
    AL = key code.  Will be 0 for extended keys.  In this case,
    repeat the interrupt, and AL will contain the extended code.
-------------------------------------------------
```

```
------------------------------------------------
Operation:  Clear keyboard buffer then read character.
Version:  DOS 1.0 -
Interrupt:  21h
Function:  12
Called With:
    AH = 12
    AL = 1, 7, 8, or 10
        The buffer is cleared, then the function whose number is
        in AL is called.  If a lot of time has elapsed since the
        last key was read, the keyboard buffer could be filled.
        This function clears out all the keys and starts fresh.
        Use this when it is important that any keys read are
        struck at the time of the read.  Do not use this function
        if you want to be able to process a backlog of commands
        entered while the system was processing.
Returns With:
    Whatever the function indicated in AL would return with.
------------------------------------------------
```

Pressing the Insert, Caps Lock, Num Lock, and Scroll Lock keys toggles a flag. You can check these flags, as well as if the shift, control, or alt keys are currently pressed with the following interrupt.

These flags are stored in a BIOS variable which is simply read by the interrupt. The format is:

Keyboard Status Flags

Bit	Hex	Meaning
0	1	Set if right shift key depressed
1	2	Set if left shift key depressed
2	4	Set if control key depressed
3	8	Set if alt key depressed
4	10	Set if Scroll Lock on
5	20	Set if Num Lock on
6	40	Set if Caps Lock on
7	80	Set if Insert on

```
------------------------------------------------------
Operation:  Report status of Insert, Caps Lock, Num Lock, and
            Scroll Lock states.
            Report if shift, control, or alt keys are pressed.
Version:  BIOS
Interrupt:  16h
Function:  2
Called With:
    AH = 2
Returns With:
    AL = keyboard status byte
------------------------------------------------------
```

READING STRINGS

There is one interrupt for reading strings. It works very well,
except in memory resident utilities. You may want to write your
own string-reading routine using one of the character-reading
interrupts.

You can also read strings with the file access routines discussed
in Chapter 17.

```
------------------------------------------------------
Operation:  Read string from standard input device.
        Waits for characters.
        Echoes.
        Processes control characters and DOS editing keys.
        Only reports normal codes.
        Reads characters until a return.
Version: DOS 1.0 -
Interrupt:  21h
Function:  10
Called With:
    AH = 10
    DS:DX = pointer to an input buffer
    DS:DX[0] = size of buffer
Returns With:
    DS:DX[1] = length of input string
    DS:DX[2.....] = input string, terminated by a return
```
    This interrupt reads from the standard input device until a
    return is encountered. Editing keys such as backspace are
    processed. The resulting string is stored in the buffer area
    as it is read. Set byte 0 to the size of the buffer minus
    one. The input string, including the return character, can be
    up to one less than this length. For example, to read a
    string up to 254 characters long, allocate 256 bytes for the
    buffer and store 255 in byte 0. The interrupt returns the
    length of the string, not including the return, in byte 1. If
    the string is longer than the buffer, DOS will beep and
    discard characters until the return.
```
------------------------------------------------------
```

LIGHT PEN

The light pen is a very useful input device. Light pens attached directly to the graphics card can be read with this interrupt. Resolution is generally not precise. Fancier light pens have better resolution.

```
-------------------------------------------------
Operation:  Read the position and status of the light pen.
Interrupt:  10h
Function:   4
Call With:
    AH = 4
Returns With:
    AH = 0 if pen switch not depressed
    AH = 1 if pen switch depressed
    If AH = 1 then
        DH = row   (0 - 24)
        DL = column  (0 - 79)
        CH = line  (0 - 199)
        BX = horizontal position (0 - 319 or 0 - 639)
    If AH = 0 then
        BX, CX, and DX are destroyed
-------------------------------------------------
```

MOUSE

The mouse is a very useful pointing input device. This discussion follows the Microsoft mouse standard. In order to use mouse interrupts, the mouse driver software, which comes with the mouse, must be installed. Check for the presence of a mouse before you use the mouse interrupts.

When the mouse is initialized, it is assumed to be in the middle of the screen. As it is moved, the mouse driver keeps track of its position. The position can be read by an interrupt. In addition, the mouse driver can automatically display a cursor on the screen as the mouse is moved. A different function reports the status of the mouse buttons.

```
-----------------------------------------------------
Operation:  Check if mouse is installed.
            Determine number of buttons.
            Reset mouse.
Version:  MOUSE
Interrupt:  33h
Function:  0
Called With:
    AX = 0
Returns With:
    AX = -1 if mouse installed
       =  0 if mouse not installed
    DX = number of buttons
    In addition, the mouse position is reset to the center of the
    screen, the mouse cursor is not displayed, the default mouse
    cursors are used, light pen emulation is enabled, and the
    default movement ratios are used.
-----------------------------------------------------
```

The mouse can be used with any of the screen modes. The way
screen position is reported and the type of cursor used depend
on the screen type. The screen positions in text modes and
medium and high resolution graphics modes always range between 0
and 199 in the y direction and 0 and 639 in the x direction.
The position values are compensated for the screen resolution.

Screen Mode	Mouse Coordinates
0-1	x coordinate = 16 * screen column
	y coordinate = 8 * screen row
2-3	x coordinate = 8 * screen column
	y coordinate = 8 * screen row
4-5	x coordinate = 2 * screen x coordinate
	y coordinate = screen y coordinate
6	x coordinate = screen x coordinate
	y coordinate = screen y coordinate
7	x coordinate = 8 * screen column
	y coordinate = 8 * screen row
14-16, 48	x coordinate = screen x coordinate
	y coordinate = screen y coordinate

```
-----------------------------------------------------
Operation:  Get mouse position.
            Get mouse button status.
Version:  MOUSE
Interrupt:  33h
Function:  3
Called With:
    AX = 3
Returns With:
    BX = button status.

        Bit         Meaning
        0           Set if left button depressed
        1           Set if right button depressed
    CX = x coordinate
    DX = y coordinate
-----------------------------------------------------
```

```
-----------------------------------------------------
Operation:  Set mouse position.
Version:  MOUSE
Interrupt:  33h
Function:  4
Called With:
    AX = 4
    CX = new x coordinate
    DX = new y coordinate
-----------------------------------------------------
```

Normally, the mouse is free to move anywhere on the screen. The following two interrupts set bounds for where it can move.

```
-----------------------------------------------------
Operation:  Set mouse x bounds.
Version:  MOUSE
Interrupt:  33h
Function:  7
Called With:
    AX = 7
    CX = minimum x bound
    DX = maximum x bound
-----------------------------------------------------
```

```
-----------------------------------------------------
Operation:  Set mouse y bounds.
Version:  MOUSE
Interrupt:  33h
Function:  8
Called With:
    AX = 8
    CX = minimum y bound
    DX = maximum y bound
-----------------------------------------------------
```

The mouse driver can automatically display a cursor at the mouse's position. In text modes, this cursor either changes the attribute or moves the hardware cursor. The attribute cursor is defined by a **screen mask** and **cursor mask**. The screen mask preserves certain of the character's original attributes. The cursor mask selects which attributes are changed. Both are word values. The low byte of the screen mask should be ffh; the low byte of the cursor mask, 0h. Logically, the attribute and character bytes for the character position under the cursor are ANDed with the screen mask then XORed with the cursor mask.

The hardware cursor is the same as that set with interrupt 10h (see Chapter 14).

In graphics modes, the cursor is also composed from a screen and cursor mask. Again, the screen mask is ANDed to the screen, and the cursor mask is XORed. For graphics, the masks are bit-mapped blocks.[1] Each word contains pixel information for one row; the table starts with the top row.

Mode	Cursor Size	Bits per Cursor Pixel
4-5	8 by 16	2
6, 14-16, 48	16 by 16	1

Each graphics cursor also has a **hot spot**. This part of the cursor is used to determine the coordinates over which the mouse lies. The hot spot value is between -16 and 16.

```
-----------------------------------------------
Operation:  Set graphics cursor.
Version:  MOUSE
Interrupt:  33h
Function:  9
Called With:
    AX = 9
    BX = hot spot x position
    CX = hot spot y position
    ES:DX =   pointer to screen and cursor masks.  These are
              contiguously placed with the screen mask first.
-----------------------------------------------
```

---

[1]For more information on bit-mapped graphics and masks, refer to Advanced IBM PC Graphics.

```
--------------------------------------------------
Operation:  Set text cursor.
Version:  MOUSE
Interrupt:  33h
Function:  10
Called With:
    AX = 10
    BX = 0 to select attribute cursor
       = 1 to select hardware cursor
    CX = screen mask or hardware cursor scan line start
    DX = cursor mask or hardware cursor scan line end
--------------------------------------------------
```

When the mouse is initialized, the mouse cursor is not displayed. This status can be toggled.

```
--------------------------------------------------
Operation:  Make mouse cursor displayed.
Version:  MOUSE
Interrupt:  33h
Function:  1
Called With:
    AX = 1
--------------------------------------------------
```

```
--------------------------------------------------
Operation:  Make mouse cursor not displayed.
Version:  MOUSE
Interrupt:  33h
Function:  2
Called With:
    AX = 2
--------------------------------------------------
```

The mouse software keeps track of the number of physical positions the mouse is moved. Each physical position corresponds to 1/200th of an inch. Initially, two physical position changes correspond to one mouse screen position change.

```
--------------------------------------------------
Operation:  Determine number of physical positions moved.
Version:  MOUSE
Interrupt:  33h
Function:  11
Called With:
    AX = 11
Returns With:
    CX = number of x positions moved since last function 11 call.
        Positive numbers mean right.
    DX = number of y positions moved since last function 11 call.
        Positive numbers mean down.
--------------------------------------------------
```

```
-----------------------------------------------------
Operation:  Set physical to screen movement ratios.
Version:  MOUSE
Interrupt:  33h
Function:  15
Called With:
    AX = 15
    CX = number of physical positions to indicate a change of 8 x
         coordinates.  The initial setting is 8.
    DX = number of physical positions to indicate a change of 8 y
         coordinates.  The initial setting is 16.
    The high bit for CX and DX must be 0.  The minimum value is 1.
-----------------------------------------------------
```

If desired, the mouse can emulate a light pen.

```
-----------------------------------------------------
Operation:  Set light pen emulation.
Version:  MOUSE
Interrupt:  33h
Function:  13
Called With:
    AX = 13
-----------------------------------------------------
```

```
-----------------------------------------------------
Operation: Stop light pen emulation.
Version:  MOUSE
Interrupt:  33h
Function:  14
Called With:
    AX = 14
-----------------------------------------------------
```

KEY PROGRAMMING POINTS

- The keyboard reading interrupts differ in the way they report keystrokes, wait for keystrokes, echo keystrokes, and process Ctrl-Break.

- The DOS interrupts read from the standard input device. The BIOS interrupts read from the keyboard.

- There are many mouse-related functions. They include interrupts to determine if the mouse is present, to control the mouse cursor, to control and check the mouse position, and to adjust the mouse movement sensitivity.

CHAPTER 16

THE PSP
AND PARAMETER PASSING

The **program segment prefix** (PSP) is a block of 256 bytes that DOS places before the beginning of every program. In COM files, the PSP is located at CS:0. When writing assembly code for a COM file, always start it with an **org 100h** statement to leave room for the PSP. In EXE files, the code starts at CS:0, and DS and ES initially point to the PSP.

The PSP contains a variety of information necessary for program operation. Among other things, it contains the command line parameters and a work space for DOS to store information about what parts of the disk a program is using. Command line parameters are parameters entered following a program's name. For example, if you typed **format b:/v,** then **b:** and **/v** would be command line parameters.

Early versions of DOS accessed files by something called a **file control block** (FCB). Starting with DOS 2.0, DOS uses a much easier method involving **file handles.** But all of the old FCB interrupts were still kept to insure upward compatibility. Much space in the PSP is reserved for FCB-style file access.

Let's look at the format of the PSP:

Byte	Contents
0-1	INT 20h instruction (Program terminate). This has two uses. An assembly language program can terminate by using one of several interrupts, or it can start with:

```
push ds
xor ax,ax
push ax
```

then finish with:

```
retf
```

When a program starts, ds points to the PSP. The far return will read ds:0 off of the stack. This points to the beginning of the PSP, where the program terminate instruction is located.

The second use of this location is as a safety feature for programs with unresolved external locations. These are set by the linker to 0. Thus, branching to them terminates the program.

2-3   Segment address of the end of available memory.

5-9   A long call to the DOS function dispatcher. (INT 21h). The word at location 6 contains the number of bytes available in the code segment.

10-13   Copy of the terminate program routine's address. This points to the routine that is executed when a program terminates. Usually the terminate routine is part of COMMAND.COM. But a program can change the routine to be used. The pointer in the PSP is a copy of the terminate address set up before the program started. When the program terminates, the address in the terminate location is restored from the PSP copy and the unrestored terminate address is jumped to. This is used when EXECing one program from within another. The EXECed program's terminate address is set to return to the location following the EXEC interrupt, and the PSP copy is set to the terminate address for the calling program. When the EXECed program finishes, the terminate address for the calling program will be restored. Changing this location changes the terminate address for the calling program.

14-17   Contains a copy of the ctrl-break exit address in use before the program was executed. The actual ctrl-break address is set to the location following the call to execute the program. When the program terminates, the original ctrl-break address is restored.

18-21   Contains a copy of the critical error exit address. Used to restore the actual critical error exit address when the program terminates.

22-43   DOS work area.

44-45	Segment of the environment. The environment, a set of ASCIIZ strings containing the environment settings, such as PROMPT and PATH information, starts at this segment, offset 0. Information can be passed to a program through the environment. For example, a variable could be set in the environment to indicate the drive in which to store temporary files.
46-79	DOS work area.
80-82	Assembly code for: int 21h retf
85-127	File control block areas.
128	Length in bytes of command line parameters.
129-255	Command line parameters.
128-255	Default disk transfer area.

When parameters are entered on the command line, they are copied to location 129 in the PSP. I/O redirection information is removed. Location 128 stores the number of characters entered on the command line, the first of which is a space.

To read the parameters, scan the data stored starting at location 129. Be sure to remove leading and intermediate blanks. Also check that enough parameters have been entered. You may want to set up defaults or terminate if enough parameters weren't entered. Check the length byte to see when the command line ends. A return also indicates the command line end. You will see examples of reading the command line parameters in MOVE.ASM and DIR2.ASM.

Locations 128-255 also serve as the default **disk transfer area** (DTA). This is a section of memory used by a few interrupts that deal with disk files, such as the directory search interrupts. The old FCB style file access method used the DTA as a storage buffer for disk information. If your program uses interrupts which use the DTA, process the command line parameters before you use these interrupts. You can also copy the parameters to a different area or relocate the DTA.

Several parts of the PSP are used for DOS work areas. These store data that DOS uses to keep track of what it is doing. When memory resident utilities use disk interrupts, they must reset the PSP. This is discussed in Section III.

The get PSP interrupt is also useful for reading PSP information in an EXE file.

```
--------------------------------------------------
Operation:  Get address of PSP.
Version:  Function 81:  Undocumented.  DOS 2.0 -
          Function 98:  DOS 3.0 -
Interrupt:  21h
Function:  81 or 98
Call With:
    AH = 81 or 98
        Both of these functions do the same thing.
Returns With:
    BX = segment of PSP.
--------------------------------------------------
```

```
--------------------------------------------------
Operation:  Set address of PSP.
Version:  Undocumented.  DOS 2.0 -
Interrupt:  21h
Function: 80
Call With:
    AH = 80
    BX = segment of PSP to change to.
Note:  The primary use of this function is for memory resident
utilities.  Be sure to save the address of the old PSP before
changing.
--------------------------------------------------
```

```
--------------------------------------------------
Operation:  Get address of DTA.
Version:  DOS 2.0 -
Interrupt:  21h
Function:  47
Call With:
    AH = 47
Returns With:
    ES:BX = pointer to the DTA.
--------------------------------------------------
```

```
--------------------------------------------------
Operation:  Set address of DTA.
Version:  DOS 1.0 -
Interrupt:  21h
Function:  26
Call With:
    AH = 26
    DS:DX =   pointer to the new location for the DTA.  Should not
              be so close to a segment bound as to cause wrap
              around.
--------------------------------------------------
```

KEY PROGRAMMING POINTS

- The PSP appears before all programs. It contains a variety of DOS variables and the command line parameters.

CHAPTER 17

DISK FILES

Accessing files from Assembly Language is unbelievably simple. For many operations, such as deleting or renaming a file, you simply give DOS the file's name, call an interrupt, and it's done.

To read from or write to a file, start by **opening** the file. Give DOS the file's name and DOS returns a **file handle**--a two-byte number which uniquely identifies the file. Then, call the read, write, or position interrupts, specifying the file by its handle. When you are finished manipulating a file, **close** it. This flushes all the internal buffers for that file, fully updates the directory, and frees the file handle.

You can have several active handles at one time. Also, the following handles are always defined and open:

Handle	Device
0	Standard input device (normally keyboard)
1	Standard output device (normally screen)
2	Standard error device (always screen)
3	Standard auxiliary device
4	Standard printer (LPT1 or PRN)

You may use any of the file access interrupts with these handles where they make sense. For example, you can use the write interrupt with handle 1 to send a block of text to the screen. If you use handle 4, it would send the text to the printer. Likewise, you could use handle 0 to read a string from the keyboard. Note that I/O redirection changes what the standard input and output devices are. When you open files, the handles are numbered starting with 5.

When you give DOS a file name, you pass it a pointer to an ASCIIZ string. This is the drive, path, file name, and extension, all in ASCII characters and followed by a hex 0. For example, to set up a file name, you could use:

```
failsafe db    'c:\utilities\failsafe.com', 0
```

The case of letters doesn't matter. If the drive or path is omitted, the default is used.

When reading from or writing to a file, specify a buffer area where the data will be loaded or read from. This location can be anywhere. If possible, load the data directly to where you will be using it. Up to 64K can be read or written at a time. If you will be reading large amounts of data at a time, use a memory allocation call (see Chapter 20) to set up the buffer area instead of setting aside space within your program. This will greatly reduce your program's disk size. The buffer is specified by a segment: offset. If the read or write is longer than the space left in the segment, the data is written or read across the segment bound to the next memory location. It docs not wrap around to the segment beginning. For example, suppose your buffer starts at 1000:FFF0h, and you are reading 100 bytes from disk. The first 16 bytes will be stored in 1000:FFF0h-1000:FFFFh, the next 84 (54h) in 1100:0000h-1100:0054h. If the data wrapped around, the first 16 bytes would be stored in 1000:FFF0h-1000:FFFFh and the next 84 in 1000:0000h-1000:0054h.

The file accessing interrupts signal that an error occurred by setting the carry flag. The error code is returned in AX. For DOS 2.1, directly check for the error code for functions 38h-57h. The carry is not reliable.

Error Code	Meaning
1	Invalid function number
2	File not found
3	Path not found
4	No available handles (too many open files)
5	Access denied
6	Invalid handle
7	Memory control blocks destroyed
8	Insufficient memory
9	Invalid memory block address
10	Invalid environment
11	Invalid format
12	Invalid access code
13	Invalid data
14	Not used
15	Invalid drive
16	Can't remove current directory
17	Not same device
18	No more files found

DOS 3.0 introduced a more advanced error signalling. After an error in a DOS call, the carry flag is set and an error code is returned in AX. If you want, you can simply check the carry and look at the error code. To get more information, issue interrupt 21h, function 89. The error code could be different than that originally in AX.

Error Code	Meaning
1	Invalid function number
2	File not found
3	Path not found
4	No available handles
5	Access denied
6	Invalid handle
7	Memory control blocks destroyed
8	Not enough memory
9	Invalid memory block address
10	Invalid environment
11	Invalid format
12	Invalid access code
13	Invalid data
14	Reserved
15	Invalid drive
16	Can't remove current directory
17	Not same device
18	No more files found
19	Write protected
20	Unknown unit
21	Drive not ready
22	Invalid command
23	CRC error
24	Bad request
25	Seek error
26	Unknown media type
27	Sector not found
28	Out of paper
29	Write error
30	Read error
31	General error
32	Sharing violation
33	Lock violation

Error Code	Meaning
34	Invalid disk change
35	File control block unavailable
36	Sharing buffer overflow
37-49	Reserved
50	Network request not supported
51	Remote computer not listening
52	Duplicate name on network
53	Network name not found
54	Network busy
55	Network device no longer exists
56	BIOS command limit exceeded
57	Network adaptor hardware error
58	Incorrect network response
59	Unexpected network error
60	Incompatible remote adaptor
61	Full print queue
62	Not enough space for print file
63	Print file deleted
64	Network name deleted
65	Access denied
66	Incorrect network device type
67	Network name not found
68	Too many network names
69	BIOS session limit exceeded
70	Temporary pause
71	Network request not accepted
72	Redirection paused
73-79	Reserved
80	File exists
81	Reserved
82	Cannot make directory entry
83	Critical error handler failure
84	Too many redirections
85	Duplicate redirection
86	Invalid password
87	Invalid parameter
88	Network device fault

Error Class	Meaning
1	Out of resource
2	Temporary problem
3	Permission problem
4	Internal software error
5	Hardware failure
6	System software error
7	Application software error
8	Item not found
9	Invalid format
10	Item locked
11	Media failure or wrong disk
12	Item already exists
13	Unknown

Recommended Action	Meaning
1	Retry
2	Retry in a while
3	Ask user to reenter request
4	Abort and cleanup
5	Abort immediately, don't cleanup
6	Ignore
7	Ask user to perform remedial action, then retry

Cause	Meaning
1	Unknown or not specific
2	Block device
3	Network device
4	Serial device
5	Memory

```
-----------------------------------------------
Operation:  Get error information.
Version:  DOS 3.0 -
Interrupt:  21h
Function:  89
Called With:
     AH = 89
     BX = 0
Returns With:
     AX = error code
     BL = recommended action
     BH = error class
     CH = cause
     CL, DX, DI, SI, DS, ES destroyed.
     Note:  DS and ES are destroyed.
-----------------------------------------------
```

OPENING FILES

There are four DOS functions for opening files. Function 60 opens a file and sets its length to 0. If the file does not already exist, a new file is created. Use this function when you want to create a completely new file or store completely new information in an old file.

Function 61 opens a file for reading or writing. The file must already exist. Any old data is left untouched; to change it, you need to write over it. Use this function when you want to read a file or want to modify parts of an old file.

Function 91, available starting with DOS 3.00, is very similar to function 60, except that if the file already exists, Function 91 will return with an error message. Use this function if you do not want to take the risk of writing over a file that already exists--that is, if you only want to create a file if one with that name doesn't already exist.

Function 90 creates a new file and picks the file name. Like function 91, it is available starting with DOS 3.00. The name is chosen so that it is not the same as the name of any other file in the directory where it will be placed. You can use this to create a file containing temporary information without having to worry about overwriting an existing file. Be sure to keep the name DOS chooses if you intend to erase the file from within your program.

You do not need to open handles 0-4. None of these interrupts will create subdirectories.

```
--------------------------------------------------
Operation:  Open a file.
            Creates a new file if file does not already exist.
            Sets length to 0  (clears old file).
Version:  DOS 2.0 -
Interrupt:  21h
Function:  60
Called With:
    AH = 60
    CH = 0
    CL = file attribute.  Uses the same format as the directory
         attribute byte.  Do not set subdirectory or volume bits.
         Bit       Meaning
         0         Read-only
         1         Hidden
         2         System
         Set CL to zero for normal files.

    DS:DX = pointer to ASCIIZ filename.
Returns With:
    AX = file handle or error code
    Carry set if error.  Error codes are 3 (path not found), 4 (no
    free handles), and 5 (access denied).
--------------------------------------------------
```

```
--------------------------------------------------
Operation:  Open a file.
            File must already exist.
            Length not changed (unless it is made longer by appended
            data).
Version:  DOS 2.0 -
            Access code bits 3 - 7 for DOS 3.0 -
Interrupt:  21h
Function:  61
Called With:
    AH = 61
    AL = access code.  This code sets how the file will be used.
    Only bits 0 - 2 need to be set for DOS 2.0 or systems without
    networking or multi-tasking.
            Bits      Meaning
            0 - 2     Access Mode.
                      000  Read only
                      001  Write only
                      010  Read and Write access
            3         Reserved.
                      Always set to 0.
```

4 - 6   Sharing Mode. Sets what to do if there is an
              attempt to open the file more than once. (That
              is, by more than one concurrently operating
              program.) This is used to insure data
              integrity.
              000 compatibility mode. Access denied to
              other processes. Can be opened more than once
              by current process.
              001 deny read/write. Access denied to other
              processes. Cannot be opened more than once by
              current process.
              010 deny write. Access denied to processes
              who attempt to open the file for writing.
              011 deny read. Access denied to processes who
              attempt to open the file for reading.
              100 deny none. Access given to all other
              processes.
7   Inheritance Mode.
              0 if child processes inherit access to this
              file automatically. All sharing and access
              restrictions are inherited.
              1 if child processes do not inherit access to
              this file automatically.

Note that the settings are arranged so that programs written
with DOS 2.0 (and thus only set the low 3 bits) will have the
most natural access by default.

    DS:DX = pointer to ASCIIZ filename.
Returns With:
    AX = file handle or error code.
    Carry set if error. Error codes are 2 (file not found), 4 (no
    free handles), 5 (access denied), 12 (invalid access code).

Operation: Create a file with a unique name.
        DOS chooses the name.
Version: DOS 3.0 -
Interrupt: 21h
Function: 90
Call With:
    AH = 90
    CH = 0
    CL = file attribute. Same format as that in directory.
    DS:DX = pointer to ASCIIZ string containing path name for new
    file. If string is null, new file will be placed in current
    directory. If path is not null, terminate the string with a
    \, followed by thirteen 0 bytes. DOS will fill in a 12
    character filename after the \. If you plan to erase the file
    from the program, be sure to keep this name area intact, as
    you will need it for the erase file interrupt.

```
Returns With:
    AX = file handle or error code.
    DS:DX = pointer to ASCIIZ filename.
    Carry set if error.
--------------------------------------------------

--------------------------------------------------
Operation:  Open a file.
         Creates a new file.
         Returns error if file already exists.
Version:  DOS 3.0 -
Interrupt:  21h
Function:  91
Called With:
    AH = 91
    CH = 0
    CL = file attribute.  Uses the same format as the directory
         attribute byte.
    DS:DX = pointer to ASCIIZ filename.
Returns With:
    AX = file handle or error code
    Carry set if error.
--------------------------------------------------
```

READING, WRITING, AND POSITIONING

Reading, writing, and positioning all require open file handles.
When a file is opened, its **file pointer** is set to 0. This pointer
indicates which part of the file will be read or written next.
Each time the file is read from or written to, the file pointer is
advanced to the end of the section just accessed. If you are
sequentially writing to a file, just repeatedly issue the write
interrupt. You do not need to keep track of or modify file
position. To do random writing or reading or to append to a file,
use the positioning interrupt to change the file pointer.

The read and write interrupts return the number of bytes
read/written. If this is not the amount attempted, the end-of-
file was reached, the disk was full, or an end-of-line (return)
was reached when reading from the standard input device.

You can use the read interrupt to read a string from the keyboard. Set CX either to the maximum length of the string you want to read. The keyboard or standard input device will be read until a return or end of file (control z) is pressed or until the string length is read in. Examine AX to determine the actual length of the string.

```
--------------------------------------------------
Operation:  Read from a file.
            File pointer moved to end of section read.
Version:  DOS 2.0 -
Interrupt:  21h
Function:  63
Called With:
    AH = 63
    BX = file handle
    CX = number of bytes to read
    DS:DX = buffer location
Returns With:
    AX = number of bytes actually read or error code.
    Carry set if error.  Error codes are 5 (access denied) and 6
    (invalid handle).
--------------------------------------------------
```

```
--------------------------------------------------
Operation:  Write to a file.
            File pointer moved to end of section written.
Version:  DOS 2.0 -
Interrupt:  21h
Function:  64
Called With:
    AH = 64
    BX = file handle
    CX = number of bytes to write
    DS:DX = buffer location
Returns With:
    AX = number of bytes actually written or error code.
    Carry set if error.  Error codes are 5 (access denied) and 6
    (invalid handle).
--------------------------------------------------
```

```
--------------------------------------------------
Operation:  Position file pointer.
Version:  DOS 2.0 -
Interrupt:  21h
Function:  66
Called With:
    AH = 66
    AL = Movement method.
        0  Move offset bytes from the beginning of the file.
        1  Move offset bytes from the current file pointer
        location.
        2  Move offset bytes beyond the end of the file.

        Use method 2 with an offset of 0 to determine the size of
        the file.  File size is returned in DX:AX, as indicated
        below.  If you move beyond the end of a file and write,
        the new material will start at the file pointer.
        Whatever was on the disk between the old end of file and
        the file pointer will become part of the file.  You may
        want to clear this section.
    BX = file handle
    CX:DX = offset to move, in bytes.  CX is high word.
Returns With:
    DX:AX = new offset of pointer, or with AX = error code.
    Carry set if error.  Error codes are 1 (invalid movement
    method) and 6 (invalid handle).
--------------------------------------------------
```

MOVING AND RENAMING FILES

To rename a file, pass it the original name and the new name. If the first name starts with a drive name, the second name must also start with a drive name, and the drive names must be the same. The new name can also specify a new path location for the file. That is, this function will move a file from one subdirectory to another. Subdirectories can be renamed but not moved.

This function works on one file at a time.   * and ? cannot be used in the file names.

In Chapter 18, you will use this interrupt to create a utility-- MOVE--which renames files and moves them across directories.

```
----------------------------------------------------
Operation:  Move and rename a file.
Version:  DOS 2.0 -
Interrupt:  21h
Function:  86
Call With:
    AH = 86
    DS:DX = pointer to ASCIIZ original name
    ES:DI = pointer to ASCIIZ new name
Returns With:
    AX = error code
    The original directory entry is cleared by setting the first
    character to e5h and the attribute byte to zero.
    Carry set if error.  Error codes are 3 (path not found), 5
    (access denied), and 17 (not same drive).
----------------------------------------------------
```

ERASING FILES

To erase a file, call the following interrupt with the file's name.
If the file is a read-only file, subdirectory file, or a volume name,
it will not be erased. To erase a read-only file, first change its
attribute to a normal file (see next interrupt discussion).

This function will only erase one file at a time. It cannot be called
with * or ? in the file name.

```
----------------------------------------------------
Operation:  Erase a file.
            Will not erase read-only files.
Version:  DOS 2.0 -
Interrupt:  21h
Function:  65
Call With:
    AH = 65
    DS:DX = pointer to ASCIIZ name
Returns With:
    AX = error code
    Carry set if error.  Errors are 2 (file not found) and 5
    (access denied).
----------------------------------------------------
```

CHANGING A FILE'S ATTRIBUTE, DATE, AND TIME

The attribute changing interrupt gives you some flexibility
in manipulating a file's attribute. As a means of
protection, it won't change the subdirectory or volume bits.
To change these, use a utility such as EXPLORER.

The close handle interrupt automatically updates a file's date, time, and archive bit if the file was opened for writing.

```
--------------------------------------------------
Operation:  Get or change a file's attributes.
            Will not change subdirectory or volume bits.
Version:  DOS 2.0 -
Interrupt:  21h
Function:  67
Call With:
    AH = 67
    AL = Operation.
        Value     Meaning
        0         Read attribute
        1         Set attribute
    CL = attribute, if setting attribute.  Attribute codes are the
    same as those stored in the directory.  Subdirectory and volume
    bits should be 0.
    DS:DX = pointer to ASCIIZ filename
Returns With:
    AX = error code
    CL = attribute, if reading attribute.  Attribute codes are the
    same as those stored in the directory.
    Carry set if error.  Error codes are 2 (file not found), 3 (path
    not found), and 5 (access denied).
--------------------------------------------------
```

```
--------------------------------------------------
Operation:  Get or change a file's date and time.
            File must be open.
            Change takes place when file closed.
Version:  DOS 2.0 -
Interrupt:  21h
Function:  87
Called With:
    AH = 87
    AL = Command Code.
        Value     Meaning
        0         Read date and time
        1         Set date and time
    BX = file handle
    CX = time, if setting date and time.  Format is that used in
    the directory.  Set to:  (hour SHL 11) + (minute SHL 5) +
    (second SHR 1).
    DX = date, if setting date and time.  Format is that used in
    the directory.  Set to:  ((year - 1980) SHL 9) + (month SHL 5)
    + day.
```

```
Returns With:
    AX = error code
    CX = time, if reading date and time.  Format is that used in
    the directory.
    DX = date, if reading date and time.  Format is that used in
    the directory.
    Carry set if error.  Error codes are 1 (invalid command in AL)
    and 6 (invalid handle).
```

INPUT/OUTPUT CONTROL FOR DEVICES

There is a special interrupt to deal with input/output
control for devices (IOCTL). This interrupt is set up to
interface with the device drivers and can handle most device
I/O. It accesses logical devices (such as drive A or C) and
handle devices (such as files). Control data and actual
information can be sent to the devices. The IOCTL interrupt
gains power with each DOS version.

The IOCTL functions are either for querying or accessing
devices. You'll look at the basic query and access
functions here. The more advanced query functions will be
discussed in Chapter 24.

The basic query function returns information in the
following format. Note that there are two tables, one for
devices and one for files.

Query Results for Files

BIT 7 = 0

Bit	Meaning
0-3	Low 4 bits of device number (0 = A, 1 = B, etc.)
5	High bit of device number
6	Clear if written to.

Query Results for Devices

BIT 7 = 1

Bit	Meaning
0	Set if console input device
1	Set if console output device
2	Set if null device
3	Set if clock device
4	Reserved
5	Set if in binary mode.
6	Set if end-of-file on input.
8-13	Reserved
14	Set if can process control strings.
15	Reserved

In **binary mode** data is sent to a file without modification. The alternative is **ASCII mode,** in which control-Z signals an end of file; carriage return/linefeed combinations are converted to linefeed when input; and linefeeds are converted to carriage return/linefeeds when output.

```
--------------------------------------------------
Operation:  Get device information.
Version:  DOS 2.0 -
Interrupt:  21h
Function:  68
Called With:
    AH = 68
    AL = 0
    BX = handle
Returns With:
    DX = device information, as outlined above.
--------------------------------------------------
```

```
--------------------------------------------------
Operation:  Set device information.
Version:  DOS 2.0 -
Interrupt:  21h
Function:  68
Called With:
    AH = 68
    AL = 1
    BX = handle
    DH = 0
    DL = device information to set for low byte of query result.
    Note that the high byte cannot be changed.
--------------------------------------------------
```

```
--------------------------------------------------
Operation:  Get input status.
Version:  DOS 2.0 -
Interrupt:  21h
Function:  68
Called With:
    AH = 68
    AL = 6
    BX = handle
Returns With:
    AL = For file:
       = 0 after end of file reached
       = ffh until end of file reached
        For devices:
       = 0 not ready
       = ffh ready
--------------------------------------------------


--------------------------------------------------
Operation:  Get output status.
Version:  DOS 2.0 -
Interrupt:  21h
Function:  68
Called With:
    AH = 68
    AL = 7
    BX = handle
Returns With:
    AL = For file:
       = 0 after end of file reached
       = ffh until end of file reached
        For devices:
       = 0 not ready
       = ffh ready
--------------------------------------------------
```

There are two types of devices--**character devices** and **block devices.**
Character devices are devices such as the screen and disk files. They
receive information character by character. Block devices are devices
such as disk drives. They receive information in chunks.

```
--------------------------------------------------
Operation:  Read from character device.
Version:  DOS 2.0 -
Interrupt:  21h
Function:  68
Called With:
    AH = 68
    AL = 2
    BX = handle
    CX = number of bytes to read
    DS:DX = pointer to buffer in which to store data
Returns With:
    AX = number of bytes read
--------------------------------------------------


--------------------------------------------------
Operation:  Write to character device.
Version:  DOS 2.0 -
Interrupt:  21h
Function:  68
Called With:
    AH = 68
    AL = 3
    BX = handle
    CX = number of bytes to write
    DS:DX = pointer to data to write
Returns With:
    AX = number of bytes written
--------------------------------------------------


--------------------------------------------------
Operation:  Read from block device.
Version:  DOS 2.0 -
Interrupt:  21h
Function:  68
Called With:
    AH = 68
    AL = 4
    BL = drive number.  0 = default, 1 = A, and so on.
    CX = number of bytes to read
    DS:DX = pointer to buffer in which to store data
Returns With:
    AX = number of bytes read
--------------------------------------------------
```

```
-------------------------------------------------
Operation:  Write to block device.
Version:  DOS 2.0 -
Interrupt:  21h
Function:  68
Called With:
    AH = 68
    AL = 5
    BL = drive number.  0 = default, 1 = A, and so on.
    CX = number of bytes to write
    DS:DX = pointer to data to write
Returns With:
    AX = number of bytes written
-------------------------------------------------
```

```
-------------------------------------------------
Operation:  Read a track from a device.
Version:  DOS 3.2 -
Interrupt:  21h
Function:  68
Called With:
    AH = 68
    AL = 13
    BL = drive number.  0 = default, 1 = A, and so on.
    CL = 97
    CH = 8
    DS:DX = pointer to a command block, where:
            Byte       Meaning
            0          set to 0
            1-2        side
            3-4        track
            5-6        first sector to read
            7-8        number of sectors to read
            9-10       offset of buffer to place read data
            11-12      segment of buffer to place read data
-------------------------------------------------
```

```
-------------------------------------------------
Operation:  Write a track to a device.
Version:  DOS 3.2 -
Interrupt:  21h
Function:  68
Called With:
    AH = 68
    AL = 13
    BL = drive number.  0 = default, 1 = A, and so on.
    CL = 65
    CH = 8
```

```
DS:DX = pointer to a command block, where:
     Byte      Meaning
     0         set to 0
     1-2       side
     3-4       track
     5-6       first sector to write
     7-8       number of sectors to write
     9-10      offset of data to write
     11-12     segment of data to write
```

KEY PROGRAMMING POINTS

- DOS versions 3.0 and up return detailed information if an error occurred while performing an interrupt function.

- Open a disk file before using it. When a file is opened, it is assigned a unique handle number.

- The standard input/output devices are always open.

- Normally files are accessed sequentially. Move the file pointer to access files randomly.

- Files can be moved across directories.

- The IOCTL function gives complete control of I/O devices.

CHAPTER 18

TERMINATION
AND A PROGRAM EXAMPLE

After a program has finished, it should restore the computer to the state in which it started, unless, of course, the purpose of the program was to change the state of the computer. For example, if you switched to the graphics screen, you might want to switch back to text. As a more drastic example, if you disabled the keyboard and started a tone on the speaker, you should reenable the keyboard and turn off the speaker. You do not need to restore any registers to their initial states and do not need to clean up the stack.

Once you have taken care of any restorations, call one of the termination interrupts. Among other things, these interrupts restore certain interrupt values from the PSP and flush file buffers. They also return a **return code**. The return code is a number which can be used to signal the parent program. This can be checked by a batch file with the ERRORLEVEL command or from a parent program with interrupt 21h, function 77, as discussed in a later chapter.

By convention, return a zero if the program completed successfully and a different number if there was an error. The return code can also be used to indicate what action a program undertook.

There are two termination functions. Use function 49 for memory resident programs (see Section III).

```
-----------------------------------------------------
Operation:  Terminate a program and stay resident.
            Program remains resident in memory.
            Allocated memory not freed.
Interrupt:  21h
Function:   49
Called With:
     AH = 49
     AL = return code
     DX = number of paragraphs to keep resident.
Returns With:
     Terminates.  Does not return to program that made the
     interrupt.
-----------------------------------------------------
```

```
--------------------------------------------------
Operation:  Terminate a program.
Interrupt:  21h
Function:   76
Called With:
    AH = 76
    AL = return code
Returns With:
    Terminates.  Does not return to program that made the
    interrupt.
--------------------------------------------------
```

MOVE--A PROGRAMMING EXAMPLE

Now let's tie all these concepts together with a program called
MOVE. MOVE is built around interrupt 21h, function 86--the move
and rename interrupt. MOVE renames files and also transfers them
between subdirectories. Using MOVE, you can straighten up a disk
without copying and erasing files--a much longer process that
leads to fragmentation and won't work on filled disks.

You can also use MOVE to move subdirectories around--a terrific
feature for reorganizing disks, especially hard disks. First, use
EXPLORER to toggle the directory attribute on the subdirectories
you want to move. Save this change. Then, use MOVE to give them
their new locations. Finally, use EXPLORER to remark them as
subdirectories.

MOVE is used by entering:

```
move old_name new_name
```

New_name can have a different path than old_name. If old_name
starts with a drive name, then new_name must start with the same
drive name. For example,

```
move b:\utilities\failsafe.com \f.com
```

is not valid, while the following is:

```
move b:\utilities\failsafe.com b:\f.com
```

MOVE first checks the PSP for the command line parameters--the old and new file names. If it can't find the right number of parameters, it prints an error message and terminates. If there are enough parameters, it makes the parameters ASCIIZ strings, sets up the registers for the move and rename file function, and executes the interrupt. It then displays a message. MOVE terminates with a return code of 0 if it is successful and a 1 if it is not.

MOVE is set up to be a COM file. Thus, it starts with an **org 100h** to leave room for the PSP. Because it only uses the code segment, there is no data segment. Note that the variables are placed at the front of the code, preceded by a jump instruction to go to the main body. This makes the variables easier to find, and makes the assembling process more efficient.[1] The code starts by setting up the segment registers. Actually, this is not necessary. When COM files are executed, all four segment registers point to the PSP. By contrast, when EXE files are executed, DS and ES point to the PSP, and CS, IP, SS, and SP are set to the values given by the linker. By making the segment setup explicit in the code, the program operation is clearer.

Note also that each subroutine has only one **ret**, and the main code only terminates at one point. This configuration makes the program easier to follow and debug.

You should recognize the disp_msg routine from Chapter 14. Note how the text messages include carriage returns and line feeds and are terminated by 0's. Find_next_space and find_next_char are used to read through the parameters.

Here's the code:

The code for MOVE is located in move.asm. move.com can be run immediately.

---

[1]The assembler doesn't have to make possibly incorrect guesses about variable sizes.

```
;MOVE.ASM
;
;This program moves files from one directory to another, renaming
;them in the process.
;
;The format is:   MOVE  old_name new_name
;
;If a drive name is specified in old_name, new_name must have the
;same drive_name.
;
;This is set up to be a .COM file.
;

;--------------CONSTANTS---------------

PARAM_START         equ     81h
PARAM_LENGTH        equ     80h
SPACE               equ     20h
RETURN              equ     0dh
FORE_COLOR          equ     3


;-------------BEGINNING--------------

code                segment
                    assume  cs:code,ds:code
                    org     100h            ;make this a .COM file
move:               jmp     main_code


;-------------DATA-------------------
;
;Note: data is placed here to make assembling more efficient
;

old_name            dw      ?
new_name            dw      ?
old_attr            dw      ?
improper_name_msg db         'Improper file name', 0ah, 0dh
                  db         '0 files moved', 0ah, 0dh, 0
missing_msg         db       'Requires source and test file names', 0ah, 0dh
                    db       '0 files moved', 0ah, 0dh, 0
ok_msg              db       '1 file moved', 0ah, 0dh, 0




;-------------MAIN CODE--------------


main_code:          mov     ax,cs    ;set up segment registers
                    mov     ds,ax
                    mov     es,ax
```

```
;.................................
;
; Get the parameters
;
;.................................
                mov     cl,ds:[PARAM_LENGTH]
                mov     ch,0
                mov     bx,PARAM_START
                jcxz    missing_filename  ;no params
                call    find_next_char    ;find old_name
                jcxz    missing_filename  ;no params
                mov     old_name,bx
                call    find_next_space   ;find end, to make ASCIIZ
                jcxz    missing_filename  ;no new_name
                mov     [bx],byte ptr 0   ;make ASCIIZ
                call    find_next_char
                jcxz    missing_filename  ;no new_name
                mov     new_name,bx
                call    find_next_space
                mov     [bx],byte ptr 0
;.................................
;
; Do the move
;
;.................................
move_it:        mov     dx,old_name       ;perform DOS interrupt
                mov     di,new_name
                mov     ah,56h
                int     21h
                jnc     move_ok           ;check for error
;.................................
;
; Display messages and return with error code
;
;.................................
improper_names: lea     dx,improper_name_msg ;display message
                mov     al,1
                jmp     move_end
missing_filename: lea   dx,missing_msg
                mov     al,1
                jmp     move_end
move_ok:        lea     dx,ok_msg              ;print message
                mov     al,0
move_end:       call    disp_msg
                mov     ah,4ch                 ;terminate
                int     21h
```

```
;-------------SUBROUTINES-------------

;find_next_space
;    returns offset of next space or return or 0
;        starting offset in BX
;        count in CX
;        result returned in BX
;        CX decremented by characters examined
;

find_next_space    proc    near
                   push    ax
f_n_s_loop:        mov     al,[bx]            ;load character
                   cmp     al,SPACE           ;is it a space?
                   je      found_space
                   cmp     al,RETURN          ;is it a return?
                   je      found_space
                   cmp     al,0               ;is it a 0?
                   je      found_space
                   inc     bx                 ;keep on looking
                   loop    f_n_s_loop
found_space:       pop     ax
                   ret
find_next_space    endp




;find_next_char
;    returns offset of next non-space, non-return, non-0 character
;        starting offset in BX
;        count in CX
;        result returned in BX
;        CX decremented by characters examined
;

find_next_char     proc    near
                   push    ax
f_n_c_loop:        mov     al,[bx]            ;load character
                   cmp     al,SPACE           ;is it a space?
                   je      cont_loop
                   cmp     al,RETURN          ;is it a return?
                   je      cont_loop
                   cmp     al,0               ;is it a 0?
                   je      cont_loop
                   jmp     found_char
cont_loop:         inc     bx                 ;keep on looking
                   loop    f_n_c_loop
found_char:        pop     ax
                   ret
find_next_char     endp
```

```
;disp_msg
;       displays an ASCIIZ message
;       offset of message in DS:DX
;

disp_msg        proc    near
                push    ax
                push    bx
                push    si
                mov     bl,FORE_COLOR
                mov     si,dx               ;point to string
d_m_loop:       mov     al,[si]             ;load character
                cmp     al,0                ;check for end
                je      d_m_end
                mov     ah,0eh              ;print char service
                int     10h                 ;print it
                inc     si
                jmp     d_m_loop
d_m_end:        pop     si
                pop     bx
                pop     ax
                ret
disp_msg        endp


code            ends
                end     move
```

Enter this code and save it as move.asm. Compile it and correct any mistakes. Then link it. Ignore the no stack warning. Use EXE2BIN to make it a COM file. The whole process is:

```
masm move;
link move;
exe2bin move
rename move.bin move.com
```

Now try it out. Rename files and directories. Move files across directories. Use MOVE and EXPLORER to move a directory. First, toggle the directory attribute with EXPLORER. Then, move the directory, which now looks like a file, using MOVE. Finally, reset the directory attribute with EXPLORER.

When a file is moved, the original directory entry for the file is cleared by setting the first character to e5h (the erased file indicator) and by clearing the attribute byte. No other data is changed, and the file allocation table isn't touched. You can take advantage of this to set up multiple paths for the same directory. After moving a directory, as discussed in the preceding paragraph, restore the original entry. That is, replace the e5h with the original character and set the directory bit in the attribute byte. The original directory will contain the same files it used to contain, and so will the moved directory.

For example, suppose you keep the results of your company's accounts in the directory \BUSINESS\FINANCES\BALSHEET. To make them easier to access, you move the whole directory to the root level, calling it \BALSHEET. By restoring the entry for \BUSINESS\FINANCES\BALSHEET, both directories will point to your company's balance sheets.

KEY PROGRAMMING POINTS

- To end a program, restore the system status if necessary. Then use a termination interrupt.

- Programs should check that input is in the proper format.

- COM files start with **org 100h.**

- Place variables at the beginning of programs to make assembling more efficient.

CHAPTER 19

DIRECTORIES

The DOS disk interrupts treat directories as separate entities. This prevents programs which are set up to operate on normal files, such as word processors, from accidentally clobbering the crucial information stored in a directory. A separate set of functions exists just to service directories. In this chapter, you will see how to create and remove directories, determine and change the current directory, and search directories. Finally, you will tie these concepts together with a utility: DIR2.

CREATING AND DELETING DIRECTORIES

The interrupts to create and delete directories operate just as DOS's MKDIR and RMDIR commands. Only empty directories can be removed. The current directory and root directory cannot be removed.

```
--------------------------------------------------
Operation:  Create a subdirectory.
Version:  DOS 2.0 -
Interrupt:  21h
Function:  57
Call With:
    AH = 57
    DS:DX = pointer to ASCIIZ name of directory to create.  Path
    name can be from root or current directory.
Returns With:
    AX = error code
    Carry set if error.  Error codes are 3 (path not found) and 5
    (access denied).
--------------------------------------------------


--------------------------------------------------
Operation:  Remove a subdirectory.
        Must not be the root or current directory.
        Must be an empty directory.
Version:  DOS 2.0 -
Interrupt:  21h
Function:  58
Call With:
    AH = 58
    DS:DX = pointer to ASCIIZ name of directory to remove.  Path
    name can be from root or current directory.
Returns With:
    AX = error code
    Carry set if error.  Error codes are 3 (path not found), 5
    (access denied), and 16 (cannot remove current directory).
--------------------------------------------------
```

CURRENT DIRECTORY

The current directory is the default directory used in file and directory creation and in searching. For example, if you attempt to open b:worms, DOS will look for a file named worms in the current b drive directory. On the other hand, an attempt to open b:\worms will cause DOS to look for a file named worms in the b drive root directory.

```
-------------------------------------------------
Operation:  Get current directory.
Version:  DOS 2.0 -
Interrupt:  21h
Function:  71
Call With:
    AH = 71
    DL = drive number.  0 = default, 1 = A, etc.
    DS:SI = pointer to a 64 byte area of user memory.  Be sure to
    set aside room for this area in your data space.  DOS will
    fill it in with the ASCIIZ name of the current directory.
Returns With:
    AX = error code
    DS:SI = pointer to the ASCIIZ name of the current directory.
    Note: the registers' values are not changed, but the 64 byte
    data area is filled in.  The current directory name starts
    with the name of the root directory.  The drive and first \
    are not included.
    Carry set if error.  Error code is 15 (invalid drive number in
    AL).
-------------------------------------------------

-------------------------------------------------
Operation:  Change current directory.
Version:  DOS 2.0 -
Interrupt:  21h
Function:  59
Call With:
    AH = 59
    DS:DX = pointer to ASCIIZ directory to make the current
    directory.  Path name can be from root or current directory.
Returns With:
    AX = error code
    Carry set if error.  Error code is 3 (path not found).
-------------------------------------------------
```

SEARCHING DIRECTORIES FOR FILES

Use two interrupts to search directories for files. Call the
first interrupt with the name pattern for which you are searching.
Wild card characters are fully supported. For example, you could
use patterns such as **b:utilities\failsafe.com** or ***.e?e**. This
interrupt finds the directory to search, expands the file portion
of the pattern name (for example, from *.e?e to ????????e?e), and
looks for the first matching entry. After using this interrupt,
use the second interrupt to continue searching. Both interrupts
return an error message if they cannot find a matching file.

You can choose whether to search only for normal files or for
hidden, system, and directory files as well. You can also search
for the volume name.

When the file is found, data is returned telling its name, size,
date of creation, and other information. This data is stored in
the DTA. If you need to use the command line parameters, make
sure that you process or copy them before you begin a directory
search.

The format of the information stored in the DTA follows. If you
change it at any time during the directory search, the search
process will be modified. For example, you can change the
matching pattern to start a search for one pattern and end it with
another. A word of warning: the use of the first 21 bytes is
undocumented. Change the values there with caution and be
especially cautious if you tinker with the drive or file pointers.

Byte	Meaning
0	Drive. 1 = A, 2 = B, etc.
1-12	Matching pattern. This does not include drive or path information. *'s are expanded to ?'s, and spaces are inserted as necessary. The period separating name and extension is not included. The matching pattern is used for a direct comparison against the name entry in the directory. Will not match to erased files.

Byte	Meaning
14-15	Position of filename in directory. The first directory entry is 0, the second 1, and so on. Erased file and volume positions are included in this count. For example, suppose you search for all files, and the first file matched is the volume. It will have position 0. Then there is an erased file. It will not be matched. Then there is a normal file. It will have position 2.
16-17	Directory (path) position.
18-20	Reserved.
21	Attribute of file found. In same format as that used in the directory.
22-23	File's time. In same format as that used in the directory.
24-25	File's date. In same format as that used in the directory.
26-29	File's size in bytes. Low word then high word.
30-43	ASCIIZ name of matched file. Includes period between name and extension if extension not blank. Not padded with blanks. That is, DIR2.COM, not DIR2 .COM

Remember, when using the directory search interrupts, use the find first matching file and then the find next matching file.

```
-------------------------------------------------
Operation:  Find first matching file in directory.
Version:  DOS 2.0 -
Interrupt:  21h
Function:  78
Call With:
    AH = 78
    CH = 0
    CL = file attribute code. Format is the same as the attribute
        byte in the directory. Use 0 for searching for normal
        files only. Set the hidden, system, or subdirectory bits
        to include those files in the search. If the volume bit
        is set, only the volume entry will be found.
    DS:DX =  pointer to ASCIIZ file pattern. Can include drive
        and path name. Path can be from current or root
        directory. A full filename pattern must be given.
        For example, b: is invalid while b:* is valid.
Returns With:
    AX = error code
    File information stored in DTA as discussed above.
    Carry set if error. Error codes are 2 (file not found) and 18
    (no more matching files).
-------------------------------------------------
```

```
------------------------------------------------------
Operation:  Find next matching file in directory.
        Interrupt 21h, function 78 must have been called first.
Version:  DOS 2.0 -
Interrupt:  21h
Function:  79
Call With:
    AH = 79
Returns With:
    AX = error code
    File information stored in DTA as discussed above.
    Carry set if error.  Error code is 18 (no more matching
    files).
------------------------------------------------------
```

DIR2 -- A DIRECTORY SEARCHING UTILITY

DIR2 uses the directory searching interrupts. It is similar to
DIR except that it also searches for hidden, system, and directory
files. As an option, it will only print hidden or directory
files. Another option pauses the display every screen.

To use DIR2, type:

```
dir2  file_pattern -options
```

Both the file pattern and options are optional. If a file pattern
is included, it must contain a file name pattern, not just a path.
Options are h, d, and p. The options must be preceded by a -. H
and d cannot be used together. H causes only hidden files to be
printed while D causes only directory files to be printed. P
pauses the screen after it is filled; the search continues after a
key is struck. Only the names of files are printed. Directory
entries are indicated by a <DIR>.

For example, to look at all directories on the B drive with names
starting with m, use:

```
dir2 b:m*.* -d
```

To examine all files in the NAMES subdirectory of the current
directory, use:

```
dir2 names\*.*
```

DIR2 is based around the find first and find next directory entry functions. First, it searches the command line parameters. If it can't find a file pattern, it uses a default of *.*. If it can't find any options, it assumes all files should be printed without screen pauses. Options can be specified in any order. The h and d options are mutually exclusive, though it is simple to change this limitation.

As the parameters are checked, the file pattern is turned into an ASCIIZ string. Then, the DTA location is found using the find DTA interrupt.[1] Next, the find first entry interrupt is called. If this call is not successful, an error message is printed. If it is successful, the matching file name is printed, and the find next entry interrupt is called until no more matches are found. The search attribute byte is set to match all; the attribute is checked if the h or d flag was set.

A variable keeps track of the number of lines printed. If the pause option is set, every 24 lines a "Hit any key to continue" message is displayed, and the routine halts to wait for a keystroke. This is done using the BIOS read keyboard interrupt.

After the name is printed, "<DIR>" appears if the file is a subdirectory. A carriage return and line feed are then printed to move to the next line.

Note that defaults are assigned for missing parameters and that case is not important for the options.

The print_it routine is placed outside the main_loop. In terms of flow, it really belongs inside the main loop block because it is not a subroutine. But it only has one exit point, and by moving it outside the main loop, the loop structure is clearer.

As with MOVE, the return code is 1 if there was an error; otherwise, it is 0.

---

[1]The default is location 80 in the PSP. Using this interrupt is not necessary but adds a nice touch. If many people are working on a programming project or if DTA's are changed, checking for the location is more important.

Here's the code:

```
The code for this program is
dir2.asm.  dir2.com is ready to run.
```

```
;DIR2.ASM
;
;This program examines the disk directory and like DIR prints out
;names matching a pattern.  As an option, it will print out only
;hidden or directory files.  It also has an option to pause after
;every 24 lines.
;
;The format is:   DIR2 [file pattern] [- or / [h or d] [p]]
;
;For example,   DIR2 C:*.COM -hp   will list all hidden .COM files
;on the C drive, pausing every 24 lines.  Only one flag (- or /)
;should be used, even if there are several options.
;
;This is to be set up as a .COM file.
;


        ;--------------CONSTANTS---------------

PARAM_START      equ      81h
PARAM_LENGTH     equ      80h
SPACE            equ      20h
RETURN           equ      0dh
FORE_COLOR       equ      3
FLAG1            equ      '/'
FLAG2            equ      '-'
LINES_PER_PAGE   equ      24
ON               equ      1
OFF              equ      0
ALL              equ      0ffh
DIR_ONLY         equ      10h
HIDDEN_ONLY      equ      2



        ;--------------BEGINNING---------------

code             segment
                 assume cs:code,ds:code
                 org      100h            ;make this a .COM file
dir2:            jmp      main_code       ;go to main code
```

```
;--------------DATA--------------------
;
;Note: data is placed here to make assembling more efficient
;

pattern          dw      ?
attr_mask        db      ALL
pause_option     db      OFF
default_name     db      '*.*', 0
error_msg        db      '0 files found', 0ah, 0dh, 0
pause_for_key    db      '----Hit any key to continue----', 0
dir_msg          db      '        <DIR>',0
new_line         db      0ah, 0dh, 0


;--------------MAIN CODE---------------

main_code:       mov     ax,cs               ;set up segment registers
                 mov     ds,ax
                 mov     es,ax
;...............................
;
; Get the parameters
;
;...............................
                 mov     cl,ds:[PARAM_LENGTH]
                 mov     ch,0
                 mov     bx,PARAM_START
                 jcxz    set_defaults        ;no params
                 call    find_next_char      ;find pattern or option flag
                 jcxz    set_defaults        ;no params
                 mov     al,[bx]             ;what is char?
                 cmp     al,FLAG1            ;is it a flag?
                 je      options_def_name    ;yes => read options, and
                 cmp     al,FLAG2            ;get the default pattern
                 je      options_def_name
                 mov     pattern,bx          ;pattern starts here
                 call    find_next_space     ;find end, to make ASCIIZ
                 mov     [bx],byte ptr 0     ;make ASCIIZ
                 jcxz    start_loop          ;no options, use defaults
                 call    find_next_char
                 jcxz    start_loop          ;no options, use defaults
                 mov     al,[bx]             ;is the character an
                 cmp     al,FLAG1            ;option flag?
                 je      rd_option           ;read the options
                 cmp     al,FLAG2
                 je      rd_option
                 jmp     start_loop
;...............................
;
; Call routines to read in options or defaults
;
;...............................
```

```
set_defaults:    call    get_default_name
                 jmp     start_loop
options_def_name: call   read_options
                 call    get_default_name
                 jmp     start_loop
rd_option:       call    read_options
;.................................
;
; Search through directory as long as possible, printing file names
; if they match the pattern and options.
;
;.................................
start_loop:      mov     si,0              ;si = line count
                 mov     ah,2fh            ;get DTA address, which will
                 int     21h               ;be 80.  Check it anyway.
                                           ;result in ES:BX
                 mov     ax,4e00h          ;find first matching file
                 mov     dx,pattern
                 mov     cx,1ah            ;match to all
                 int     21h
                 cmp     al,0              ;was there an error?
                 je      main_loop         ;no.
                 lea     dx,error_msg      ;an error.
                 call    disp_msg
                 mov     al,1              ;error return code
                 jmp     dir2_end

main_loop:       cmp     attr_mask,ALL     ;display all files?
                 je      print_it          ;yes, so print name
                 mov     al,es:[bx]+21     ;look at file attribute
                 and     al,attr_mask      ;see if it matches option
                 jne     print_it          ;yes, so print name
cont_match:      mov     ax,4f00h          ;look for next matching file
                 int     21h
                 cmp     al,0              ;no more files?
                 je      main_loop
                 mov     al,0              ;successful finish
dir2_end:        mov     ah,4ch            ;terminate
                 int     21h

;.................................
;
; Print file name, pause for keystroke if necessary,
; then return to loop.
;
;.................................
```

```
print_it:          cmp    pause_option,ON        ;check for pause?
                   jne    p_cont
                   cmp    si,LINES_PER_PAGE      ;time to pause?
                   jne    p_cont
                   lea    dx,pause_for_key       ;yes, display message
                   call   disp_msg
                   mov    ah,0                   ;wait for keystroke
                   int    16h
                   lea    dx,new_line            ;advance to a new line
                   call   disp_msg
                   mov    si,0                   ;reset count
p_cont:            mov    dx,bx                  ;offset of file name
                   add    dx,30
                   call   disp_msg               ;print it
                   test   es:[bx]+21,byte ptr DIR_ONLY
                                                 ;is it a subdirectory?
                   jz     p_new_line
                   lea    dx,dir_msg
                   call   disp_msg
p_new_line:        lea    dx,new_line            ;advance to a new line
                   call   disp_msg
                   inc    si                     ;increment line count
                   jmp    cont_match             ;continue with search



;--------------SUBROUTINES-------------

;read_options
;    examines command line characters following BX to set options.
;

read_options       proc   near
                   push   ax
                   inc    bx            ;look at char following flag
                   mov    al,[bx]
                   call   check_options
                   inc    bx            ;look at next char
                   mov    al,[bx]
                   call   check_options
                   pop    ax
                   ret
read_options       endp
;check_options
;    given a character in AL, sets pause_option or attr_mask
;    accordingly
;
```

```
check_options    proc    near
                 cmp     al,'p'
                 je      set_pause
                 cmp     al,'P'
                 je      set_pause
                 cmp     al,'h'
                 je      set_hidden
                 cmp     al,'H'
                 je      set_hidden
                 cmp     al,'d'
                 je      set_dir
                 cmp     al,'D'
                 je      set_dir
                 jmp     c_o_end
set_pause:       mov     pause_option,ON
                 jmp     c_o_end
set_hidden:      mov     attr_mask,HIDDEN_ONLY
                 jmp     c_o_end
set_dir:         mov     attr_mask,DIR_ONLY
c_o_end:         ret
check_options    endp

;get_default_name
;    Because no pattern was given, just use current directory
;    in default drive. (*.*)
;

get_default_name proc    near
                 push    ax
                 lea     ax,default_name
                 mov     pattern,ax
                 pop     ax
                 ret
get_default_name endp




;**
;**
;**    Place find_next_space, find_next_char, and disp_msg here.
;**    Their code is in MOVE.ASM  (Chapter 18).
;**
;**

code             ends
                 end     dir2
```

Enter this code and save it as dir2.asm. Assemble it and correct any typos. Link it and convert it to a COM file. Then try it out. Be sure to try the switches.

KEY PROGRAMMING POINTS

- There are separate DOS functions to deal with directories.

- The current directory is the default for file creation and directory searching.

- Start a directory search with the find first function. Then, repeatedly issue the find next function. These functions store information in the DTA.

CHAPTER 20

MEMORY

There are three types of RAM: conventional, extended, and expanded. **Conventional memory** is the memory you normally deal with--the first megabyte. Of this, the first 640K is not reserved. **Extended memory** is the next fifteen megabytes. This memory is only available starting with the AT and is not addressable by DOS 1.0-3.2. **Expanded memory** is page-banked memory that is added with a special memory expansion card, such as the Intel Above Board.

CONVENTIONAL MEMORY

When a program is loaded, all free memory is allocated to it. This means that as long as you are in a single user environment, you are safe to use any unreserved memory area--within the first 640K--for data storage. But this is inelegant and prevents the use of child programs. If you need to use large areas of memory for data or plan to spawn child programs, you must first free all the memory your program doesn't use. When you need to use a big block of memory, issue a memory request. DOS keeps track of what memory is free and assigns a portion to the program. When you are finished using that portion, free it.

There are three interrupt functions to control memory, all part of interrupt 21h. All deal with memory in groups of 16 bytes (one paragraph). Function 72 allocates memory. Call it when you need memory for data. It is just like the C **alloc** function. Function 73 frees memory that was allocated by function 72. Be sure to free all allocated memory before program termination. Function 74 modifies the size of a memory block. Before you use any of the other memory functions, you must use this function to shrink the amount of memory allocated to the program from all free memory to the program's size. To do this, you will need to figure out where the program ends. For single segment programs, place a label at the end; for multiple segment programs, place a dummy segment at the end. If you use the label approach, divide the offset by 16, add it to the segment value, and increment the result to get the ending segment.

DOS keeps track of memory with a linked list that stores the first paragraph[1] in a memory block, its size, and whether it is free.

---

[1]A paragraph is a block of 16 bytes. Paragraphs are numbered sequentially starting with 0 at byte 0 of conventional memory. The paragraph number is the same thing as a segment number, except that it refers to a 16-byte block instead of a 64K-byte block.

When you use the memory function calls, DOS scans this list to find either the block you want to free or modify or a free block it can allocate.

```
--------------------------------------------------
Operation:  Allocate memory.
Version:  DOS 2.0 -
Interrupt:  21h
Function:  72
Call With:
    AH = 72
    BX = number of paragraphs to allocate
Returns With:
    AX = starting paragraph of allocated block or error code
    BX = if there was an error, size of largest available block,
    in paragraphs.
    Carry set if error.  Error codes are 7 (memory control blocks
    destroyed) and 8 (insufficient memory).
--------------------------------------------------
```

```
--------------------------------------------------
Operation:  Free allocated memory block.
        Block must have been allocated.
Version:  DOS 2.0 -
Interrupt:  21h
Function:  73
Call With:
    AH = 73
    ES = starting paragraph of block to free
Returns With:
    AX = error code
    Carry set if error.  Error codes are 7 (memory control blocks
    destroyed) and 9 (invalid memory block address).
--------------------------------------------------
```

```
--------------------------------------------------
Operation:  Modify size of memory block.
        Can shrink or expand.
        Block must have been allocated.
Version:  DOS 2.0 -
Interrupt:  21h
Function:  74
Call With:
    AH = 74
    ES = starting paragraph of block to modify
    BX = new size, in paragraphs
```

Returns With:
    AX = error code
    BX = if error on attempt to expand block size, set to maximum
    possible size for the block.
    Carry set if error. Error codes are 7 (memory control blocks
    destroyed), 8 (insufficient memory), and 9 (invalid memory
    block address).

The easiest way to address memory allocated with these calls is to
load the starting paragraph number into a segment register.
Offset zero in that segment is the first byte in the block.

If you have allocated a block but can't expand it to the size you
want, try to allocate a new block of the desired size. If
successful, copy the old information to the new block and free the
old block.

To determine the total amount of memory available, point ES to
the PSP, and try to expand the block by ffffh paragraphs. This
will cause an error, and the amount of free memory will be
returned in BX. Remember to free up memory that the program
doesn't use if you want a meaningful answer. (If you don't, you
will get zero.)

You can use the following interrupt to determine the total
amount of conventional memory. It checks the hardware setup
switches.

Operation: Report amount of conventional memory installed on
              computer.
Version: BIOS
Interrupt: 12h
Call With:
    NA
Returns With:
    AX = kilobytes of memory installed

EXTENDED MEMORY

Extended memory only exists starting with the AT.

```
--------------------------------------------------
Operation:  Determine amount of extended memory
Version:  AT BIOS
Interrupt:  15h
Function:  136
Call With:
    AH = 136
Returns With:
    AX = kilobytes of extended memory
--------------------------------------------------
```

EXPANDED MEMORY

Expanded memory is added with an expanded memory board. Several megabytes can be added, but only a small portion can be accessed at one time. A certain part of conventional memory is set aside as an expanded memory window. Portions of the expanded memory are addressed via this window. All program instructions that deal with memory locations in the window memory addresses are modified by the expanded memory board hardware to address the portion of expanded memory mapped to the window. Interrupts are used to control which section of memory to address.

For example, suppose you have one megabyte of expanded memory and the window size is 16K. To search through all of expanded memory, you would use an interrupt to look at the first 16K, process it, look at the next 16K, process it, and so on. Only 16K of the expanded memory would be available at one time. Suppose that the window started at C000:0000 and that the second 16K of expanded memory were mapped to this window. If a program looked at memory location C000:0001h, it would see the value stored at location 4001h (byte 1 in the second 16K) of expanded memory. If a program changed the value at memory location C000:0017h, it would change the value stored in location 4017h of expanded memory.

There are several different manufacturers of expanded memory boards with different standards for using the memory. This book discusses the Lotus/Intel/Microsoft Expanded Memory Specification, called the EMS, which is the most widely accepted and used.

With the EMS, up to 8M bytes of memory can be addressed via 4 contiguous 16K windows. These windows are located in high memory (above 640K). Their location can be determined by an interrupt call. All expanded memory function calls are through interrupt 67h.

Using the expanded memory is similar to using files and conventional memory. When you need expanded memory, issue an interrupt request to allocate a certain amount of memory in units of 16K. The interrupt returns a handle number by which you reference that memory block. The expanded memory management software (EMM) controls which physical expanded memory pages are used for the block; you see the block as a contiguous set of pages numbered from 0 on up. To examine the memory, specify the handle and the page number. Also, specify in which of the four windows you want to access the information.

For example, suppose you want to use expanded memory to store images from the graphics screens for animation. You have five pictures that you want to sequence through. Assuming they are not compressed, each takes 16K. So you request five blocks of 16K. Suppose the handle number is 7. To look at the second picture, ask to look at the second page of handle 7. Of course, this page could physically reside anywhere in expanded memory. Suppose the windows start at segment c000h, and you map the page to the third window. Then, you can address the graphics information through memory locations c800:0000h-c800:3fffh.

As another example, suppose you wanted to store a 128K array in expanded memory. Issue an allocation request and get a handle. To look at an array element, figure its offset within the block, divide this by 16K to get the page, and then request to look at that page. You could also map four of the array pages to windows at the same time. In this fashion, you can address 64K of the array at once.

Once you are finished with a block of expanded memory, free it.

The application program must keep track of what windows it is using so as not to overwrite important data.

Before a program uses expanded memory, it should check that the expanded memory management device driver is installed and that an expanded memory board is present and operational. Then it should find the starting location of the windows.

To see if the software driver is installed:

1) Find the address interrupt 67h points to. This is discussed in more detail in Chapter 23 and Section III. Use interrupt 21h, function 53:

```
mov  ah,53      ;read value for interrupt
mov  al,67h     ;67h and return location in
int  21h        ;es:bx
```

2) Compare the 8 bytes starting at offset 10 within this routine (ES:000Ah) to the ASCII string EMMXXXX0.

3) If the 8 bytes are the same, the expanded memory manager software is installed, and you can use any of the expanded memory board interrupts.

As mentioned, all expanded memory interrupts are through interrupt 67h. The function number is placed in AH. An error code is returned in AH:

Error Code	Meaning
0	No error.
128	Malfunction in EMM software.
129	Malfunction in EM hardware.
130	Not used.
131	Invalid handle.
132	Invalid function code.
133	No available EMM handles (all are in use).

Error Code	Meaning
134	Page mapping context error.
135	Not enough expanded memory pages.
136	Not enough free memory pages.
137	Can't allocate 0 pages.
138	Request for a page greater than the number of pages allocated to the handle.
139	The physical memory page to which the handle's page is mapped is invalid.
140	No room to save the expanded memory board status.
141	Expanded memory board status information already associated with this handle number.
142	No status information is associated with this handle number.
143	Invalid subfunction.

Let's examine the major expanded memory interrupts. Remember, you must first check that the expanded memory software driver is installed before you use any of these interrupts. If the driver is not installed and you call these, your computer may hang. Also, do not use the expanded memory handles for DOS handles or vice versa. There is no correlation, and you might get unexpected results.

```
-------------------------------------------------
Operation:  Check expanded memory board status.
Version:  EMS
Interrupt:  67h
Function:  64
Call With:
    AH = 64
Returns With:
    AH = error code.  Error codes are 128, 129, and 132.  If the
    board is installed and working, there will be no error (0).
-------------------------------------------------
```

```
--------------------------------------------------
Operation:  Get window location.
Version:  EMS
Interrupt:  67h
Function:  65
Called With:
    AH = 65
Returns With:
    AH = error code.  Error codes are 128, 129, and 132.
    BX = segment where windows start.  First window is at offset
    0; second, at offset 4000h; third, at offset 8000h; and
    fourth, at offset c000h.
--------------------------------------------------


--------------------------------------------------
Operation:    Determine number of free and total expanded memory
              pages.
          A page is 16K.
Version:  EMS
Interrupt:  67h
Function:  66
Call With:
    AH = 66
Returns With:
    AH = error code.  Error codes are 128, 129, and 132.
    BX = number of free pages.
 .  DX = total number of pages.
--------------------------------------------------


--------------------------------------------------
Operation:  Allocate expanded memory pages.
        Pages are referenced by the handle returned.
Version:  EMS
Interrupt:  67h
Function:  67
Call With:
    AH = 67
    BX = number of pages to allocate
Returns With:
    AH = error code.  Error codes are 128, 129, 132, 133, 135,
    136, and 137.
    DX = handle
--------------------------------------------------
```

```
--------------------------------------------------------
Operation:  Get expanded memory page.
            Maps a page belonging to a handle to a window.
            The data is addressed via the window's memory address.
Version:  EMS
Interrupt:  67h
Function:  68
Call With:
    AH = 68
    AL = window number  (0 - 3)
    BX = page to get.  The first page for the handle is 0, the
    next is 1, and so on.
    DX = handle
Returns With:
    Page data addressable through window location.
    AH = error code.  Error codes are 128, 129, 131, 132, 138,
    139.
--------------------------------------------------------
```

```
--------------------------------------------------------
Operation:  Free expanded memory block.
Version:  EMS
Interrupt:  67h
Function:  69
Call With:
    AH = 69
    DX = handle of block to free.  Frees all pages allocated to
    handle.
Return With:
    AH = error code.  Error codes are 128, 129, 131, 132, and 134.
--------------------------------------------------------
```

There are also several utility functions. You can use these to make a utility akin to EXPLORER which examines expanded memory. To display blocks allocated to a handle, find all handles and their sizes. Then, window through their data. Include the ability to decode directory information. To look at the free memory, keep allocating it to blocks. Start with as large a block as you can; if you can't allocate one that size, decrease the request a page at a time until you can. This way, you will use as few handles as possible and will be able to examine all free memory. Be sure to free the blocks you allocate.

```
----------------------------------------------------
Operation:  Get version number of EM software driver.
Version:  EMS
Interrupt:  67h
Function:  70
Call With:
   AH = 70
Returns With:
   AH = error code.  Error codes are 128, 129, and 132.
   AL = version number.  High hexit is major version (that is, 3
   in 3.1); low hexit is minor version (that is, 1 in 3.1).
----------------------------------------------------
```

```
----------------------------------------------------
Operation:  Determine number of active handles.
Version:  EMS
Interrupt:  67h
Function:  75
Call With:
   AH = 75
Returns With:
   AH = error code.  Error codes are 128, 129, 131, and 132.
   BX = number of handles.  BH always 0.
----------------------------------------------------
```

```
----------------------------------------------------
Operation:  Determine block size.
Version:  EMS
Interrupt:  67h
Function:  76
Call With:
   AH = 76
   DX = handle
Returns With:
   AH = error code.  Error codes are 218, 129, 131, and 132.
   BX = number of pages allocated to handle.  Less than or equal
   to 512 and greater than 0.
----------------------------------------------------
```

```
-----------------------------------------------------
Operation:  Get array of all handle sizes.
Version:  EMS
Interrupt:  67h
Function:  77
Call With:
     AH = 77
     ES:DI = pointer to the data area where the results will be
     stored.  Size of the area must be at least 4 * (number of
     active handles) bytes.  This will never exceed 1K.  The area
     should not cross over the ES segment boundary.  For example,
     if the array is 10 bytes long, don't place it at ES:FFF8h.
Returns With:
     AH = error code.  Error codes are 128, 129, and 132.
     BX = number of active handles.  BH will always be 0.
     ES:DI = pointer to array containing size information.  The
     register values will not change, but the data will be filled
     in.  There will be BX entries, each 2 words long, starting at
     DI + 0.  The first word in each pair is the handle number; the
     second, its size.
-----------------------------------------------------
```

Special care must be taken when using expanded memory from
memory resident routines and device drivers. They must save
any handles they allocate and deallocate them when necessary.
When they access expanded memory, they need to save the
current status of the expanded memory board--the information
about what data is addressed by each window. They may want to
load information about the status of the board when they were
last using it. Before they terminate, they must restore the
status to what is was before they were called.

Saving and restoring the status is done with two interrupts.
Both of these require that a handle number is passed to them.
To prevent possible conflict, this handle number should be
owned (that is, initiated) by the resident routine.

The resident routine may want to allocate all the expanded
memory it needs when it is loaded and use this block when the
routine is called. If so, use the handle for this block when
saving and restoring the expanded memory board status.

Several expanded memory boards can be used by one computer.
The status save and restore interrupts save and restore the
status of all of these boards.

```
--------------------------------------------------
Operation:  Save expanded memory board status.
Version:  EMS
Interrupt:  67h
Function:  71
Call With:
    AH = 71
    DX = handle with which to associate status.  Handle should be
    owned by the routine that is saving the status.
Returns With:
    AH = error code.  Error codes are 128, 129, 131, 132, 140, and
    141.
--------------------------------------------------
```

```
--------------------------------------------------
Operation:  Restore expanded memory board status.
Version:  EMS
Interrupt:  67h
Function:  72
Call With:
    AH = 72
    DX = handle with which status to restore is associated.
    Status should have been associated with this handle using
    function 71.
Returns With:
    Old state (window mapping) restored.
    AH = error code.  Error codes are 128, 129, 131, 132, and 142.
--------------------------------------------------
```

The EMS standard also supports multi-tasking environments.
For a full discussion of this and some Assembly Language
sketches, refer to the LIM EMS manual.

KEY PROGRAMMING POINTS

- The three types of memory are conventional, extended, and
  expanded.

- When a program is loaded, all memory is allocated to it.
  Free all memory that it doesn't use.

- Use of extended memory is limited with DOS versions up to
  and including 3.2.

- Expanded memory is page banked and mapped to a high memory window.

- The EMS standard contains many functions for allocating, using, and freeing expanded memory.

CHAPTER 21

DISK SECTORS
AND DRIVE INFORMATION

As you saw in EXPLORER, there are two ways to access individual disk sectors--with BIOS calls and with DOS calls. The BIOS calls reference disk locations by side, track, and sector; the DOS calls just use a sector number. BIOS calls deal with absolute disk locations; they ignore partition bounds. DOS calls deal with relative locations. Sector 0 refers to the first sector in the current partition. Sectors cannot be read outside the current partition.

In general, DOS calls are easier to use because they deal with relative sectors, and you do not need to decide when to switch sides and tracks. Use BIOS calls when you need to access sectors outside of the current partition.

Note that the DOS read and write interrupts return with the original flags left on the stack. After calling the interrupts, you must clean these flags off the stack. Either check the flags for an error indicator and then **popf,** or pop the flags into a dummy location. If you do not clear the flags off the stack, the subroutine return address will be incorrect.

```
-------------------------------------------------
Operation:  Read disk sectors.
            DOS sector numbering scheme.
            Returns original flags on stack.
Version:  DOS 1.0 -
Interrupt:  25h
Call With:
     AL = drive.  0 = A, 1 = B, 2 = C, etc.
     DS:BX = pointer to area in which to store the read
     information.
     CX = number of sectors to read
     DX = first sector to read
Returns With:
     AX = error code.  (See table following discussion of next
     interrupt.)
     Carry set if error.
     All registers except segment registers may be destroyed.
     Original flags returned on stack.
-------------------------------------------------
```

```
---------------------------------------------------
Operation:  Write disk sectors.
            DOS sector numbering scheme.
            Returns original flags on stack.
Version:  DOS 1.0 -
Interrupt:  26h
Call With:
    AL = drive.  0 = A, 1 = B, 2 = C, etc.
    DS:BX = pointer to area from which to read the information to
    write to disk.
    CX = number of sectors to write
    DX = first sector to write to
Returns With:
    AX = error code.
    Carry set if error.
    All registers except segment registers may be destroyed.
    Original flags returned on stack.
---------------------------------------------------
```

For interrupts 25h and 26h, the following error codes apply:[1]

Value in AH	Meaning
2	Unknown error
3	Disk is write protected
4	Bad sector number
8	Bad CRC
64	Couldn't access track
128	Drive did not respond

Value in AL	Meaning
0	Disk is write protected
1	Invalid drive number
2	Drive not ready
4	Bad CRC
6	Couldn't access track
7	Unrecognizable disk format
8	Sector not found
10	Write error
11	Read error
12	General unknown error

---

[1]The DOS 2.0 Technical Reference Manual reports different AH codes for some of the hardware errors. Rely on the AL codes.

The following two interrupts are the BIOS disk read and write interrupts. If more than one sector is being read or written, the sectors must be on the same side and track.

```
--------------------------------------------------
Operation:  Read disk sectors.
        BIOS sector numbering scheme.
        Sectors must be on same side and track.
Version:  BIOS
Interrupt:  13h
Function:  2
Call With:
    AH = 2
    AL = number of sectors to read.  Should not be 0.
    ES:BX = pointer to area in which read information will be
    stored.
    CL = low six bits are the sector number.  High two bits are
    high two bits of the track number.
    CH = low eight bits of track number.
    DL = drive number.  0 - 3 for floppies, 80h - 87h for hard
    drives.
    DH = side
Returns With:
    AH = error code  (see table which follows)
    Carry set if error.
--------------------------------------------------
```

```
--------------------------------------------------
Operation:  Write disk sectors.
        BIOS sector numbering scheme.
        Sectors must be on same side and track.
Version:  BIOS
Interrupt:  13h
Function:  3
Call With:
    AH = 3
    AL = number of sectors to write.  Should not be 0.
    ES:BX = pointer to area from which to read information that
    will be written to disk.
    CL = low six bits are the sector number.  High two bits are
    high two bits of the track number.
    CH = low eight bits of track number.
    DL = drive number.  0 - 3 for floppies, 80h - 87h for hard
    drives.
    DH = side
Returns With:
    AH = error code  (see table which follows)
    Carry set if error.
--------------------------------------------------
```

The error codes for the BIOS disk read and write interrupts are:

Value	Meaning
1	Bad command
2	Sector address mark not found
4	Sector not found
9	DMA failure
10	Bad sector
11	Bad track
16	Bad ECC (parity error)
17	Data error detected and corrected. Data is most likely good.
32	Disk controller failed
64	Couldn't access track
128	Drive did not respond
170	Drive not ready
187	Unknown error
204	Write fault

DISK INFORMATION

Some drives, such as the AT high density floppy drives, can detect
if a disk has been changed. Two AT interrupts deal with this; one
determines what type of drive a drive is, and the other reports if
a disk has been changed.

```
--------------------------------------------------
Operation:  Get disk type
Version:  AT BIOS
Interrupt:  13h
Function:  21
Call With:
    AH = 21
    DL = drive number
Returns With:
    AH = drive type
            Value       Meaning
            0           no drive
            1           floppy drive, cannot sense disk changes
            2           floppy drive, can sense disk changes
            3           hard disk
    CX:DX = if hard disk, number of sectors on the hard disk.
--------------------------------------------------
```

```
-----------------------------------------------------
Operation:  Check for changed disk.
Version:  AT BIOS
Interrupt:  13h
Function:  22
Call With:
    AH = 22
    DL = drive number (0 or 1)
Returns With:
    AH = 6 if disk was changed, 0 otherwise.
    Carry set if disk changed.
-----------------------------------------------------
```

The get disk information calls provide useful information about the disk. The format of the information returned by function 50 is:

Byte	Meaning
0	Drive number. 0=A, 1=B, and so on.
2-3	Bytes per sector
4	Sectors per cluster-1
5	$\log_2$(sectors per cluster)
6-7	Sectors in boot record
8	Copies of FAT
9-10	Number of entries in root directory
11-12	First sector in data area
13-14	Last cluster number
15	Sectors in FAT
16-17	First sector in root directory
18-21	Internal
22	Disk type byte

```
-----------------------------------------------------
Operation:  Get disk information.
Version:  DOS 2.0 -
Interrupt:  21h
Function:  54
Call With:
    AH = 54
    DL = drive.  0 = default, 1 = A, etc.
Returns With:
    AX = sectors per cluster.  ffffh if invalid drive.
    BX = number of free clusters
    CX = bytes per sector
    DX = total number of clusters
-----------------------------------------------------
```

```
--------------------------------------------------
Operation:  Get disk information.
Version:  Undocumented.  DOS 2.0 -
Interrupt:  21h
Function:  50
Called With:
    AH = 50
    DL = drive number.  0 = default, 1 = A, and so on.
Returns With:
    AL = 0 if drive exists
       = ffh if error
    DS:BX = pointer to disk information block.
    Note:  the DS segment register is changed.
--------------------------------------------------
```

KEY PROGRAMMING POINTS

- BIOS calls reference absolute disk locations using side, track, and sector numbers. DOS functions reference sectors relative to the partition start and use logical sector numbers.

- High density drives sense when disks have been changed.

- Several interrupts provide disk information. Generally, it is better to use these rather than read the boot record.

CHAPTER 22

SUBPROGRAMS
AND OVERLAYS

A subprogram--or child--is one that is invoked by another program. The child is loaded into memory following its parent and is executed. When finished, control returns to the parent. An overlay is like a child, but it is not executed. Any routine located in the overlay can be called by the parent.

Subprograms are very useful for making integrated packages. As discussed before, the parent program can call any other program, such as a word processor, during the middle of operation. When the child program ends, the parent continues running from where it left off. Subprograms can also be used to execute DOS commands from within a program. Use COMMAND.COM as the child program. Enter the DOS command **exit** to return to the parent program.

Use overlays for large programs. If possible, break the large program into a general controller and a set of self-contained modules. For example, if you are writing on a word processor, you can have a module for cut and paste functions and a module for search functions. When a particular module is needed, the general controller loads it in as an overlay if it is not already in memory. Any routines in that module can then be used.

Before executing a child program, the parent must free up all memory it doesn't use, as discussed in Chapter 20. The child will destroy all registers, including the stack registers. Only cs and ip will be restored. Thus, you should **push** all registers that you need saved, including ds and es. Save the ss and sp registers in variables located in the code segment. When the child returns, restore ss and sp and **pop** the other registers. When the child program is loaded, a PSP is automatically created for it. The termination and control-break vectors are set to the parent statement following the interrupt that created the child. The PSP termination and control-break address copies contain the vectors that the parent program uses. When the child program terminates, it restores the parent's terminate and control-break vectors. The child returns a return code as long as it terminated with interrupt 21h, function 76, as discussed in Chapter 18. Use interrupt 21h, function 77, as discussed in this chapter, to read this code.

All handles used by the parent can be used by the child unless they were opened with inheritance off (see interrupt 21h, function 61, AL bit 7).

The interrupt that creates a child program uses a table of parameters with the following format:

Offset	Contents
0-1	Segment where environment string begins. The environment must start at offset 0 within this segment. The environment is a set of ASCIIZ strings, such as VERIFY = ON. The last ASCIIZ string in the environment must be followed by another 0 byte. To use the parent's environment, fill this table entry with 0 (that is, set bytes one and two to zero).
2-3	Offset of command line parameters.
4-5	Segment of command line parameters. These parameters are in the same format as those entered on a command line and placed in the PSP. The first byte pointed to should contain the number of characters in the command line parameters. The parameters should be terminated by a return character (ASCII 13). If there are no command line parameters, fill bytes 2-5 with zeros.
6-7	Offset of FCB 1
8-9	Segment of FCB 1
10-11	Offset of FCB 2
12-13	Segment of FCB 2. FCB's were needed for the old style of file access. As long as you use the methods discussed in this book (handle methods), you will not need FCBs and should fill bytes 6-13 with zeros.

When overlays are loaded, their code is not executed, and a PSP is not created. Before overlays are used, the parent program must have freed all memory that it didn't use, just as for calling child programs. Allocate a memory block large enough for the biggest overlay. Call the overlay code as a far procedure.

The overlay function requires a parameter table with the following format:

Offset   Contents

0-1   Segment where overlay is to be loaded. Overlay will
                be loaded starting at offset 0 within this segment.
1-2   Relocation adjustment factor. Use the same value as
                that value in bytes 0-1.

The overlay may contain any number of segments, including its own
stack segment. Segment registers must be changed by the overlay
to point to its own segments.

```
Operation:  Load and run child program or load overlay.
Version:  DOS 2.0 -
Interrupt:  21h
Function:  75
Called With:
    AH = 75
    AL = command code.
          Value      Meaning
          0          Load and run child program
          3          Load overlay
    ES:BX = pointer to parameter table.  If the command code is 0,
    use the child program style parameter table; if 3, use the
    overlay style parameter table.
    DS:DX = pointer to ASCIIZ name of child/overlay file.  Can
    include drive and path.
Returns With:
    AX = error code
    Carry set if error.  Error codes are 1 (invalid command code
    in AL), 2 (file not found), 5 (access denied), 8 (insufficient
    memory), 10 (invalid environment), and 11 (invalid table
    format).
    If a child program was loaded and run, all registers except
    for CS and IP will be destroyed.
```

```
--------------------------------------------------
Operation:  Retrieve return code from child program.
            Code can only be retrieved once.
Version:  DOS 2.0 -
Interrupt:  21h
Function:  77
Call With:
   AH = 77
Returns With:
   AL = return code
   AH = code indicating way child terminated.
            Value     Meaning
            0         normal termination
            1         termination by control break
            2         termination due to critical error
            3         terminated and stayed resident
--------------------------------------------------
```

KEY PROGRAMMING POINTS

- Programs can invoke child programs.

- Child programs destroy all registers before returning to the parent.

- Child programs can use any parent handles opened with inheritance on.

- Overlay code is not executed. It can be accessed by far calls. Overlay procedures are responsible for adjusting the DS and ES registers as necessary.

CHAPTER 23

INTERRUPTS
DEALING WITH INTERRUPTS

When an **int** instruction is executed, the address of the interrupt routine is loaded from a table stored in memory beginning at segment 0, offset 0 (0000:0000h). Each table entry is composed of the offset and segment of the routine for the corresponding interrupt. There is room for 256 entries. See Chapter 27 for more details.

You can use interrupts to examine or change the addresses stored in the interrupt table. In general, you only need to do this to set up or check for memory resident utilities or device drivers. For example, you must find the address of the code for interrupt 67h to see if the expanded memory board software driver is installed.

```
---------------------------------------------------
Operation:  Determine address for interrupt routine.
Version:  DOS 2.0 -
Interrupt:  21h
Function:  53
Call With:
    AH = 53
    AL = number of interrupt to check
Returns With:
    ES = segment of interrupt routine
    BX = offset of interrupt routine
---------------------------------------------------


---------------------------------------------------
Operation:  Set address for interrupt routine.
Version:  DOS 1.0 -
Interrupt:  21h
Function:  37
Call With:
    AH = 37
    AL = number of interrupt to set
    DS = segment of new interrupt routine
    DX = offset of new interrupt routine
---------------------------------------------------
```

KEY PROGRAMMING POINTS

• The interrupt table contains addresses of all interrupt routines.

• You can redirect the interrupt vectors to point to new interrupt routines. This is discussed in Section III.

CHAPTER 24

SYSTEM AND DEVICE
INFORMATION

You have seen several interrupts determining the type of hardware or information about disks. In this chapter, you will examine a few more.

```
-----------------------------------------------
Operation:  Determine system set up.
Version:  BIOS
Interrupt:  11h
Call With:
    NA
Returns With:
    AX = equipment list.
            Bit        Meaning
            0          Set if floppy drives attached
            1          Not used   (PC)
                       Math co-processor installed   (AT)
            4-5        Initial video mode
                       Value       Meaning
                       1           40 x 25 text, color card
                       2           80 x 25 text, color card
                       3           80 x 25 text, monochrome card
            6-7        Number of diskette drives.  Add one.  Valid
                       only if bit 0 is 1.
            9-11       Number of RS-232 ports
            12         Set if game adaptor installed   (PC)
                       Not used   (AT)
            13         Not used   (PC)
                       Set if internal modem installed   (AT)
            14-15      Number of printers
-----------------------------------------------
```

To determine the type of computer, look at the byte in location ffff:000eh.

Value	Computer
252	AT
253	PCjr
254	XT
255	PC

```
-----------------------------------------------
Operation:  Determine DOS version.
Version:  DOS 2.0 -
Interrupt:  21h
Function:  48
Call With:
    AH = 48
Returns With:
    AL = major version number (3 in 3.10)
    AH = minor version number (10 in 3.10).  In numeric format.
    BX, CX destroyed.
-----------------------------------------------
```

```
--------------------------------------------------
Operation:  Determine current drive.
Version:  DOS 1.0 -
Interrupt:  21h
Function:  25
Call With:
   AH = 25
Returns With:
   AL = number of current drive.  0 = A, 1 = B, 2 = C, etc.
--------------------------------------------------
```

The switch character is the character used to indicate options on a DOS command line. Normally it is /, as in FORMAT B:/V.

```
--------------------------------------------------
Operation:  Determine or set DOS switch character.
Version:  Undocumented.  DOS 2.0 -
Interrupt:  21h
Function:  55
Call With:
   AH = 55
   AL = command code.
      Value     Meaning
      0         Determine switch character
      1         Set switch character
   DL = new switch character, if setting.
Returns With:
   DL = switch character, if determining switch character.
--------------------------------------------------
```

```
--------------------------------------------------
Operation:  Determine date.
Version:  DOS 1.0 -
Interrupt:  21h
Function:  42
Call With:
   AH = 42
Returns With:
   AL = day of week.  0 = Sunday, 1 = Monday, etc.
   CX = year.  (1980 - 2099)
   DL = day of the month.  (1 - 31)
   DH = month number.  1 = January, 2 = February, etc.
--------------------------------------------------
```

```
------------------------------------------------
Operation:  Set date.
Version:  DOS 1.0 -
Interrupt:  21h
Function:  43
Call With:
    AH = 43
    CX = year.
    DL = day of month.
    DH = month.  1 = January, 2 = February, etc.
Returns With:
    AL = 0 if operation successful.
       = ffh if invalid, no change.
------------------------------------------------


------------------------------------------------
Operation:  Determine time.
Version:  DOS 1.0 -
Interrupt:  21h
Function:  44
Call With:
    AH = 44
Returns With:
    CL = minute.  (0 - 59)
    CH = hour.  (0 - 23)
    DL = hundredths of seconds.  (0 - 99)
    DH = second.  (0 - 59)
------------------------------------------------


------------------------------------------------
Operation:  Set time.
Version:  1.0 -
Interrupt:  21h
Function:  45
Call With:
    AH = 45
    CL = minute.
    CH = hour.
    DL = hundredths of seconds.
    DH = second.
Returns With:
    AL = 0 if operation successful
       = ffh if invalid, no change
------------------------------------------------
```

DEVICE INFORMATION

The IOCTL interrupt gives more information about devices than the elemental queries discussed in Chapter 17.

```
--------------------------------------------------
Operation:  Check for removable media.
Version:  DOS 3.0 -
Interrupt:  21h
Function:  68
Called With:
    AH = 68
    AL = 8
    BL = drive number.  0 = default, 1 = A, and so on.
Returns With:
    AX = 0 if removable
       = 1 if fixed
       = 15 if invalid drive number
--------------------------------------------------


--------------------------------------------------
Operation:  Check if device is local or remote.
Version:  DOS 3.1 -
Interrupt:  21h
Function:  68
Called With:
    AH = 68
    AL = 9
    BL = drive number.  0 = default, 1 = A, and so on
Returns With:
    DX = bit 12 set if remote
--------------------------------------------------


--------------------------------------------------
Operation:  Check if handle is local or remote.
Version:  DOS 3.1 -
Interrupt:  21h
Function:  68
Called With:
    AH = 68
    AL = 10
    BX = handle
Returns With:
    DX = bit 15 set if remote
--------------------------------------------------
```

```
----------------------------------------------------
Operation:  Check number of drive letters assigned to device.
Version:  DOS 3.2 -
Interrupt:  21h
Function:  68
Called With:
    AH = 68
    AL = 14
    BL = drive number.  0 = default, 1 = A, and so on.
Returns With:
    AL = 0 if only one drive letter for this device
       = otherwise, drive number for last drive letter used to
         access device
    Carry set if error, error code returned in AX.
----------------------------------------------------
```

The following interrupt returns extensive device information:

Byte	Meaning
0	0 if a build BPB parameter block is returned.
	1 if a default BPB parameter block is returned.
1	Device type:

Value	Meaning
0	5.25" double density disk
1	5.25" high density disk
2	3.5" disk
3	8" single density disk
4	8" double density disk
5	Fixed disk
6	Tape drive
7	Other

Byte	Meaning
2	Device Attributes:

Bit	Meaning
0	Set if media is fixed
1	Set if diskette change can be detected

Byte	Meaning
3-4	Number of tracks
5	Media type in drive. 0 indicates default type.
6-7	Bytes per sector
8	Sectors per cluster

Byte	Meaning
9-10	Reserved sectors (boot record)
11	Number of FATs
12-13	Number of entries in the root directory
14-15	Number of sectors
16	Disk type byte
17-18	Sectors per FAT
19-20	Sectors per track
21-22	Sides
23-26	Hidden Sectors

```
--------------------------------------------------
Operation:  Get device information.
Version:  DOS 3.2 -
Interrupt:  21h
Function:  68
Called With:
    AH = 68
    AL = 13
    BL = drive number.  0 = default, 1 = A, and so on.
    CL = 96
    CH = 8
Returns With:
    DS:DX = pointer to parameter block.
    Note:  DS will be changed.
--------------------------------------------------
```

KEY PROGRAMMING POINTS

● Several interrupts provide important system and device information.

CHAPTER 25

MISCELLANY

This chapter lists a variety of interrupts that don't fall under other classifications. Many of them are very useful.

The **active byte** counts the number of DOS function calls currently being processed. It is very useful for memory resident utilities (see Chapter 37).

```
---------------------------------------------------
Operation:  Find active byte.
Version:  Undocumented.  DOS 2.0 -
Interrupt:  21h
Function:  52
Call With:
    AH = 52
Returns With:
    ES = segment of active byte
    BX = offset of active byte.
    Note:  ES is changed.  ES:BX points to a byte value.
---------------------------------------------------
```

```
---------------------------------------------------
Operation:  Print the screen.
            Same as hitting shift-print screen.
Version:  BIOS
Interrupt:  5h
Call With:
    NA
Returns With:
    The screen is printed.
---------------------------------------------------
```

The DOS BREAK ON command forces DOS to check for control-break before it executes any DOS interrupts. This is very useful for breaking out of programs.

```
---------------------------------------------------
Operation:  Determine or set control-break status.
Version:  DOS 2.0 -
Interrupt:  21h
Function:  51
Call With:
    AH = 51
    AL = command code
            Value     Meaning
            0         Determine status
            1         Set status
    DL = status, if setting. 0 for OFF, 1 for ON.
Returns With:
    DL = status, if determining.  0 for OFF, 1 for ON.
---------------------------------------------------
```

KEY PROGRAMMING POINTS

- The active byte is very useful for memory resident utilities that use DOS calls.

- Setting BREAK ON makes it easier to break out of programs.

SECTION III

MEMORY RESIDENT UTILITIES

In this section, you will learn about memory resident utilities. You will examine the details of how interrupts work and see how to redirect them. You will examine the resident and non-resident portions and particular details of writing keyboard-activated routines and pop-ups. You will see how to coexist with DOS and applications. You will also examine detection, communication, dormancy, and deinstallation. Throughout, your concern will be with writing cooperative, well-behaved routines.

You can greatly enhance your computer with memory resident utilities. Keyboard enhancers, print spoolers, pop-up notepads, and on-line spelling checkers are all examples of such utilities.

Note: The letter "l" and the number "1" are represented in the program code by the same character. **In no case is the letter "l" used as a variable name.**

CHAPTER 26

INTRODUCTION TO
MEMORY RESIDENT UTILITIES

Memory resident utilities are perhaps the most exciting and important type of utility. They allow complete computer customization and give powerful background features. Unlike regular utilities, once loaded, memory resident utilities are always present. They can be called at any time, even when another program is operating. Thus, if you have an idea while you are in the middle of a spreadsheet, you can jot it down on a computer note pad with **Sidekick**. If a program you are working on malfunctions, you can examine it with **FAILSAFE** and even break out if it is hung. **PROTECT,** which you will build, customizes the computer; once it is loaded, the hard disks are safe from reformatting.

Memory resident utilities work by redirecting interrupts; they replace the routine called when an interrupt occurs. Sometimes they just redirect an interrupt--such as the one called every time a key is pressed--to see when to spring into action. For example, **FAILSAFE** redirects the keyboard interrupt to see if the Ctrl-Alt-Left shift keys have been hit. Sometimes, memory resident utilities redirect interrupts to modify the way the interrupts operate. For example, **PROTECT** modifies the BIOS and DOS disk access interrupts so they will not format a hard disk.

Memory resident utilities bring great power, but they also bring great programming responsibility. Most application programs and operating systems aren't designed with memory resident utilities in mind, so you must be very careful to design your memory resident utilities so their operation doesn't disrupt the operation of other programs. Likewise, you must design your memory resident utilities so they will function with and not disrupt other memory resident utilities.

The results of uncooperative programming are drastic: stacks overflow, programs hang, screens garble, and disks crash. In this section, you will see how to write cooperative memory resident utilities. You will see how interrupts work, explore the basic parts of memory resident utilities, and see what features to add and avoid to make them work with other programs and utilities.

KEY PROGRAMMING POINTS

- After being loaded, memory resident utilities stay in memory and can be activated at any time.

- Memory resident utilities redirect interrupts.

CHAPTER 27

INTERRUPTS

Every time an interrupt is activated--whether by a hardware action, such as a key press, or a software **int** call--a special machine language routine is called. The location of this routine is found in the **interrupt table.** This table starts at offset 0000:0000h. There are 256 entries, each containing the offset and segment of the interrupt routine corresponding to that entry. When the computer is booted, the interrupt table is initialized to default values. If you change an interrupt table entry to point to a routine you have written, your routine will be called every time the interrupt is activated.

Before we discuss interrupts in more detail, examine the interrupt table. This will give you more complete knowledge of the range of interrupts.

To compute the address of an interrupt's entry, multiply the interrupt number by four. Remember that the first word in the entry is the offset and the second is the segment of the interrupt routine.

Interrupt #		Machine	Type	Interrupt
(D)	(H)			
0	00		H	Divide by zero
1	01		S	Single step
2	02		H	Non-maskable interrupt
		PC	H	8087 action
3	03		S	Break point
4	04		S	Arithmetic overflow
5	05		IG	Print screen (called by 9)
		AT	H	Bound exception (no BIOS support for this condition)
8	08		H	Clock tick
		AT	H	Lidt exception (no BIOS support for this condition)
9	09		H	Key struck
		AT	H	80287 segment overrun (no BIOS support for this condition)
10	0A		H	I/O Channel action
		AT	IG	Called by 71H

Interrupt#		Machine	Type	Interrupt
(D)	(H)			
11	0B		H	COM1 action
		AT	H	COM2 action
12	0C		H	COM2 action
		jr	H	Modem action
		AT	H	COM1 action
13	0D	XT	H	Fixed disk action
		jr	H	Video vertical retrace
		AT	H	LPT2 action
		AT	H	80286 segment overrun (no BIOS support for this condition)
14	0E		H	Diskette action
15	0F		H	LPT1 action
16	10		S	BIOS video services
17	11		S	BIOS equipment list
18	12		S	BIOS memory size
19	13		S	BIOS disk services
20	14		S	BIOS communication services
21	15		S	BIOS cassette services
		AT	S	BIOS joystick, timer, sys req other AT extensions
22	16		S	BIOS keyboard services
23	17		S	BIOS printer services
24	18		S	Activate ROM BASIC
25	19		IG	Warm boot (called by 9)
26	1A		S	BIOS time and date
27	1B		IG	Control Break (called bt 0)
28	1C		IG	Clock tick (called by 8)
29	1D		T	Video control parameters
30	1E		T	Disk control parameters
31	1F		T	Graphics characters for ASCII 128-255
32	20		S	DOS program terminate
33	21		S	DOS services
34	22		S	Routine to jump to after program termination
35	23		S	Routine that DOS uses for control-break handling (called by 21H)

Interrupt #		Machine	Type	Interrupt
(D)	(H)			
36	24		S	Routine that DOS uses for critical errors
37	25		S	DOS disk read
38	26		S	DOS disk write
39	27		S	Terminate, stay resident
40	28		H	Called when DOS is free
47	2F		S	Multiple-use program interface interrupt
51	33	MOUSE	S	Mouse interrupts
64	40	XT,AT	S	Points to diskette interrupt routines when a hard disk is installed
65	41	XT,AT	T	Fixed disk parameters
68	44	jr	T	Graphics characters for ASCII 0-127
72	48	jr	S	Translate keyboard codes
73	49	jr	T	Keyboard translation table
74	4A	AT	IG	Alarm (called by 70H)
96	60		S	Available for use
.	.		.	
.	.		.	
103	67		S	
		EMS	S	Expanded memory management interrupts for the EMS standard
112	70	AT	H	Real time clock
113	71	AT	H	Redirected IRQ2
117	75	AT	H	Math coprocessor action
118	76	AT	H	Hard disk action
128	80			Reserved for BASIC
.	.			
.	.			
240	F0			

H=hardware   IG=generated by other interrupts
S=software   T=table

Note: IG interrupts can also be called directly with an **int** instruction.

TYPES OF INTERRUPTS

As you can see from the interrupt table, there are several
different types of interrupts. The most important classes are
hardware, software, and **table** interrupts.

Hardware interrupts are initiated by a particular hardware action:
the striking of a key, the ticking of the clock, or some hardware
problem. There are two types of hardware interrupts: those
related to peripherals (8-fh, on the AT, also 70h-77h) and those
related to the microprocessor or non-peripheral hardware
difficulties (0 and 2; on the AT, also 5, 8, 9, and dh). The
peripheral-based interrupts are called **maskable interrupts.** The
non-peripheral interrupts are called **non-maskable interrupts.**

With the maskable interrupts, the hardware sends an interrupt
request (IRQ) to the processor. The processor stops its current
task and takes care of the interrupt request by executing the code
pointed to in the interrupt table. Because several hardware
interrupts can (and frequently do) occur at the same time, the
hardware interrupts are given priority levels. If the processor
is currently handling an interrupt request, it will only process
new interrupts of a higher priority level.

The non-maskable interrupts are given the highest priority level.
After them come interrupts 8-fh, in that order. On an AT, the
maskable priority is 8, 9, 70h-77h, bh-fh (ah is used to pass
control to 70h-77h).

Maskable interrupts allow peripherals to operate asynchronously
from the processor. The processor can send an instruction to the
peripheral and continue processing. The peripheral processes the
instruction and initiates an interrupt if it needs attention.
Thus, the processor doesn't need to continually poll the
peripherals to see if they need some type of handling (for
example, polling to see if a key has been struck); the peripheral
just sends a signal when it has information for the processor.
This saves much CPU time.

The IBM PC family uses a special chip--the 8259--to handle peripheral interrupts. This chip uses a bit mask to mask off any interrupt requests of lower priority than the one currently being handled. This mask is set when the interrupt request is received and must be reset by software when the interrupt processing is finished.

Software interrupts aren't prioritized. They are called by the machine language **int** instruction. When the **int** instruction is executed, the flags are pushed onto the stack, the segment and offset of the return address (line after the **int**) is pushed on the stack, the interrupt flag is cleared (maskable interrupts are disabled), and the address of the interrupt routine is loaded from the interrupt table and jumped to. It is equivalent to:

```
PUSHF
CLI
CALL DWORD PTR 0000:4*interrupt number
```

Exit interrupt routines with the **iret** instruction. It returns to the calling routine and pops the flags off the stack. To modify the flags, use a **ret 2** instead of the **iret**. You will probably also want to do a **sti** if you use the **ret 2**.

Table interrupts are never called by software or hardware. They simply point to tables of important information.

USING THE INTERRUPT TABLE

Changing the way hardware and software interrupts are processed allows for powerful enhancements. Use the interrupt table to determine interrupts you may want to change. If you plan to enhance the function of an interrupt rather than use it to check for a trigger, consult the appropriate references if possible.
For hardware interrupts, look at the BIOS listing so you can see how IBM processes the interrupt. Then, add your own routine. With software interrupts, make sure you know what they are called with, what they return, and what they change, so the replacement will be compatible.

If possible, redirect the interrupts with DOS function calls 37 and 53 (Chapter 23). If you cannot do this--for example, if you are redirecting an interrupt from within a memory resident routine--**cli**, then set the interrupts directly. Each interrupt address takes up four bytes, so the table entry for an interrupt starts at four times the interrupt number.

In the next few chapters, you will examine how to change and use several of these interrupts to create memory resident utilities.

KEY PROGRAMMING POINTS

- Interrupts invoke routines pointed to by the interrupt table.

- There are hardware, software, and table interrupts. Hardware interrupts can be maskable or non-maskable.

- Maskable interrupts are prioritized.

- Modifying the interrupt table allows interrupt features to be customized.

CHAPTER 28

ELEMENTS OF
A MEMORY RESIDENT UTILITY

A memory resident utility works by taking over an interrupt vector. Every time that interrupt is used, the memory resident utility can check for special activation conditions. If these are met, the utility swings into action. If they are not met, the interrupt acts as it normally would.

Once loaded, the utility code stays resident; the memory used by the utility will not be used by any other program. Thus, the utility code will operate any time the interrupt it is tied to is activated, even if applications or other memory resident utilities are running.

There are two main portions to a memory resident utility: the **non-resident section** and the **resident section.** The non-resident section contains all the code to load and set up the utility. It checks if the utility has already been installed, checks and sets up any system configuration information, displays an installment message, redirects interrupts, and then exits, leaving the code resident.

At a minimum, the resident section needs to check for activation, execute its special routines if activated, and return. Often, it will also need to call the interrupt routine it replaced. For the utility to perform certain actions, it may need to examine or change the machine setup, check the system and DOS status, and interact with other interrupts.

To prevent crashes, the resident section must completely restore the state the computer was in before the utility was called. It also must use as little of the stack as possible and, in many cases, stay active for as short a time as possible. Further, the code must be reentrant. That is, it must assume that the activating interrupt may be called many times while the routine is executing.

There are many things to keep in mind when writing memory resident utilities. For instance, it can be very difficult to debug a memory resident utility. Programs such as DEBUG and SYMDEB are often of little help. You may want to get a memory resident debugger or FAILSAFE. To make the debugging process easier, include text variable names before each variable. For example, you could use:

```
                db    'x_position'
x_position      dw    ?
```

With FAILSAFE, it is simple to search for these text messages and check the variable value. This can be done after the utility has been installed, while it is active, or from inside some other application. If the value is incorrect, you can then change it to debug other sections of the code.

You may also want to print out messages occasionally. For example:

`Now attempting to save file`

or:

`DOS active, can't save file`

Unless absolutely necessary, make the resident routines as clean and cooperative as possible. Don't assume particular hardware configurations or change BIOS variables. Don't assume the routine is the only resident routine. You can't assume it is the first or last to process an interrupt, and you must be very careful about changing and examining system status. If you are writing a keyboard expander, you must consider conflicting hot keys. Pop-ups may need to consider multi-tasking systems.

Also, plan your routine so that it will not be overly difficult to remove or deactivate.

If possible, make the utility a COM file. The easiest way to do this is to use only one segment (group) and start the program with an **org 100h.** EXE files can also be made resident, but placing the non-resident section last and choosing the resident size is more difficult. Also, remember that with EXE files CS:0 points to the program start while with COM files CS:0 points to the PSP.

Chapter 29 will discuss the non-resident section in detail. Chapters 30-37 will discuss the resident section.

KEY PROGRAMMING POINTS

- Memory resident utilities have a resident and non-resident section. Both must follow guidelines to function properly.

- If possible, make resident utilities COM files.

CHAPTER 29

THE NON-RESIDENT SECTION

The non-resident section does not remain in memory after the program is loaded. Its primary functions are to make sure the utility can be loaded, to load it, and to set up any type of configuration variables.

Place the non-resident section at the end of the program, and jump to it from the first line of the program. When programs are made resident, only the front portion remains in memory. Since the non-resident section is in the rear, it will not be kept in memory. This leaves more room for other utilities and applications. Nothing in the non-resident section is ever needed after the utility is made resident.

The non-resident or **installation** section should start by checking if the utility has already been loaded. A utility should not be allowed to load twice; each time it is loaded, it takes up more memory. If the utility is properly designed, loading it twice will not cause any conflicts, though interrupt calls will go through an unnecessarily long chain, and more stack space will be used. Poorly designed programs could malfunction if loaded twice.

To see if the utility has already been installed, include an identifying name in the resident data section. Place the name right after the sequence of jumps to the installation section and communication routine (discussed further in later chapters). Place a 0 after the name so that it won't match names of which it is a subset. For example:

```
start:          jmp    install
communicate:    jmp    comm_routine
ame             db     'FAILSAFE',0      0
```

Before you finish installing the routine, you will use one of the user-definable interrupts (60h-67h) to point to **communicate.** The name field begins three bytes after this. To see if the utility has already been installed, compare the name field in the utility being loaded to the data starting three bytes after that pointed to by any non-zero, user-definable interrupts. If a match is found, the utility has already been loaded. If this is the case, print out an error message and stop.

While looking for a matching name, keep the number of the last unused user-definable interrupt found. This will be used when the pointer to the name is set up. If there are no free interrupts, there is no way to mark that the utility has already been loaded or to easily communicate with it. Print out a message stating this warning.

Next, print out a message stating that the utility is being installed. This has two purposes. First, it ensures that you know what is loaded. Second, it gives you a chance to control-break out of the utility before any permanent changes have been made.

Next, check any unchanging system status information that your program needs. For example, if your program needs to undergo certain routines dependent upon the machine type, presence of a math co-processor, or DOS version, determine the status in the installation section and store the results in a variable for the resident section. If your program can only run if certain hardware is installed, such as an extended memory board, check for that hardware here. If you do not find it, print an error message and stop.

If there is any user installation input, such as a password, process it here. This may involve reading the command line parameters or getting input from the disk or keyboard.

Read and save the old vectors for any interrupts that you will redirect. You will need these for chaining and deinstallation.

Next, free the copy of the environment. Find its location by examining the PSP and using the free memory function of interrupt 21h. Whenever a program is loaded, a copy of the environment is made and passed to it. This copy is not useful for memory resident utilities because the environment may change after they are loaded. Removing the copy gives more memory for other programs.

Redirect the interrupts to your own interrupt routines. Start by using a free user-definable interrupt to point to the communicate jump (and thus the name field). Next, redirect any software interrupts. Then, redirect any hardware interrupts. If you use the clock interrupt, redirect it last. By redirecting vectors in this order, the chance is minimized that an interrupt routine, such as one tied to the clock interrupt, will be activated before any of its supporting interrupt routines are put into place.

Finally, terminate and stay resident. Pass a return code through the terminate interrupt to indicate whether the utility was successfully loaded.

AN EXAMPLE--VIDEOTBL

Let's examine a memory resident routine with just the bare essentials. This one replaces the video parameters table. Since it sets up a table, it doesn't need any complicated resident code --just the table itself.

This program is very useful. Many non-IBM graphics boards have problems with screen position in graphics modes or monochrome modes. They may shift the screen too far to the left or right, or the screen may scroll off the top and bottom. By changing the appropriate numbers in the table, you can automatically adjust for the particular graphics board you have. Unlike **MODE**, the adjusted parameters are always in effect--not just after the **MODE** command.[1]

VIDEOTBL has a very simple installation section. There is no need to save the location of the old table or to see if it has already been installed.

After you have looked at VIDEOTBL, be sure to look at the installation section of PROTECT found in Chapter 33. (Before proceeding with program code, see special on letter "l" and number "1" at the beginning of this section.)

---

[1]For a discussion of the actual values to use, see Advanced IBM PC Graphics, the IBM Technical Reference Manual, or the IBM Options and Adapters Manual.

```
;VIDEOTBL.ASM
;
;This program replaces the video parameter table.  The new set of
;values is used to adjust for a particular graphics board or
;monitor. For example, the values used here are to adjust for a
;Tecmar Graphics Master Board.
;
;The table stays resident in memory.  It does not check to see if
;another table was previously entered.
;
;This program is set up to be a .COM file.
;

;--------------CONSTANTS----------------

TABLE_LEN       equ     64


;--------------BEGINNING---------------
code            segment
                assume cs:code,ds:code
                org     100h
video_table:
                jmp     set_int

;---------NEW VIDEO TABLE DATA--------

table:
                db      38h,28h,2dh,0ah,1fh,  6,19h,1ch   ;40 x 25
                db       2,  7,  6,  7,  0,  0,  0,  0
                db      71h,50h,5ah,0ah,1fh,  6,19h,1ch   ;80 x 25
                db       2,  7,  6,  7,  0,  0,  0,  0
                db      38h,28h,2ah,0ah,7fh,  6,64h,70h   ;graphics
                db       2,  1,  6,  7,  0,  0,  0,  0
                db      61h,50h,52h,0fh,19h,  6,19h,19h   ;mono
                db       2,0dh,0bh,0ch,  0,  0,  0,  0

;--------------MAIN CODE------------

set_int:
                mov     ax,cs           ;set up segment registers
                mov     ds,ax
                lea     dx,table        ;set up interrupt to point
                mov     ah,37           ;to new video table
                mov     al,1dh
                int     21h
                mov     ah,49           ;terminate and stay resident
                mov     al,0            ;no error
                lea     dx,set_int      ;Keep everything up to
                mov     cl,4            ;the paragraph containing
                shr     dx,cl           ;the main code.
                inc     dx
                int     21h
code            ends
                end     video_table
```

KEY PROGRAMMING POINTS

- Place the non-resident section at the end of the code.

- Make sure the utility is not already loaded.

- Print an installation message.

- Check unchanging system information.

- Save old vectors.

- Free the environment.

- Set the communication vector and redirect vectors.

- Terminate and stay resident.

CHAPTER 30

THE RESIDENT SECTION

The resident section contains a section for variables and interrupt handlers. Each interrupt handler contains a section to check for activation, a section to chain to other interrupts, and sections for special processing if the routine is activated.

As mentioned, the resident section should start with a jump to the installation section, then a jump to the communication routine. The variables section should follow. Start with a text identifier followed by any other version information you wish to include. Set up room for saving the old interrupt vectors for any interrupts you change. Follow with internal variables and then text messages. The order is not crucial, but will make it easier for you to find information when you debug. To make assembling more efficient, the variables section must appear right after the two jumps or in a separate object module with all variables declared as external.

THE INTERRUPT HANDLERS

The interrupt vectors are redirected to routines called interrupt handlers. Whenever a redirected interrupt is activated, one of these routines is called.

The first parts of an interrupt handler are the activation and chaining sections. The order in which they should occur depends on the application. **Activation** is the process of determining whether the memory resident utility should become active. For example, a pop-up might check for a particular key combination. **Chaining** is the process of calling the interrupt the handler replaced. Chaining is important because it gives other interrupt handlers tied to the interrupt a chance to activate. Further, hardware interrupts often need to do some special hardware processing and resetting of the 8259. If it is possible to enhance the original interrupt function without completely replacing the original hardware manipulation, it is much better to have the interrupt handler enhance and chain to the original handler.

Depending on the redirection of the interrupt and the application, it may be necessary to chain before or after checking for activation. Chain first if the activation check examines a system status indicator modified by the original interrupt. For example, suppose you redirected the keyboard interrupt to check for the simultaneous pressing of the left and right shift keys. Before you use interrupt 16h to check for this (Chapter 15), the variable must be updated by the keyboard interrupt handler. Thus, you must chain to the old interrupt before checking the status.

In other cases, activation does not depend on some status set by the redirected interrupt but depends on some other status. In these cases, you may need to process before you chain to the interrupt. First check for activation, then chain. For example, suppose you write a utility to modify DOS so that every time a file is erased, it is moved to a hidden directory instead. Redirect interrupt 21h and check the registers for the erase file function call. If it is found, change the registers to indicate a move (rename) call, and chain to the old interrupt 21h.

There are also cases where the new handler is always active. Again, you need to decide whether to chain before or after processing or not at all. Often, this will depend on the application. For example, suppose you have written a utility to take input from some type of non-standard input device, such as a home brew three-dimensional joystick. Convert movement from this device to cursor keystrokes, and place them in a special buffer. Then, redirect interrupt 16h so that every time a program looks for a key, you can feed it one of the cursor keystrokes from the special buffer. If you want the cursor strokes from the three-dimensional joystick to have priority, every time there is a int 16h call, see if there are any keystrokes waiting in the special buffer. If there are, return from the interrupt with the next special buffer keystroke. If there aren't, chain to the old int 16h call. But, suppose you want to give the keyboard a higher priority. In this case, chain to the int 16h call (switching function 0 calls to function 1 calls), and if no keystrokes are available, check the special buffer.

As a general rule, if activation depends on some hardware status set by the redirected interrupt, chain first and then check for activation. If activation depends on some other source or on the registers, chain last if the application requires it. If the application doesn't require chaining last, chain first, because it is more cooperative.

Usually, hardware interrupts are redirected so that system status can be checked for some type of triggering indicator. In Chapter 34, you will examine using the keyboard as a trigger. Usually, software interrupts are redirected to modify the way the interrupt operates. Here, the registers are usually checked for activation. Both types can also be redirected to detect activation flags.

If the triggering condition is not met, pass control down the chain.

CHAINING

When chaining, make sure all registers and flags are set as the routine you are calling expects. You are simulating an **int** call, so the interrupt flag must be cleared and the flags pushed on the stack. The called routine will end with an **iret**. If you want to regain control after chaining to the old interrupt handler, use a **call:**

```
pushf
cli
call dword ptr cs:old_interrupt
```

If you don't want to regain control after chaining, use a **jmp:**

```
restore system status
pop off any registers you have used
cli
jmp dword ptr cs:old_interrupt
```

If your interrupt switches one software function call with another, as in the example with deleting files, you may want to reissue the interrupt instead of chaining. This gives all other utilities a chance to modify your request. If you reissue, make sure your routine is reentrant.

CLI AND STI

When an interrupt handler is called, the interrupt flag is cleared. This means that no other maskable interrupts can occur. The interrupt flag should be kept off during operations that must not be disrupted, such as the switching of interrupt vectors; however, keeping interrupts shut out for a long time can be hazardous, especially if peripherals--such as modems--are being used in the background. Reallow interrupts as soon as possible by issuing a **sti.**

REENTRANCY

If it's possible for the interrupt to reoccur before the handler is finished processing the interrupt, then the routine must be made reentrant. This means that the routine must be able to be called again--from its beginning--even if the routine is currently active.

As an example, suppose you redirect the keyboard interrupt, and the new routine, if activated, also reads information from the keyboard. In this case, the keyboard interrupt will be called again while the first keyboard interrupt is still being processed. Even if your routine didn't have keyboard calls, a different interrupt handler, such as one based on the clock interrupt, could have sprung into action and asked for keyboard input. Also, you could be holding down a key. Just checking for the activation sequence is not enough--you could be holding down the activation keys, causing them to auto-repeat.

As another example, suppose you enhance a disk write interrupt. While you are processing one disk write interrupt, another one may come through, perhaps from a memory resident utility run off the clock interrupt. It is crucial that both disk writes work perfectly.

Always assume that your routine needs to be reentrant, even if the routine it is replacing is not, or you can't think of an application where it will be reentrantly called. The makers of DOS didn't assume reentrancy, and, as you'll see in Chapter 37, this leads to great programming difficulties for memory resident utilities.

Let's look at a few examples of what happens if your routines are not reentrant. As a simple example, suppose you enhance the disk write interrupt and temporarily store the sector number in an internal variable. Suppose this routine is called again before the first one is finished. The first disk sector number will be lost; it will be set to the second. When the second request is finished and control returns to the first, disk integrity will be destroyed.

As another example, suppose you write a pop-up notepad that triggers every time the left and right shift keys are pressed simultaneously. Because it's a pop-up, you save the background screen so you can restore it when finished. (See Chapter 36.) Suppose that while you are typing a message on this notepad, you accidentally press the two shift keys instead of the question mark. The pop-up routine is called again, and you save the screen so you can restore it. This time, however, you saved the screen with the notepad already on it. The original screen is lost.

As a final example, suppose you redirected the clock interrupt. Every time the clock ticks, you save all the registers on the stack and begin processing. Suppose processing takes a long time under certain conditions and doesn't finish before the next clock tick. More registers will be pushed onto the stack. Eventually, the stack will overflow.

In the first and second examples, the program malfunctioned because it stored critical information in a variable that was overwritten. In the second and third examples, the program should have checked for prior activation.

There are two ways to make routines reentrant. The first is best for very short, quick routines. Never use variables for storing information--just use registers. Make sure that the registers are saved when the routine begins and restored when the routine ends. PROTECT and BIOS use this method.

The second is best for longer routines and, in particular, hardware interrupt handlers, such as pop-up routines. In this case, set an internal status variable to indicate when the routine is inactive. If the routine is not inactive, immediately pass control down the chain with a **jmp.** This does not use any stack space. If the routine is inactive, set the status to CHECKING in case the interrupt is reissued before the activation check is complete. Then check for activation. Chain with a **call** where appropriate. Change the status to ACTIVE or INACTIVE.

By checking for inactivity specifically, you can have many status settings to indicate different types of activity. Some of these will be discussed in the following chapters.

Here's an example from the code for FAILSAFE:

```
new_kybd_9_int  proc    far
                cmp     cs:status,INACTIVE  ;can FAILSAFE be called?
                je      nk9_1               ;yes
;....................................
;
; FAILSAFE is already active.  Chain immediately.  Do not use
; up stack space with a pushf and call.  Do not return.
;
;....................................
                jmp     dword ptr cs:old_kybd_9_int

;....................................
;
; FAILSAFE can be activated.  Chain, then check for activation.
;
;....................................
nk9_1:          mov     cs:status,CHECKING  ;indicate checking
                pushf                       ;prepare to chain
                call    dword ptr cs:old_kybd_9_int  ;chain
                sti                         ;allow interrupts

;
; Check for activation here
;


;
; IF NOT ACTIVE:
;

                cli                         ;not active
                mov     cs:status,INACTIVE  ;reset status
                iret                        ;return


;
; IF ACTIVE:  set status to ACTIVE, begin processing
;
```

PREPARING FOR PROCESSING

Once you have determined that the utility has been triggered, you must prepare for processing. Begin by pushing any registers that you will change. If your routine will be active for a long time, temporarily disable the control-break processing vectors (1Bh and 23h). This prevents unexpected hangs due to the control-break routines assuming a particular environment.

Do not use the DOS functions to disable these interrupts. DOS is not reentrant and might crash the system (see Chapter 37). Instead, you must access the table directly. Be sure to **cli** first to prevent peripheral interrupts from occurring while only part of the new interrupt address has been entered.

```
;
; This segment is for accessing the interrupt table
;


int_table          segment      at 0h
                   org          1bh*4
BIOS_CTRL_C        dw           ?,?
                   org          23h*4
DOS_CTRL_C         dw           ?,?

int_table          ends


;this part is in the normal code segment

old_bios_ctrl_c  dw       ?,?
old_dos_ctrl_c   dw       ?,?


;redirect to this routine to disable an interrupt

disable_int:      iret      ;don't do any processing if disabled


;this routine disables the control-break vectors
```

```
disable_breaks    proc   near
                  push   ds         ;temporarily save these registers
                  push   ax
                  xor    ax,ax    ;ax <- 0
                  assume ds:int_table   ;point to int table
                  mov    ds,ax
                  cli               ;prevent interrupts from occurring
                  mov    ax,BIOS_CTRL_C ;save old vectors
                  mov    cs:old_bios_ctrl_c,ax
                  mov    ax,BIOS_CTRL_C[2]
                  mov    cs:old_bios_ctrl_c[2],ax
                  mov    ax,DOS_CTRL_C
                  mov    cs:old_dos_ctrl_c,ax
                  mov    ax,DOS_CTRL_C[2]
                  mov    cs:old_dos_ctrl_c[2],ax
                  lea    ax,disable_int ;now disable them
                  mov    BIOS_CTRL_C,ax
                  mov    DOS_CTRL_C,ax
                  mov    ax,cs
                  mov    BIOS_CTRL_C[2],ax
                  mov    DOS_CTRL_C[2],ax
                  sti               ;allow interrupts
                  pop    ax
                  assume ds:code ;or what it used to point to.
                                 ;If unknown, assume nothing
                  pop    ds
                  ret
disable_breaks    endp
```

Restore these vectors before you leave the routine.

If your routine uses a lot of stack space, you may be tempted to redirect the stack. Do this with extreme caution, and avoid it if possible. Remember that many other interrupt routines may activate while your routine is processing, and your routine may be reentrantly called many times. You must create a large enough stack to account for this. To be safe, provide at least 800 bytes above what your routine uses. Keep track of the old SS and SP values. These must be stored in variables--not on the stack. If the portion of the routine that switches the stack can be entered more than once, you must keep a counter of the number of entrances and exits. Increment the counter as soon as the routine is entered, and decrement it just before leaving. Only switch to the new stack on entrances when the counter is 1 (the first time in), and only switch the old stack on exits when the counter is 1 (the last time out). Remember to **cli** before you switch stacks.

Switching the stack is dangerous. Other routines may have placed data on your stack. You must not delete this information when you switch to the original stack. Further, other routines could redirect the stack as well. You must not reset their stack to the original stack. On the other hand, if they switch back to your stack and you're not active, you must restore to the original stack. If at all possible, do not switch stacks.

Application programs should be responsible for maintaining a large stack, but many of them do not. If possible, minimize your use of the stack. If you write application programs, create a large stack.

Finally, your routine may need to examine and modify the system status. For example, utilities that write to or read from the screen may need to check what type of screen and what page is currently active (See Chapters 13 and 36). If you change this status, be sure to save the old status and restore it before you finish. Use BIOS calls whenever possible. Avoid writing directly to ports. If you do write directly to ports, be sure to update the appropriate BIOS variables.

At this point, your utility can begin processing.

ACCOUNTING FOR WARM BOOTS

There are two ways to reboot the system. One is to hold down the control-alt-delete key combination. This goes through the system start-up checks, resets low memory, reloads the boot record from disk, reloads all the hidden system files and DOS files, and so forth. It is almost the same as turning the computer off and back on. The other method is to issue an interrupt 19h. This initiates a similar process that skips the system checks and starts by loading in the boot record. Thus, the low memory variables are not restored. It is much less drastic.

Some utilities reconfigure system information flags and then reboot the system so DOS will reload with the new configuration information. Among other things, this enables you to change the amount of memory DOS sees and to keep the utility resident.

When the system is rebooted in this fashion, all DOS addressable memory is considered free. DOS reloads and reinitializes portions of the interrupt table. DOS versions 2.0-3.0 reinitialize interrupts 20h-27h while versions 3.1 and 3.2 reinitialize vectors 0fh-3fh. IBMBIO.COM reinitializes interrupts 0-fh.

Thus, the memory where your routines reside is freed, but the interrupt vectors pointing there are not necessarily changed. To be safe, you need to redirect interrupt 19h--the reboot interrupt. When this interrupt occurs, you must restore any interrupt vectors you have changed, including the reboot interrupt, and then jump to the old reboot interrupt. This ensures that your routines--and any other redirected interrupt routines loaded after them--will not be called when an interrupt occurs after they have been cleared from memory.

As with redirecting the control-break vectors, you must access the interrupt table directly. Simply restore the old interrupt values that you saved, including the reboot interrupt and the communication/name marker interrupt.

THE COMMUNICATION INTERRUPT

In Chapter 29, you placed a jump before the name marker to a routine called **comm_routine**. Then, you redirected one of the user-definable interrupts to point to this jump. You can use this interrupt to communicate with the memory resident utility from an outside program.

The resident utility sets up different communicating functions and checks and processes these when the communication interrupt is called. The outside utility calls the communication interrupt to use these functions.

First, the outside utility searches the user-definable interrupts for the one pointing to the utility, as identified by the name marker. This search is the same as checking to see if the utility is installed. Then, the outside utility issues the interrupt, coding the desired function in the AH register.

For example, FAILSAFE's communication routine has functions to report status, change the trigger key, and deactivate or reactivate FAILSAFE. The report status feature is function 0. Suppose FAILSAFE used interrupt 62h for communications. To get the status, you would:

```
mov  ah,0      ;get status of FAILSAFE
int  62h       ;communicate interrupt
```

To make your routine process these outside world commands, set up **comm_routine** appropriately. It should check for a valid function request and do the processing. For example, here's an excerpt from FAILSAFE's code:

```
;---------------------COMMUNICATION INTERRUPT------------------
;
; Redirected user definable interrupt for communicating with
; FAILSAFE.
;
; Called with:
;   AH = 0  Get status
;     Returns:
;     AH = status flag
;     AL = keyboard mask
;     ES:BX = pointer to version number
;
;   AH = 1  Set keyboard mask
;     AL = new keyboard mask
;
;   AH = 2  Deactivate
;
;   AH = 3  Activate
;

comm_routine    proc    near
                sti                         ;re-enable interrupts
                cmp     ah,0                ;get status?
                jne     c_r_1               ;nope
;....AH = 0 Get status
                mov     ah,cs:status        ;status
                mov     al,cs:key_mask      ;keyboard mask
                push    cs                  ;segment of version number
                pop     es
                lea     bx,version          ;offset of version number
                jmp     c_r_iret            ;return
```

If you don't have any communicate functions, simply **iret**:

```
comm_routine proc  near
             iret
comm_routine endp
```

KEY PROGRAMMING POINTS

- Place variables at the beginning of the program.

- Interrupt handlers contain sections for activation checking, chaining, and processing. The order of chaining and activation checking depends on the application.

- Keep interrupts enabled when possible.

- Make interrupt handlers reentrant. Either store all data in registers or keep a status byte.

- Disable control-break interrupts if the routine will be active for a long time. Process the table directly.

- Restore all vectors if the computer is rebooted.

- Use the communication interrupt to communicate with the resident utility.

CHAPTER 31

THE PROCESSING SECTION

There are a few guidelines for writing the processing section.
First, try to minimize stack use. This helps prevent any stack
overflow problems. Also, try to keep the code as short as
possible. Minimize the time that interrupts are disabled.
Remember, even if interrupts are enabled, interrupts with a lower
priority are shut out until the 8259 receives the end-of-interrupt
command. Thus, be especially careful of time if you do not chain
to a hardware interrupt until after processing or if there is a
background communications line open.

Avoid using write-only ports. The status of the port may have
been set by the application or some other utility. Unless you are
guaranteed of its previous status, changing it could be hazardous.

Also, avoid writing to BIOS variables, such as the keyboard shift
status byte. Other programs may read them or expect them in a
particular format. Further, some utilities may replace the
standard BIOS locations. For example, many keyboard enhancers use
an internal keyboard buffer. Writing directly to the BIOS buffer
could be either ineffectual or disastrous. Whenever possible, use
the BIOS interrupts.

If you do write directly to a port, such as to the 6845 chip, be
sure to update all appropriate BIOS variables. It is not enough
to simply restore the status when you exit the interrupt. Other
interrupt handlers triggered while yours is active could depend on
the BIOS variables.

Avoid using DOS functions, at least until you have read Chapter
37. In general, they are not reentrant and will cause overwrites
of important DOS variables. Effects range from strange characters
on the screen to complete hangs.

If you are doing any critical processing, such as changing status
bytes, BIOS variables, or redirecting interrupts, be sure to **cli**
first. This will prevent interrupts from disrupting these events.
As soon as possible, **sti** so that normal interrupt processing can
continue.

Never assume anything. Do not assume that page 0 of the display screen is currently in use or that you can use other pages for scratch buffers. Do not assume that areas in DOS for programmer use are free. If you need a scratch buffer, set one aside. If you write to a screen, first check for the active page with a BIOS call.

Remember, there could always be other utilities active at the same time, and an application program could be using unmarked or normally free memory areas. Further, the program could be running on a PC compatible, so hardware results and BIOS variables could be quite different. Thus, whenever possible, use BIOS routines to check or change system status. If your routine is machine-critical, check the machine before you load the utility.

KEY PROGRAMMING POINTS

- Minimize stack use.

- Minimize the amount of time interrupts are disabled or masked out.

- Avoid write-only ports.

- Avoid changing BIOS variables.

- Avoid DOS functions.

- Do not assume a particular system setup or status.

CHAPTER 32

LEAVING
AN INTERRUPT HANDLER

As with the processing section, there are a few guidelines to follow when leaving an interrupt handler. You must leave the system in exactly the same state as you found it. If you changed the screen mode or active page, be sure to reset it. Likewise, restore the palette, the break status, or anything else you may have changed.

Next, restore the stack if you changed it. Likewise, restore any interrupts you temporarily redirected. If you use a variable to indicate active or inactive status, adjust it as appropriate. Then, pop any registers you pushed onto the stack and **iret**.

If you redirect a hardware interrupt, be sure that the 8259 receives the end-of-interrupt instruction. If you chain to earlier interrupts, assume this is done. If you don't, be sure to clear the 8259 for further use. Do this by sending 20h to port 20h.

If you need to return messages by flags, such as to fake a BIOS error, do the following:

```
set the flags

sti
ret 2
```

If not, leave with an **iret**.

KEY PROGRAMMING POINTS

- Restore system status before leaving.

- Restore all registers and clean the stack.

- Restore any temporarily redirected interrupts.

- Adjust the status byte.

CHAPTER 33

AN EXAMPLE—PROTECT

In this chapter, you'll see how to create a memory resident utility to protect hard disks from accidental reformatting, called PROTECT. If you are a hard disk user, especially if you are in an office, you should type in and assemble PROTECT. It could easily save you from an expensive disaster. You can also buy PROTECT in ready-to-run and source form on the <u>Advanced DOS Guide Diskette</u>.

Once PROTECT is installed, you needn't worry about hard disk reformatting. If you try reformatting your hard disk, FORMAT will chug along until it actually begins to do damage. At this point, it will stop dead, display an error message, and return to DOS. If a malicious program attempts to do a low-level reformatting with BIOS calls, it will also be stopped. The only way to reformat your disk is through direct programming of the disk controller.

PROTECT will illustrate most of the points discussed so far in Section III. It will check if it's already loaded, display an installation message, and free the environment. It will be reentrant and will deinstall if the system is rebooted. It will also redirect several interrupts.

HOW FORMATTING WORKS

Before you look at the routine, you must first understand a bit more about how formatting works. There are two types of formatting--**high-level** and **low-level**. Low-level formatting is done to floppy disks or by programs that maliciously destruct a hard disk. It amounts to clearing out all the data on every sector on the disk, except for a few sector marks. This is done with BIOS call 13h, function 5. Once a disk is formatted this way, the data is irretrievable.

High-level formatting is done by the DOS FORMAT command to a hard disk. First, the whole disk is read to search for bad sectors. This is what takes the most time and is why the disk whirs for a while. At any point during this period, you can control-break out, and the disk will be unchanged. Once FORMAT is finished scanning the disk, however, it uses DOS disk calls to rewrite the boot record, the FAT, and the root directory. Once this has started, all file information on the disk is effectively lost.

The sectors in the data area are not changed. If you are skillful, you can probably recreate most text files using EXPLORER. First, set up a dummy entry in the root directory, using the erased indicator as the first character. Then, search through the disk, adding together the old file fragments with the retrieve erased file feature. You may also want to write a program to automatically search the disk and print out the location of data fragments.

HOW PROTECT WORKS

PROTECT works by redirecting the BIOS and DOS disk write routines. If a BIOS call is used to reformat a hard disk track, it returns an error indicating that the track cannot be accessed. If the program checks for this error, the program will most likely terminate with an error message. If it doesn't check, the format doesn't take place anyway. Likewise, if the DOS disk write call is used to write to sector 0 on a hard disk--the boot record--an unusable sector message is returned. Because this is the first damage FORMAT tries to do, it sees that it can't write to the disk and stops with an error message.

As it is set up, PROTECT stops low-level formatting to any hard disk and high-level formatting only on drive C. It is easy to change the code to protect against either type of formatting for different drive combinations.

THE PROTECT CODE

Let's examine the code. Note the segment to define the interrupt table and the PSP definition of the environment pointer. Note how constants are used to make the code more readable. Also, note the **org 100h**, the jump to the installation section, and the jump to the communication section. Examine how PROTECT checks if it is already installed and how it prints appropriate messages. Look at the order in the installation routine--printing the message, freeing the environment, setting up the marker, setting up the redirected interrupts, and then switching the interrupts and terminating. Examine the actual redirected interrupts. See how they check for activation, chain, and terminate. Also note the redirected reboot interrupt.

Examine how the resident and non-resident sections are set up.
Note how the display message procedure and the error messages are
in the non-resident section because they are only used during
program installation.

```
The code for this program is found in
protect.asm.  The ready-to-use
version is protect.com.
```

```
;PROTECT.ASM
;
;This program prevents fixed disks from being reformatted.  It
;replaces the BIOS and DOS disk-access interrupt.  The DOS
;FORMAT command starts by rewriting the boot record.  If an
;attempt to do so is made, a fatal error is returned, thus
;stopping the format.  This program also protects against low
;level BIOS formats by also returning a fatal error if there is
;an attempt to format a hard disk.  For all other cases, the old
;disk routine is called.
;
;This program deinstalls when the system is rebooted.
;
;This program stays resident.  It is set up to be a .COM file.
;
;Interrupts 13h, 19h, and 26h are redirected.
;
;
;Note:  This program is only set up to protect the C drive against
;DOS reformatting.  Thus, external disks can be formatted without
;problem. To protect more drives, modify the procedure
;new_dos_write.  You might want to specify the drive(s) to be
;protected through command line parameters.
;
```

```
;----------------CONSTANTS-----------------

DISK_INTR            equ     13h
REBOOT_INTR          equ     19h
DOS_WRITE            equ     26h
FREE_INT1            equ     60h
FREE_INT_LAST        equ     67h
DISK_ENTRY           equ     DISK_INTR*4
REBOOT_ENTRY         equ     REBOOT_INTR*4
DOS_WRITE_ENTRY      equ     DOS_WRITE*4
FORMAT_CMD           equ     5
C_DRIVE              equ     2
BAD_TRACK            equ     40h
BAD_TRACK_LO         equ     6
FORE_COLOR           equ     3
RETURN               equ     0dh
LINEFEED             equ     0ah

;-------------DUMMY SEGMENT----------------

;................................
;
; Set up a dummy segment heading pointing to the interrupt
; table.
;
;................................

int_table            segment at 0
int_table            ends




;----------------BEGINNING-----------------

code                 segment
                     assume  cs:code
                     org     44              ;here is the environment
environ_addr         dw      ?               ;pointer
                     org     100h            ;make this a .COM file
protect:             jmp     install         ;install interrupt


;----------------DATA----------------------

communicate:         jmp     comm_routine
program_name         db      'PROTECT',0
copyright            db      '(C) Michael I. Hyman 1986 '
version              db      'V1.0',0
old_disk_intr        dw      ?,?
old_reboot_intr      dw      ?,?
old_dos_write        dw      ?,?
ident_intr           db      DOS_WRITE
IDENT_LENGTH         equ     OFFSET copyright - OFFSET program_name
```

```
;---------------NEW INTERRUPT ROUTINES-----


;.................................
;
; This routine replaces the BIOS disk interrupt.  If the interrupt
; call is to format a hard disk, it returns a bad track error;
; otherwise, the control is passed along the interrupt chain.
;
; Note that this routine is called with the command in AH and
; the drive in DL.  DL will be greater than 80h for hard drives.
;
;.................................




new_disk_intr     proc    far
                  cmp     ah,FORMAT_CMD   ;is it a format command?
                  jne     do_old_int      ;nope, pass control
                  test    dl,80h          ;is it for a hard disk?
                  jz      do_old_int      ;nope, pass control
                  mov     ah,BAD_TRACK    ;yes, fake a bad track error
                  stc                     ;indicate error
                  sti                     ;allow interrupts
                  ret     2               ;return, clearing old flags

do_old_int:       jmp     dword ptr cs:old_disk_intr
                                          ;pass control to old int

new_disk_intr     endp




;.................................
;
; This routine replaces the DOS disk write interrupt.
; If it is used to change sector 0 (the boot record), a
; bad track error is returned; otherwise, the control is
; passed along the interrupt chain.
;
; Note that this routine is called with the sector in DX and
; the drive in AL.  Flags must be left on the stack.
;
;.................................
```

```
new_dos_write    proc    far
                 cmp     dx,0                 ;write to boot record?
                 jne     do_old_write         ;no, do old interrupt
                 cmp     al,C_DRIVE           ;Writing to the hard disk?
                 jne     do_old_write         ;no, do old interrupt
                 sti                          ;allow interrupts
                 mov     ah,BAD_TRACK         ;fake a bad track error
                 mov     al,BAD_TRACK_LO
                 stc                          ;signal error
                 ret                          ;exit, keep stack

do_old_write:    jmp     dword ptr cs:old_dos_write
                                              ;pass control to old int

new_dos_write    endp



;..............................
;
; The following deinstalls the redirected interrupts
; if there is a soft reboot.  This keeps the vectors from
; pointing to an area of memory that no longer contains
; program code.
;
;..............................

new_reboot_intr  proc    far
                 cli                          ;don't allow interrupts
                 push    ds                   ;save old values
                 push    bx
                 assume  ds:int_table         ;point to interrupt table
                 xor     bx,bx
                 mov     ds,bx
                 mov     bl,ident_intr        ;find marker interrupt
                 xor     bh,bh
                 shl     bh,1
                 shl     bh,1
                 mov     [bx],word ptr 0      ;clear it
                 mov     [bx+2],word ptr 0
                 mov     bx,cs:old_disk_intr  ;replace disk
                 mov     ds:DISK_ENTRY,bx     ;interrupt
                 mov     bx,cs:old_disk_intr+2
                 mov     ds:DISK_ENTRY+2,bx
                 mov     bx,cs:old_reboot_intr ;replace reboot
                 mov     ds:REBOOT_ENTRY,bx   ;interrupt
                 mov     bx,cs:old_reboot_intr+2
                 mov     ds:REBOOT_ENTRY+2,bx
                 mov     bx,cs:old_dos_write  ;replace DOS write
                 mov     ds:DOS_WRITE_ENTRY,bx ;interrupt
                 mov     bx,cs:old_dos_write+2
```

```
                    mov     ds:DOS_WRITE_ENTRY+2,bx
                    pop     bx                      ;restore registers
                    assume ds:nothing
                    pop     ds
                    jmp     dword ptr cs:old_reboot_intr ;continue
new_reboot_intr     endp


;.......................................
;
; The following allows for communication between PROTECT
; and outside programs.
;
; No features are currently implemented.
;
;.......................................


comm_routine        proc    near
                    iret
comm_routine        endp



;----------------INSTALLATION SECTION--------------


install:            assume ds:code
                    push    cs                      ;set up segments
                    pop     ds
;..............................
;
;See if PROTECT is installed already
;
;..............................
                    mov     al,FREE_INT1    ;scan the interrupt table
check_loop:         mov     ah,35h          ;free range for PROTECT
                    int     21h             ;marker
                    cmp     bx,0            ;see if interrupt is in use
                    jne     compare_strings ;yes, see if it is marker
                    mov     cx,es           ;now check segment
                    cmp     cx,0
                    jne     compare_strings ;else, this vector is free
                    mov     ident_intr,al   ;remember it
                    jmp     cont_loop

compare_strings: mov     di,bx              ;es:di points to target
                    add     di,3            ;don't look at jump
                    lea     si,program_name ;ds:si points to name
                    mov     cx,IDENT_LENGTH ;see if target points to
                    repe    cmpsb           ;same string as name
                    jcxz    already_installed ;matched => installed
```

```
cont_loop:      inc     al              ;look at next interrupt
                cmp     al,FREE_INT_LAST ;time to stop?
                jne     check_loop      ;no, keep checking
                cmp     ident_intr,DOS_WRITE ;a free interrupt?
                jne     not_installed   ;yes, so install it
;...............................
;
; No free room to install communications and identifier interrupt
; vector.  Print a message and install anyway.
;
; ident_intr is initialized to the DOS write interrupt.  Thus, if
; no marker is installed, the sections which redirect during
; installation and upon rebooting will change the DOS write
; interrupt when modifying the identifier interrupt, then correct
; it when modifying the DOS write interrupt.
;
;...............................
                lea     dx,no_ident_warning
                call    disp_msg
                jmp     not_installed

;...............................
;
; Already installed, so print a message
; and terminate.
;
;...............................
already_installed: lea  dx,already_msg      ;display message
                call    disp_msg
                mov     al,1                ;indicate error
                mov     ah,4ch              ;terminate
                int     21h
;...............................
;
; Not installed, so continue
;
;...............................

not_installed:  lea     dx,start_up_msg     ;print message that
                call    disp_msg            ;protect is installed
;...............................
;
; Read old interrupts
;
;...............................
                mov     al,DISK_INTR        ;read old disk interrupt
                mov     ah,35h
                int     21h
                mov     old_disk_intr,bx    ;save it
                mov     old_disk_intr+2,es
                mov     al,REBOOT_INTR      ;read old reboot interrupt
                mov     ah,35h
                int     21h
```

```
                mov     old_reboot_intr,bx  ;save it
                mov     old_reboot_intr+2,es
                mov     al,DOS_WRITE
                mov     ah,35h
                int     21h
                mov     old_dos_write,bx
                mov     old_dos_write+2,es
;..................................
;
; Free environment
;
;..................................
                mov     ax,environ_addr     ;find environment
                mov     es,ax               ;free it
                mov     ah,73
                int     21h
;..................................
;
; Redirect interrupts
;
;..................................
                lea     dx,communicate      ;set up communication /
                mov     al,ident_intr       ;identifier interrupt
                mov     ah,25h
                int     21h
                lea     dx,new_disk_intr ;redirect disk interrupt
                mov     al,DISK_INTR
                mov     ah,25h
                int     21h
                lea     dx,new_reboot_intr ;redirect reboot interrupt
                mov     al,REBOOT_INTR
                mov     ah,25h
                int     21h
                lea     dx,new_dos_write ;redirect DOS disk
                mov     al,DOS_WRITE        ;write interrupt
                mov     ah,25h
                int     21h
;..................................
;
; Now terminate and stay resident
;
;..................................
                lea     dx,install          ;keep everything up to
                mov     cl,4                ;install
                shr     dx,cl
                inc     dx
                mov     al,0                ;no error
                mov     ah,49               ;terminate
                int     21h
```

```
;------------UTILITIES (non-resident) -----------


;disp_msg
;       displays an ASCIIZ message
;       offset of message in DS:DX
;

disp_msg        proc    near
                push    ax
                push    bx
                push    si
                mov     bl,FORE_COLOR
                mov     si,dx               ;point to string
d_m_loop:       mov     al,[si]             ;load character
                cmp     al,0                ;check for end
                je      d_m_end
                mov     ah,0eh              ;print char service
                int     10h                 ;print it
                inc     si
                jmp     d_m_loop
d_m_end:        pop     si
                pop     bx
                pop     ax
                ret
disp_msg        endp


;------------------MESSAGES (non-resident)--------------

start_up_msg    db  LINEFEED,RETURN
                db  '----------------------------------------'
                db  LINEFEED,RETURN
                db  'PROTECT is now installed.',LINEFEED
                db  LINEFEED,RETURN
                db  'Your hard disks are safe from reformatting'
                db  LINEFEED,LINEFEED,RETURN
                db  'PROTECT  V1.0    ',LINEFEED,RETURN
                db  'Copyright (C) 1986, Michael I. Hyman'
                db  LINEFEED,RETURN
                db  '----------------------------------------'
                db  LINEFEED,LINEFEED,RETURN,0
already_msg     db  LINEFEED,RETURN
                db  '----------------------------------------'
                db  LINEFEED,RETURN
                db  'Sorry--PROTECT was already installed.',LINEFEED
                db  LINEFEED,RETURN
                db  '----------------------------------------'
                db  LINEFEED,LINEFEED,RETURN,0
```

```
no_ident_warning db   LINEFEED,RETURN
                 db   '----------------------------------------'
                 db   LINEFEED,RETURN
                 db   'Warning--Many resident utilities are already'
                 db   LINEFEED,RETURN
                 db   'installed.  PROTECT will not warn you if you'
                 db   LINEFEED,RETURN
                 db   'install it twice. Communications with PROTECT'
                 db   LINEFEED,RETURN
                 db   'will be limited. '
                 db   LINEFEED,RETURN
                 db   '----------------------------------------'
                 db   LINEFEED,LINEFEED,RETURN,0


code             ends
                 end protect
```

Type in this program and assemble it. Correct any typing
mistakes. Then, convert it to a COM file with EXE2BIN. Run it.
Try loading it again. Fill in the unused interrupt 60h-67h
vectors with FAILSAFE or DEBUG. Try loading PROTECT again.

If you are adventurous, test PROTECT by trying to format your
hard disk. In case you made a typo, make a backup copy first. (I
tested it on my hard disk several times. It always worked.)
Remember, FORMAT starts by reading a lot of sectors. Don't let
this scare you.

There are many ways that PROTECT can be changed or improved.
Format protection for floppy drives and logical devices can be
added with a user interface to select and override the choices. A
more complex check could be used to halt formatting during the
verify stage. DOS-WORKS1, from Qualitas, is an excellent utility
with all of these and many more useful features. It also supports
write protection and media checking.

KEY PROGRAMMING POINTS

- Floppy disks are low-level formatted. Hard disks are high-level
  formatted.

- High-level formatting does not destroy information in the data area.

CHAPTER 34

SPECIAL NOTES ON USING THE KEYBOARD AS A TRIGGER

The keyboard is a very convenient way to signal activation for a memory resident utility. Many popular memory resident utilities base activation on the keyboard. FAILSAFE, for example, is activated by pressing Ctrl-Left Shift-Alt. Keyboard enhancers treat many key combinations as macros.

Every time a key is struck--whether a letter, shift, or arrow key--interrupt 9 is activated. The normal (BIOS) routine checks the keyboard controller, deciphers the scan code and, if appropriate, puts a character code into the keyboard buffer. It accounts for shift states, beeps if the keyboard buffer is full, and checks for control-break, control-num lock, pause, print screen, and control-alt-delete. Further, it sets special BIOS variables to indicate if certain keys, such as the shift and control keys, have been pressed. Before it exits, it resets the keyboard and interrupt controller.

Every time a request for a key is made, interrupt 16h is called. It returns with the ASCII and scan codes for the character.

There are two reasons to redirect the keyboard interrupt. The first is to check for a particular triggering key or key combination. Most pop-up utilities, such as FAILSAFE, take this approach. The triggering key is called a **hot key**. The second reason is to replace it with a different keyboard interpretation routine. You might expand the keyboard buffer or reorganize the keyboard layout. One further use, though uncommon, would be to simply check some internal variable, set by a different section of the interrupt handler, to see whether to activate.

There are two ways to check for a trigger key. The first is to check what key was just pressed every time a key is struck. This method relies on interrupt 9 and lets a utility check for activation instantly. It is a fairly simple method to use if the activation key combinations are limited.

For routines that are not so urgent or that need to check for many triggers, it is much better to tie into interrupt 16h. Every time an application or other utility looks for input, you can check for the triggering key.

CHECKING FOR TRIGGERING KEYS USING INTERRUPT 9

When a key is struck, a scan code is generated by the keyboard controller and placed in a readable I/O port. The BIOS interrupt 9 handler reads this port and places the scan code and the corresponding ASCII code into the keyboard buffer. It also sets bits to indicate status of the shift, control, and other keys.

This gives you three methods of examining keystrokes for trigger keys. The easiest method is to restrict the trigger to a combination of the insert, caps lock, num lock, scroll lock, alt, control, and left and right shift keys. For example, valid triggers would be control-alt, left shift-right shift, alt-scroll lock, and so forth.

Every time you press a key, examine the status byte to see if the trigger combination was met. There are two bytes which indicate status, located at memory locations 0000:0417h and 0000:0418h:

Byte 0000:0417h

Bit	Hex Val	Meaning
0	01	Right shift key is depressed
1	02	Left shift key is depressed
2	04	Control key is depressed
3	08	Alt key is depressed
4	10	Scroll lock state is on
5	20	Num lock state is on
6	40	Caps lock state is on
7	80	Insert state is on

Byte 0000:0418h

BIt	Hex Val	Meaning
3	08	Control Num lock state is on
4	10	Scroll lock key is depressed
5	20	Num lock key is depressed
6	40	Caps lock key is depressed
7	80	Insert key is depressed

If you have FAILSAFE, examine these bytes. Activate FAILSAFE and use the Snoop command to examine the page starting with 0000:0417h. Experiment with holding down the shift, insert, control, and other keys. At the same time, strike an arrow key to update the screen. You will see the status bytes changing.

If you plan to use these status bytes for triggering, first chain to the old interrupt 9 vector. This will ensure that the status bytes are updated and will take care of any keyboard hardware processing. Then, use BIOS interrupt 16h, function 2 to check the status (see Chapter 15). This returns byte 0000:0417h in the AL register.

Unfortunately, this restricts you to combinations of the shift, control, and alt keys. If you need to access the second keyboard status byte, read them both from memory:

```
bios_variables      segment at 0h
                    org       417h
keyboard_status     dw        ?
bios_variables      ends

                    xor       ax,ax      ;set to 0
                    push      ds
                    assume    ds:bios_variables
                    mov       ds,ax
                    mov       ax,keyboard_status
                    assume    ds:code
                    pop       ds
```

The BIOS method is preferred because the BIOS variable location may change with a different version of BIOS, and a co-resident keyboard interrupt handler may replace or not update the keyboard status byte. In either case, the BIOS interrupt would be adjusted so as to properly return the keyboard status.

Don't simply **and** out the bits that don't concern you and check the rest for the trigger condition. This will cause many key combinations to trigger your routine. For example, if you were looking for control-right shift and **and**ed out all other bits, control-right shift-left shift would also trigger your routine. Just mask off the state bits--byte 0000:0417h bits 4-7 and byte 0000:0418h bit 4.

If two coresident routines share the same trigger combination, using this method, the first one loaded will activate first. Do not change the status bytes in such a way that your program is the last program to see the combination. Let each program have its own turn. Changing the BIOS bytes could have drastic and unintentional effects. A different resident routine may have checked these bytes before you changed them and expect them in the same condition after (or during) your program's operation.

You will need to use a different technique if you want non-shift combination hot keys or need several hot keys. The best technique is to redirect interrupt 16h and watch the interrupt stream, as is discussed shortly.

For a more immediate check, you must redirect interrupt 9. There are two ways to do this: you can check the key codes that interrupt 9 places in the keyboard buffer or directly read the keyboard controller. Both of these methods have problems. We will discuss reading the buffer for completeness, though redirecting interrupt 16h is safer. Checking the input stream directly is much more troublesome and machine-dependent. This method is not recommended.

The keyboard buffer is stored in low memory as a **circular queue** of words, normally starting at 0000:041eh. A circular queue means that the buffer memory is treated as a loop. Characters are added until the end of the buffer memory is reached. Then, the characters wrap around to the beginning. To keep track of where to add a character and to determine if the buffer is full, there are two pointers. The **head** points to the next character to be read out of the buffer. This is the beginning of character information. The **tail** points to where the next character will be added to the buffer. This is the end-of-character information. If the head and tail point to the same location, the buffer is empty. If the tail points to the position right before the head, the buffer is full. When the tail passes the end of the buffer, it wraps to the beginning.

There are four BIOS variables that point to the keyboard buffer. All are word-length pointers of offsets relative to segment 0040h. Depending on your application, you may want to access them through segment 0 starting at offset 400h (0000:0400h) or through segment 40h starting at offset 0 (0040:0000h).

Keyboard Buffer Pointers

Location	Meaning
0040:0080h	Pointer to the beginning of the keyboard buffer memory area
0040:0082h	Pointer to the end of the keyboard buffer memory area
0040:001ah	Pointer to the head of the buffer
0040:001ch	Pointer to the tail of the buffer

To read the character just pressed, compare the head and tail pointers to see if a character is waiting in the buffer (they will be equal if there isn't). If one is, read the most recent character struck--that stored in the location one position before the character pointed to by the tail. Remember, the buffer is circular. If the tail points to the buffer beginning, the character to read is the character one word before the buffer end. Characters are stored as words, with the ASCII value followed by the scan code.

Unfortunately, this method has three disadvantages. First, it relies very much on the position of certain BIOS variables. More importantly, it assumes that the keyboard buffer in use is the one pointed to by the BIOS pointers. Because this buffer is so small, most keyboard enhancers replace it. Thus, the data stored in the BIOS area does not necessarily reflect the most recent characters typed in. Also, other resident keyboard processors could be in the process of modifying the BIOS data at the same time you are reading it.

You can also check the scan codes directly as they are passed through interrupt 9h. On the PC, this requires accessing the keyboard controller chip directly. It is easier on the AT. Every time interrupt 9h receives a scan code from the keyboard controller, it places the scan code in the AL register, sets the carry flag, and calls interrupt 15h, function 79. If on return the carry is clear, the scan code is discarded.

Normally, interrupt 15h, function 79 simply returns. You can redirect this function to watch the scan codes as they are sent to the keyboard controller. If a triggering combination is met, either clear the carry to discard the scan code or change AL to modify the returned keystroke.

CHECKING FOR TRIGGERING KEYS USING INTERRUPT 16H

If you need to use many different trigger keys, the best method is to redirect interrupt 16h. This is especially useful if you are writing a keyboard enhancer that replaces certain key combinations, such as Alt-A, with other strings of text. It is also a good method if you have many different types of routines to run and different triggers for each. For example, you could pop-up a calculator with Alt-C and a watch with Alt-W.

This method is not as immediate as chaining off of interrupt 9h. Your routine will only be activated if the trigger is struck when some other program is looking for input. This is fairly common. Your program will work well with DOS, word processors, and spread sheets; however, you will not be able to call it if a program is in the middle of some intense calculations.

If you have certain features you need to access immediately, tie them to the status byte, as discussed previously. If you have features that require many triggers, especially if they involve enhancements to input features, tie them to interrupt 16h.

Routines tied to interrupt 16h will be more successful with multi-tasking operating systems.

If interrupt 16h is called for function 2, simply jump to the old interrupt 16h. For functions 0 and 1, call the old interrupt. Then, examine the character code that it returns in the AX register. If it is your hot key, begin processing. If not, pass the value through (return from the interrupt).

If your program asks for input, make sure that you mark a status variable so your routine will be reentrant.

Remember, if you are triggered, the calling routine still expects a character to be returned. You can't return with garbage in the AX register. Either wait for another input or adjust AX as appropriate for your application.

With this method, all characters are examined before they get to the calling program. Further, you give utilities loaded before you the chance to activate. By keeping a record of characters previously struck, you can also use complex activation codes, such as whole words. Remember, the calling routines also will have seen the previous characters.

Using interrupt 16h is an excellent way to make a macro program. For each character request, check to see if a character from part of an expanded macro--that is, from a text message that replaces a trigger key--is in your internal macro buffer. If one is waiting, return it to the caller through ax. If one isn't, chain to the old interrupt 16h command. The only disadvantage of this method is that ill-behaved routines that directly raid the BIOS keyboard buffer will not detect your characters.

Here's an outline of what an interrupt 16h processor might look like:

```
new_interrupt_16h    proc      far
                     pushf
                     cli
                     call      dword ptr cs:old_interrupt_16h
                     cmp       ax,TRIGGER
                     jne       no_trigger

        start processing section here
        then return

no_trigger:          iret
new_interrupt_16h    endp
```

COEXISTING WITH OTHER KEYBOARD-TRIGGERED ROUTINES

There is a limited number of single key combinations, but there are many possibilities for using them. Do not assume that your program is the only keyboard-triggered utility. Allow for some method to change the triggering commands. If you have several triggering features, you can create a separate utility to choose the triggering commands and set them with the communication vector (**comm_routine**). If you only have a few triggers, allow them to be selected from the command line.

Note that if several utilities are loaded that use the same triggers, the priority each has depends on the techniques used by the different utilities.

REPLACING INTERRUPT 9

To implement certain features, such as a new layout for the keyboard, you may need to replace interrupt 9. Here, you intercept all scan codes from the keyboard port, process them, and place them in the BIOS keyboard buffer or an internal keyboard buffer.

The basic process is to intercept scan codes, check if they are depress or release codes, character or shift codes, and act appropriately. You need to translate any character codes into the ASCII code and place them in a buffer. If you use an internal buffer, you must also redirect interrupt 16h so it reads characters from this buffer.

Remember to clear the keyboard and interrupt controllers. If you plan to make a complicated keyboard replacement routine, first look over the IBM BIOS listing.

KEY PROGRAMMING POINTS

- Every time the keyboard is struck, interrupt 9 is activated.

- Interrupt 16h is called every time there is a key request.

- The keyboard buffer is a circular queue.

- Redirecting interrupt 9 allows immediate checking for hot keys. This is best for hot keys restricted to combinations of the control, alt, and shift keys.

- On the AT you can check, change, and discard scan codes as interrupt 9 processes them.

- Redirect interrupt 16h if you plan to use a wide variety of hot keys.

- Use the communication routine to change hot keys.

CHAPTER 35

SPECIAL NOTES ON ROUTINES THAT USE THE CLOCK

The clock is a powerful interrupt for three reasons. First, it has the highest maskable priority. Second, it is called regularly and frequently. Third, it tells you absolute and elapsed time.

The clock is very useful for coordinating actions among interrupts. For example, you may want your utilities, especially pop-ups, to wait until other interrupts aren't active before processing. To do this, set a variable to TRIGGERED when the trigger condition is met. Have the clock interrupt check this variable. If it detects a TRIGGERED, check if the system is ready for the utility's operation. If so, change the status to ACTIVE and begin processing.

You can also use the clock to execute routines after a specified amount of time has elapsed. For example, you can blank the screen after a few minutes of disuse or pop-up an alarm message at a particular time.

Another use is to run processes in the background. For example, you could create a program to play music in the background. For every timer tick, it would check if the next note should be played. If so, it would set up the tone generation circuitry to play the next note.

There are two clock interrupts. Interrupt 8 is called every time the clock ticks. Normally, this is 18.2 times a second. Interrupt 8 updates the system clock, and checks if the diskette motor has been running too long. If it has, it shuts it off. It then issues an interrupt 1Ch. After regaining control, it issues an end-of-interrupt command to the interrupt controller.

Interrupt 1ch is called 18.2 times a second. If your utility relies on being called at this steady pace, chain to interrupt 1ch. Remember, the EOI is not sent until after you return to the interrupt 8.

If your routine doesn't rely on being called so steadily, use interrupt 8. Chain first, then process.

When you chain to a clock interrupt, keep the routines that check for activation as short as possible. Each cycle spent in the clock interrupt is a cycle that the application program won't receive.

KEY PROGRAMMING POINTS

- The clock has the highest maskable priority.

- The clock is useful for coordinating interrupts and for running background processes.

- If possible, use interrupt 8 and chain first.

- Keep the activation checking section of a clock handler short.

CHAPTER 36

SPECIAL NOTES
ON WRITING POP-UPS

When activated, pop-up utilities pop windows onto the screen. When finished, they restore the screen to its original contents. They are memory resident pulldown windows. If you have FAILSAFE loaded, press control-shift-alt. A window will pop up onto the screen.

Be careful when writing pop-ups. Compared to other interrupts, pop-ups take control of the computer for a long time. Before you activate a pop-up, make sure you won't disrupt anything. Once activated, check the screen status and type, and save information from the old screen. When finished, restore the original screen status and contents. There are other considerations when working with multi-tasking operating systems.

WHEN TO POP UP

Before you pop up, check that no interrupts with lower priority are currently active. This way, you avoid disrupting an important hardware service, such as a disk call. Have the routine that checks for activation set the status flag to TRIGGERED. Check for this with interrupt 8. When found, examine the interrupt controller in service register (ISR). Activate and set the status flag to ACTIVE as soon as no other interrupts are processing.

To check the interrupt controller:

```
cli
mov       al, 11        ;check status of
out       20h, al       ;interrupt controller
jmp short $ + 2         ;pause for AT
in        al,20h        ;get result
sti
```

The byte returned in al will have a bit set for any interrupts that are active:

Bit	Meaning
0	Interrupt 8 active
1	Interrupt 9 active
2	Interrupt ah active
3	Interrupt bh active

Bit	Meaning
4	Interrupt ch active
5	Interrupt dh active
6	Interrupt eh active
7	Interrupt fh active

The interrupt handler that checks for activation should set the status to TRIGGERED right before leaving. This saves stack use by preventing the interrupt 8 handler from starting before the other handler has fully finished.

```
; end of interrupt handler that checks for activation
; pop registers
                cmp        cs:status,WAS_TRIGGERED
                je         new_int_x_1
                cli                             ;shut int's off
                mov        cs:status,INACTIVE   ;clear status
                jmp        new_int_x_end
new_int_x_1:    cli                             ;shut int's off
                mov        cs:status,TRIGGERED  ;triggered
new_int_x_end:  iret
```

CHECKING SCREEN STATUS AND SAVING THE SCREEN

When you activate, use interrupt 10h, function 15 to determine the screen mode and active page. Then, save the old screen information. Use BIOS calls or access video memory directly. For relatively small pop-up windows and for the most compatibility, use BIOS. Move the cursor to each location on the screen over which the window will appear, and read in the character and attribute.

For larger screens, read the video memory directly. This is a much faster technique. The disadvantages are that it requires extra memory to work with graphics screens and that by avoiding BIOS calls, it is less cooperative.

There is a special area in memory set aside to store the characters on the screen. Each word in the display memory corresponds to a character position on the screen. The first byte is the character code; the second is the attribute (see Chapter 14).

Word 0 stores information for the upper left position in the screen. Word 1 stores information for the next character over-- row 0, column 1. Then comes information for row 0, column 2. After the information for one column finishes, information for the next begins, so on an 80 column screen, the information for row 1, column 0 follows that for row 0, column 79.

Thus, to find the offset of information for a particular character position, you find:

[(position row) * (characters per row) + (position column)] * 2

You multiply by two because there are two bytes (one word) for every character position.

For the monochrome adaptor, text information starts at location b000:0000h. For the color graphics and enhanced graphics adapters, the location depends on the display page. Forty column pages each use 1000 words and eighty column pages, 2000 words. The first page starts at location b800:0000h. Thus, to find the information for a particular character, do one of the following:

For the monochrome screen, add the offset computed above to:

b000:0000h

For the graphics text screens, add the offset computed above to:

b800:0000h + (page number) * (columns per page) * 50

Because the text information is located sequentially, it is very easy to read all text behind a window with a single **movsw** or a loop of **movsw's**.

For example, to read the whole screen, you could:

```
;assumes that es points to data segment
;assumes that ds points to beginning location of screen buffer
;note -- this is the reverse of the usual situation
        lea     di,our_buffer_location    ;point to where you
                                          ;will store info
        mov     si,text_offset            ;as computed above
        mov     cx,text_length            ;depends on # of
                                          ;columns on the
                                          ;screen
        cld
        rep  movsw
```

To save information from the graphics screen, you must read the data for every pixel behind the window. The method to use depends on the screen and mode and can require much memory. Refer to <u>Advanced IBM PC Graphics</u> for more information. You may want to switch to a text screen and not worry about saving the graphics screen.

SWITCHING SCREENS

You may want to design your window layouts specifically for 80-column screens or just the 80-column text screen. If the screen is not in one of these modes, switch it using interrupt 10h, function 0 before you pop up any windows. You don't need to do this for the monochrome screen. For color screens, choose mode 2. It is the 80-column black and white text screen. On RGB monitors, it will appear in color; on composite monitors, it won't smear.

Note that if you switch modes, you will lose all information from the old screen. This is an unfortunate sacrifice, but probably an acceptable consequence. Use a different technique if you are writing for a graphics-based windows environment.

WRITING TO THE SCREEN

Once you have saved the old screen information and perhaps switched modes, pop up your window. Use BIOS calls or write directly to memory. BIOS calls are slow; using them will cause a bit of flicker because there is a pause as each character is written, yet they are more portable and will work on the graphics screen. If you are not doing much updating to the screen whenever a command is generated, using BIOS calls is probably easiest.

If you frequently update a large portion of the screen, direct memory writes will give a much better appearance. Calculate the screen memory location just as you did for reading the screen. Write the new character information to this location.

To make the display even smoother, do all of your writes to an internal buffer. When the information is ready to be displayed, move it to the screen all at once.

For example, suppose you pop a window onto the bottom 10 rows of an 80-column text screen. Set aside a 10 * 80 * 2 byte buffer to store your text information. To write a character to window row 2, column 7 (which corresponds to screen row 18, column 7), write it to byte [(2 * 80) + 7]*2 in your buffer. When all your writes are finished, copy the whole buffer to the screen with a single **rep movsw**. Of course, if your windows are not of full-page width, you must copy and read the text in a series of **rep movsw's**.

If possible, include a command to move the window location. This is easiest if you use an internal screen buffer or use BIOS calls.

PREPARING TO LEAVE

When you are finished with the pop up, be sure to restore the original mode and page, and then copy back the original screen information. The process for restoring the screen information is the same as writing to the screen. Do it directly or with BIOS calls.

POP-UPS IN MULTI-TASKING ENVIRONMENTS

Pop-ups must take special care when working in a multi-tasking environment. The major problem is context switching. When your pop-up begins, a particular application may be on the screen. The pop-up saves this screen information, but by the time the pop-up finishes, the multi-tasker may have switched to a different application, and the screen may be completely changed.

Each multi-tasker provides a different way of coordinating screens with pop-ups. For example, some provide an alternate video area to address. They take into account any information written directly to this area. Others may require a more elaborate notifying procedure. Consult the reference manuals for the particular systems you deal with.

Also, look through Chapter 37 for special notes on designing memory resident utilities to work with multi-taskers.

KEY PROGRAMMING POINTS

- Before popping up, check that no other maskable interrupts are active. You may want to coordinate the clock interrupt with the interrupt that checks for activation.

- Check screen status and save the screen before displaying a pop-up window.

- Read the screen directly or use BIOS calls.

- Restore the screen before leaving.

- In a multi-tasking environment, tie the processing section to a software interrupt. There may be special processes for popping windows on the screen.

CHAPTER 37

SPECIAL NOTES ON USING
DOS AND MULTI-TASKERS

DOS calls are an incredibly powerful way of interacting with the computer environment. Unfortunately, they are not reentrant, and you must be very careful when using them from memory resident utilities. It's not enough to trigger the utility only when it appears DOS is not busy. Even while DOS displays the command line prompt, it is using a DOS call to wait for a string input. If you make a DOS function call at the wrong time, you will overflow one of DOS's internal stacks. The results are unpredictable and hazardous.

DOS uses internal stacks and PSPs, DTAs, and FCBs to store information. DOS functions 0-12 appear to use two stacks, and the higher function calls a third. When executing DOS calls from a memory resident utility, you must preserve these stacks and storage areas.

If possible, avoid DOS calls completely. Change any DOS screen or keyboard calls to BIOS calls. Disk access, unfortunately, is too difficult to replicate with BIOS.

To get around the DOS reentrancy problem, you need to do a bit of fancy footwork based on redirecting interrupts 8h and 28h.

Interrupt 28h is repeatedly called by DOS as it waits for keyboard input. At this point, the third stack--that used for function calls above 12--is free. Thus, you can safely execute any of the higher numbered DOS calls, including the disk calls.

Redirect interrupt 8 in case an application uses DOS input infrequently. Set a status variable to tell interrupt 8 you want to execute DOS calls. When interrupt 8 detects this flag, it needs to check the DOS active byte (see Chapter 25). If this is 0, no DOS calls are outstanding; it is safe to execute any of the DOS calls. Find the location of the active byte in the non-resident section, and save this information for the resident section.

You may also want to check the interrupt controller status register to see if any other interrupts are currently being processed. Because DOS file access calls take a long time to process, delay making them if other interrupts are active.

Before you make DOS file access calls, you must switch the PSP. First, read in the current PSP, then switch the PSP to the utility's PSP. Restore the PSP before you exit. If you use any calls that use a DTA, such as the directory search calls, you must also switch the DTA.

Further, you might want to set up your own critical error handler.

MULTI-TASKING SYSTEMS

Multi-tasking systems switch back and forth between programs. During this time, they most likely swap in and out interrupt vector tables and BIOS variables.

The main problem in working with multi-taskers is that the hardware interrupts are not tied to a particular context. Thus, if you activate from an interrupt such as the timer or keyboard, the context you are in could switch. This will change the status of vectors and system variables that your routine may have already examined or planned to restore. To get around this, check for the triggering condition from hardware interrupts, and then set a flag that is checked by frequently called software interrupts. Your routine will have to wait for the next software interrupt before it activates, but the context will be in a stable state at this point.

If you check for the DOS active byte from a multi-tasker, also check from within a software interrupt. For further information on writing in a multi-tasking environment, consult the technical manuals for the various multi-taskers.

EXPANDED MEMORY

If your utility uses expanded memory, make sure that you save and restore the page map. Refer to Chapter 20.

KEY PROGRAMMING POINTS

- DOS functions are not reentrant.

- To use DOS functions, redirect interrupts 8 and 28h.

- Check the DOS active byte from interrupt 8 before making DOS calls.

- Only use DOS functions above number 12 when using interrupt 28h.

- Check the 8259 to make sure that no other interrupts are in progress.

- Temporarily redirect the PSP and, if necessary, the DTA.

- Save and restore the page maps if your utility uses expanded memory.

CHAPTER 38

DEACTIVATING, DEINSTALLING, AND AT PITFALLS

After loading a memory resident utility, you may want to temporarily shut off its operation. This might be because you plan to load another utility that uses similar commands or duplicates certain features or because you no longer want your utility's features to be active.

To do this, you should have some means of deactivating and reactivating your utility. Set up a flag to indicate if the utility is currently deactivated. If you have already set up a status variable, just add a new possibility: DORMANT. Since this will have a value other than INACTIVE, your utility will no longer trigger. Have an external utility use the communication interrupt to tell the utility to become dormant or to reactivate. If there are no free interrupts in which to install the communication interrupt, scan down the interrupt chain of an interrupt you redirected, checking the appropriate offset for the name identifier. From this, find the jump to **comm_routine**. This approach is rather tedious.

You may want to completely remove your utility from memory. This is a little more difficult. If your utility is fairly small, deactivating it is the better approach. To deinstall a utility, you must preserve chains to the old interrupts yet free up as much space as possible. To do this, you need to place all the interrupt handlers one after another and have them jump to the main routines:

```
;old interrupt vectors stored here
old_int_x       dw          ?,?
old_int_y       dw          ?,?
    .
    .
    .
;interrupts redirected to this section.
;it takes up very little memory
new_int_x:      cmp         status,DEINSTALLED
                jne         new_int_x_routine
                jmp dword ptr cs:old_int_x
new_int_y:      cmp         status,DEINSTALLED
                jne         new_int_y_routine
                jmp dword ptr cs:old_int_y
    .
    .
;variables section here
    .
    .
```

```
;interrupt processing in this section
;it could take up a lot of memory
new_int_x_routine:
    .
    .
    .
```

To deinstall the handler, set the status to DEINSTALLED. Use
the memory block modify interrupt to shrink the utilities memory
space to only the new_int_x and new_int_y routines.

Again, this is only useful if your utility is large. If it is
small, the memory block that is freed is not necessarily going to
be used again. After all, any utilities loaded after you will
still be present, and a fragment of your code will still remain.

You can also completely remove your utility by restoring all the
interrupt vectors which you modified. This will cut out any
routines loaded after the deinstalled utility. Once you do this,
you can free up all memory from your PSP on. To do this, jump to
offset 0 in your PSP. This is very dangerous. It assumes that if
any utilities are loaded after the deinstalled utility, they don't
use any interrupts which you don't. If they use other interrupts,
those interrupts will point to unused memory and the system will
hang. To be safe, you must deinstall utilities from the last
entered to the first.

AT PITFALLS

If you are writing interrupt handlers that will be used on the AT,
be careful of the low-numbered interrupts with both a hardware and
an IBM-assigned meaning, as listed in Chapter 27. For example,
interrupt 5 doubles as the print screen interrupt and the **bound**
exception interrupt. BIOS does not have any support for the **bound**
exception; it handles it as a request for a screen dump. If you
write an interrupt 5 handler, you may want to address this issue.

Also, be careful with the other conflicting interrupts.

KEY PROGRAMMING POINTS

- Use the status byte and communication interrupt to deactivate a resident utility.

- Use the status byte, communication interrupt, and shrink memory block function to deinstall a resident utility. You must structure the utility so that you can free as much memory as possible.

- Be careful of conflicting interrupts on the AT.

CHAPTER 39

SUMMARY

Cooperation is the most important part of programming memory resident utilities. Never assume anything. Always consider others. By following the guidelines presented in these chapters, you will be able to develop friendlier utility packages.

In May of 1986, many software firms collaborated in an attempt to create a standard for memory resident utilities and communication between such programs. One issue they stressed was creating a structure through which utilities could know what other utilities are present, know what interrupts and trigger keys they use, and know information for deinstallation. The meeting set various goals and brought attention to many programming issues, but as of the writing of this book, there has been no resolution and no standard.

By following the principals of cooperation, however, a standard is not so critical. If your routine can become dormant, if you have the option to select hot keys, if you check when to activate, and if you follow all the other guidelines, your program will work well and be cooperative enough for almost all situations.

Happy hacking.

BIBLIOGRAPHY

Cooper, Frolik, Greenberg, et al. DOSUNDOC.DOC. May 1986.

Hyman, Michael I. Advanced IBM PC Graphics. New York: Brady Communications Co., Inc., 1985.

IBM AT Technical Reference Manual. IBM Corp., 1985.

IBM DOS 2.0 Manual. IBM Corp., 1983.

IBM DOS 3.1 Technical Reference Manual. IBM Corp., 1985.

IBM DOS 3.2 Manual. IBM Corp., 1986.

IBM DOS 3.2 Technical Reference Manual. IBM Corp., 1986.

IBM PC Technical Reference Manual. IBM Corp., 1983.

Jourdain, Robert. Programmer's Problem Solver for the IBM PC, XT, and AT. New York: Brady Communications Co., Inc., 1986.

Jump, Dennis. Programmer's Guide to MS DOS. New York: Brady Communications Co., Inc., 1984.

Lotus Intel Microsoft Expanded Memory Specification. Version 3.20. U.S.A.: Lotus Development Corporation, Intel Corporation, Microsoft Corporation, 1985.

Microsoft C Run-Time Library Reference. Microsoft Corp., 1985.

Microsoft Mouse User's Guide. Microsoft Corp., 1986.

Microsystem Components Handbook. Volume II. U.S.A.: Intel Corporation, 1985.

Norton, Peter. Inside the IBM PC. New York: Brady Communications Co., Inc., 1986.

Norton, Peter. Programmer's Guide to the IBM PC. Washington: Microsoft Press, 1985.

Proceedings from the May 1986 Memory Resident Utilities Conference.

Rector, Russell and George Alexy. The 8086 Book. California: Osborne/McGraw-Hill, 1980.

Smith, Bob. Qualitas, Inc. Bethesda, Maryland. Interviews, October 1985 - August 1986.

Smith, James. The IBM PC AT Programmer's Guide. New York: Prentice Hall Press, 1986.

Triebl, Walter and Avtar Singh. The 8086 Microprocessor. New Jersey: Prentice Hall, Inc., 1985.

Turbo Pascal 2.0 Reference Manual. Borland International, 1984.

Turbo Pascal 3.0 Reference Manual. Borland International, 1985.

INDEX

disk transfer area 188-189
  switching 357
disk type byte 43
DOS commands--changing 134
  location 134, 136-137
DOS version 266
DTA (see disk transfer area)

E

environment 330
  freeing 297
equipment list 266
erased files 100-101
error codes--cause 196
  class 196
  disk reading and writing 251, 253
  DOS 193-197
  DOS 2.1 193
  DOS 2.x 193 DOS 3.x 194-197
  general 194-195
  recommended action 196
EXE files 149, 214
expanded memory (see memory)
extended memory (see memory)
extended keys 164

F

FAT (see file allocation table)
file allocation table 6, 50 - 54
  12 and 16-bit 51-54, 121
  decoding 52-54
  entries 50
  entry codes (12 bit) 53
  entry codes (16 bit) 54
  location 54
file attribute 65, 203-204
file chain 51
file handle 192
file pointer 200-202

files 78, 192-210
  circularly-linked 128
  closing 192
  cross-linked 128
  date 204-205
  erased 100-101
  erasing 203
  for keyboard and screen
      access 192, 201
  fragmentation 129-130
  opening 192, 197-200
  partially-linked 129
  reading 200-202
  renaming 202-203
  searching for 224-233
  space allocation 50
  standard 192
  time 204-205
  writing 200-202
formatting 322
fragmentation 129-130
freeing environment 297

G

graphics 161-162
  palette 161
  reading dot 162
  setting dot 162

H

handle--memory 240
head 4
header 325
hot key 334
hot spot 181

I

in service register 348-349
inheritance--and children 259

ORDER FORM
1·800·MANUALS

MAIL TO:
Management Information Source, Inc.
1107 N.W. 14th Avenue
Portland, Oregon 97209-2802
(503) 222-2399

PLEASE CHARGE
☐ VISA　　　　　☐ MasterCharge
☐ American Express　　☐Check Enclosed

Exp. Date _____

Acct No _____

Signature _____

Company Name _____

Attn: _____

Address _____

City _____

State/Zip _____

Phone_____

Quantity	The following books are available	Price	Total Price
	Memory Resident Utilities, Interrupts, and Disk Mgmt. with MS and PC DOS	$22.95	
	dBase III plus Power Tools	$21.95	
	Hard Disk Management	$21.95	
	Turbo Prolog: Features for Programmers	$22.95	
	The Power Of: Word Perfect (incl. version 4.2) avail. 2-1-87	$19.95	
	The Power Of: Q&A (incl. version 2) avail. 2-1-87	$19.95	
	The Power Of: Lotus 1-2-3, Release 2 Complete Reference Guide	$19.95	
	The Power Of: Lotus 1-2-3, Release 2 For Business Applications w/diskette*	$34.95	
	The Power Of: Lotus 1-2-3, Release 2 For Business Applications	$19.95	
	The Power Of: Running PC DOS	$22.95	
	The Power Of: R:Base 5000 For Business Applications with diskette*	$34.95	
	The Power Of: R:Base 5000 For Business Applications	$19.95	
	The Power Of: Financial Calculations for Multiplan with diskette*	$28.95	
	The Power Of: Financial Calculations for Lotus 1-2-3 with diskette*	$28.95	
	The Power Of: Construction Management Using Lotus 1-2-3 with diskette*	$44.95	
	The Power Of: Construction Management Using Multiplan with diskette*	$44.95	
	The Power Of: Appleworks	$19.95	
	The Power Of: Appleworks with diskette (Apple-DOS)	$34.95	
	THE MANUAL: dBase II	$14.95	
	THE MANUAL: dBase III	$14.95	
	THE MANUAL: Multiplan	$14.95	
	THE MANUAL: Wordstar	$14.95	
	THE MANUAL: Apple Works	$14.95	

Shipping & Handling_____
TOTAL PRICE_____

To save C.O.D. charges:
☐ Enclosed is a check or use one of the above major credit cards.
*MS-DOS or IBM diskette.

Shipping & Handling Charges
1 . . . . $1.50 per book
4-up . . . . $ .50 per book

ORDER FORM
1·800·MANUALS

MAIL TO:
Management Information Source, Inc.
1107 N.W. 14th Avenue
Portland, Oregon 97209-2802
(503) 222-2399

PLEASE CHARGE
- ☐ VISA
- ☐ American Express
- ☐ MasterCharge
- ☐ Check Enclosed

Exp. Date _____

Acct. No. _____

Signature _____

Company Name _____

Attn: _____

Address _____

City _____

State/Zip _____

Phone _____

Quantity	The following books are available	Price	Total Price
	Memory Resident Utilities, Interrupts, and Disk Mgmt. with MS and PC DOS	$22.95	
	dBase III plus Power Tools	$21.95	
	Hard Disk Management	$21.95	
	Turbo Prolog: Features for Programmers	$22.95	
	The Power Of: Word Perfect (incl. version 4.2) avail. 2-1-87	$19.95	
	The Power Of: Q&A (incl. version 2) avail. 2-1-87	$19.95	
	The Power Of: Lotus 1-2-3, Release 2 Complete Reference Guide	$19.95	
	The Power Of: Lotus 1-2-3, Release 2 For Business Applications w/diskette*	$34.95	
	The Power Of: Lotus 1-2-3, Release 2 For Business Applications	$19.95	
	The Power Of: Running PC DOS	$22.95	
	The Power Of: R:Base 5000 For Business Applications with diskette*	$34.95	
	The Power Of: R:Base 5000 For Business Applications	$19.95	
	The Power Of: Financial Calculations for Multiplan with diskette*	$28.95	
	The Power Of: Financial Calculations for Lotus 1-2-3 with diskette*	$28.95	
	The Power Of: Construction Management Using Lotus 1-2-3 with diskette*	$44.95	
	The Power Of: Construction Management Using Multiplan with diskette*	$44.95	
	The Power Of: Appleworks	$19.95	
	The Power Of: Appleworks with diskette (Apple-DOS)	$34.95	
	THE MANUAL: dBase II	$14.95	
	THE MANUAL: dBase III	$14.95	
	THE MANUAL: Multiplan	$14.95	
	THE MANUAL: Wordstar	$14.95	
	THE MANUAL: Apple Works	$14.95	

Shipping & Handling _____

TOTAL PRICE _____

To save C.O.D. charges:
☐ Enclosed is a check or use one of the
above major credit cards.
*MS-DOS or IBM diskette.

Shipping & Handling Charges
1 .... $1.50 per book
4-up .... $ .50 per book